Switzerland and Japan – Highlights of Their Encounter
Yearbook 2006 Swiss-Japanese Chamber of Commerce
Edited by Roger Mottini

Impressum
Editor (concept and content): Roger Mottini
Switzerland and Japan – Highlights of Their Encounter
Yearbook 2006 Swiss-Japanese Chamber of Commerce

Art Director: Kim Küng, Zurich
Project Management: Weber-Thedy Corporate & Financial Communications, Zurich
Layout, printing and distribution: Schwabe AG, Basle, auslieferung@schwabe.ch
1st Edition: 1000

ISBN-13: 978-3-7965-2235-2
ISBN-10: 3-7965-2235-1

SWITZERLAND AND JAPAN

Highlights of Their Encounter

Yearbook 2006 Swiss-Japanese Chamber of Commerce

Roger Mottini (ed)

スイスと日本　－　その邂逅の軌跡

年鑑２００６　スイス－日本商工会議所

編者　ロジャ　モッテイーニ編

SJCC Swiss–Japanese Chamber of Commerce

スイス–日本商工会議所

CONTENTS

Ladies and Gentlemen,
Dear Readers

Despite their different cultures, Switzerland and Japan have enjoyed a long history of uninterrupted friendship and mutually beneficial trade relations. It was a particular pleasure for me to visit Japan as a President of the Swiss Confederation just as our two countries were celebrating the 140th anniversary of their official relations two years ago. Indeed, with the signing of the Treaty of Friendship and Commerce in 1864, Switzerland became the first nonmaritime country to establish official ties with the island nation of Japan.

At the time of their encounter, Switzerland and Japan could hardly be more different with regard to their political and social structure. The secret of the understanding between the two countries can be summed up in two words: mutual respect. Ever since, Swiss-Japanese relations have been very good, giving proof that differences in appearance need not be an obstacle to sincere communication.

Over the years, our economic ties have reached impressive levels. Japan is Switzerland's leading economic partner in Asia and Switzerland, with about 150 firms present in Japan, is the fifth-largest foreign investor in Japan. I wish it could be the same the other way round and strongly encourage Japanese investors to have a closer look at Switzerland as a business location in the heart of Europe. Bilateral trade has also shown new dynamics in the last four years.

When I met with Prime Minister Koizumi in 2004, we agreed that both countries should strengthen economic relations by further developing favourable conditions for bilateral trade as well as for foreign direct investment. The recent establishment of a Joint Study Group to examine means of promoting these relations, including through a Free Trade Agreement, is a very positive step in this direction.

Today, like hundred forty years ago, we are living in a period of global changes. These are testing times, calling into question old habits and asking for new answers, including in the field of economic cooperation. Both our countries are prepared to bring their contribution to answer the new challenges and make sure that the values they share will continue to be relevant, providing a solid base for their future relationship as well.

The Swiss Government is confident that the excellent relations to Japan will not only last, but become even closer. I thank the SJCC for its precious contribution to this process.

Federal Councillor Joseph Deiss
Head of the Federal Department of Economic Affairs

スイス－日本　商業会議所　２００６年報への序文
関係各位及び読者の皆様

異文化をもつ国でありながら、スイスと日本は友好と相互の有益な貿易関係を、長い年月に渡り絶えることなく育んできました。二年前、スイス連邦大統領として日本を訪れました際には、日本国とスイス国、二カ国のみによる国際交流１４０周年記念を祝うことができ、真に喜ばしい訪問となりました。１８６４年の友好・通商条約証印をもちまして我国は、陸続きの国の中で初めて、島国である日本と正式な条約を結んだ国となったわけです。

当時、両国間には政治姿勢及び社会情勢に堅固たる相違がありました。にもかかわらずこの二国は理解を示し合うことができたのです。その秘密を「相互尊重」という短い言葉で表現できましょう。以来、スイスと日本の関係はとてもよいものとなりました。「相違」が、誠実なコミュニケーション形成の障害とはならない事を証ししています。

数年の間に、われわれの経済的結びつきは深く強い関係になりました。日本はスイスにとり、アジアでの経済先導パートナーであり、約１５０の企業を日本に有するスイスは日本国にとり、日本で５番目に位置する大投資国なのです。私は、日本の勇敢な投資家たちが、ヨーロッパの心臓に横たわるスイス国を、ビジネスの適切な場として注視することを願ってやみません。過去四年間の商業取引上には、新しい活動力の芽生えがみられます。

２００４年に総理大臣の小泉氏と会見した折、貿易と投資の両面において二国が一層親密さを増し、経済関係をより強靭にしていくことを確認し合いました。輸出入税を含むこれらの事柄を促進的に協議する場としてJoint Study Group が創設されましたことは、両国にとりまして前進的な第一歩と言えましょう。

今われわれは、１４０年前のように、世界規模の転換期を迎えています。試練の時代です。経済的な助け合いを含め、まず基本に戻り物事を問い、時に即した答えを生み出す時期なのです。スイスと日本は、この新しい挑戦に備え貢献する準備があり、われわれの援助が役に立ち、助け合いの輪が将来に向けて広がっていくことを信じます。

スイス連邦政府は、日本との優れた関係が保たれるばかりではなく、さらに密接になってゆくことを確信しています。両国の相互活動を支援するＳＪＣＣに感謝致します。

連邦政府閣僚　ジョセフ・ダイス
スイス連邦政府　経済省大臣

Dear Members of the Chamber,
Dear Readers

Japan and Switzerland have more than 140 years of diplomatic relations, a history of friendship and mutual respect. When the Iwakura mission visited Switzerland in the summer of 1873, shortly after the “Meiji Restoration”, the members of the mission noticed with amazement that Switzerland was already highly industrialized despite its lack of natural resources and its limited size. The key to Switzerland’s success, they acknowledged, was an education-oriented nation building. Their experiences in Switzerland confirmed their conviction that Japan should focus on the development of its human resources in order to become a modern industrialized country. This remains true until today.

Nowadays, both countries are faced with the common challenge of a globalized economy and they both share many features common to mature economies. Now as then, education in a broad sense remains the key to their efforts to cope with the fast changing world. Both nations have understood that their success is based on fully functioning democratic institutions and well-educated skilled workforce. Necessary reforms are steadily realized without social or economic disruption.

Japan and Switzerland have shown that long-lasting friendly and mutually beneficial relations are absolutely possible between the two nations with different cultures and languages. Both nations share a tradition of seeking pragmatic consensus based on respect for each other. I believe this virtue will provide the friendship between Japan and Switzerland with a solid ground for many centuries to come.

阿部信泰

Nobuyasu Abe
Ambassador of Japan to Switzerland

商工会の会員の皆様、
読者の皆様、

日本とスイスは１４０年以上にわたる外交関係、友好と相互信頼の歴史を築いてきました。岩倉使節は明治維新直後の１８７３年夏にスイスを訪問しましたが、使節団一行は、スイスが天然資源に乏しく国の大きさも限られているにもかかわらず既に高度の工業化を達成していることに驚きました。一行は、スイスの成功の鍵は教育を重視した国造りにあることを見てとり、日本が新しい工業国家になるためには人材の育成に努めなければならないことに意を強くしました。この人材育成、教育重視の姿勢は現在まで続いております。

今日、日・スイス両国はグローバル化する経済の共通の課題に直面しており、成熟した経済に共通する種々の側面を共有しております。教育は、かつても、また現在においても、変化の早い世界に対処していくための鍵であります。両国は、成功の基礎は完全に機能する民主的な諸制度と良く教育された熟練労働力にあると考えております。諸々の必要な改革は、社会的・経済的な混乱もなく着実に実施されてきました。

日本とスイスは、文化や言語が異なっても相互に利益のある良好な関係を長続きさせることは全くもって可能であることを示しております。両国は相互の信頼関係に基づき現実的な解決策を探る伝統を持っているのです。私は、日・スイス両国のこの美徳により、両国の友好関係が今後さらに何世紀にもわたり続く確固たる基礎があると確信しております。

在スイス日本大使
阿部　信泰

Dear Members and Readers

I have the pleasure to present you the yearbook 2006 in which we look back on two anniversaries in the history of Swiss-Japanese relations.

In 2004 we were able to celebrate the 140th anniversary of the first Treaty of Friendship and Commerce between Switzerland and Japan. Last year marked the 20th anniversary of the Swiss-Japanese Chamber of Commerce.

Different as the two countries might be in size and culture, they were nevertheless able to establish a friendship based on mutual respect that was to last and to flourish until today – a proud achievement in a century and a half riven by political and ideological unrest.

The founding of the Swiss-Japanese Chamber of Commerce took place at a time when Japan was approaching the height of her economic might, second only to that of the United States. Despite the setback caused by the stock crash of 1990/91 and a decade of stagnation, Japan's inherent strengths have remained intact: functioning democratic institutions, the rule of law and a market economy based on a highly skilled labor force and high technology.

The signs of accelerating growth in Japan are encouraging and the Swiss economy is well positioned to gain from Japan's new vigor. It is our aim to further the benefits derived from mutual trade and cooperation. The ongoing process of globalization is a challenge for both countries but we are convinced, that Switzerland and Japan will remain at the forefront of economic and technological progress. Despite the many new players appearing on the world market we think that the potential of the Japanese market for Swiss enterprises is still far from being exhausted.

The same can be said with regard to the opportunities which Switzerland has to offer for Japanese enterprises' intent on developing their international activities.

Despite their obvious differences in appearance, both countries rely on the highest technological and quality standards for their products. This formula has been successful in coping with the challenges of a changing world so far and it will be crucial for the well-being of both nations in the future.

We are confident that Switzerland and Japan will continue and deepen their long-standing friendship, providing our children with an example of mutual respect and sympathy as our predecessors have done so for us.

Wegmann

Henry Wegmann
President, Swiss-Japanese Chamber of Commerce

会員各位及び読者の皆様

スイスと日本の相互活動機関創設からこれまでの２年間を振り返る、２００６年報を皆様にご紹介できますことをたいへん嬉しく思います。

２００４年にわたくしたちは、スイスと日本のあいだで初めて調印された友好／通商条約の１４０周年記念を祝う事ができました。
また昨年は、スイスと日本の商工会議所設立２０周年記念を迎えております。
文化や国の規模が異なるにもかかわらず、わたしたちは、相互尊重を土台にして、今日も尚絶えることなく繁栄し続ける友好関係を築いたのです。

日本が経済力においてアメリカの次に位置付けるほどの力を養い始めていた頃に、スイスと日本の間で商工会議所が創設されました。１９９０年と９１年の株式市場倒壊や１０年不景気による逆行にもかかわらず、日本固有の頑強さは、高度な研究開発力と優れた技術を基に、民主主義社会制度としての法と経済市場を活動させ、その影響から逃れました。
日本が早い速度で威力を拡大している様子は、スイス経済に活性化を生じさせ、良い影響をもたらしたました。
相互貿易と国際交流を通し、そこから多くの恩恵を派生させることが、われわれの目的です。
世界に関与していく前進行動は、両国にとりましてもチャレンジ、つまり挑戦と言えましょう。しかし私は、このような世界状況下においても、スイスと日本が経済および技術開発において重要な位置を占めて行くであろうことを確信しています。
世界市場には、たくさんの新しい活動国が出現します。が、スイス国にとりまして、日本市場が潜在的に所有する素質は、われわれに興味を抱かせ続けます。
同じように，スイスも日本に対し、国際的活動に向けて力を注ぐことを働きかけなければならないでしょう。

明らかな相違をみせながらも両国は、生産品の優秀な技術と品質において信頼を裏切りません。この定則は、世界変動への挑戦の手本として良い結果を引き出しています。そしてこれは、スイスと日本の将来の繁栄にとり、きわめて重大な事柄です。
両国が、長い年月育んできた友好関係をさらに深めてゆき、前任者が私たちに示してくれたように、我々も後を継ぐ子供たちへ、相互尊重と思いやりの大切さを手本として残していかれることを、かたく信じます。

ヘンリー・ヴェクマン
スイス一日本商工会議所会長

THE FIRST JAPANESE MISSIONS TO SWITZERLAND
By Dr. Roger Mottini

The Tokugawa mission of 1867

With the establishment of diplomatic relations in 1864, Japanese interest in Switzerland started to develop. Within Japan, the political conflict between the followers of the feudal government around the Tokugawa Shogun and their political enemies' intent on restoring imperial rule was in its final stage. The conservative Shogunate was already on the defensive and fighting for its survival against the Southern Domains of Chōshū, Satsuma, Tosa and Hizen (Inoue 1993: 304).

Despite their political differences, however, both sides shared a keen interest to know more about the Western countries with which Japan now had diplomatic relations. The best opportunities to gather information were found at the World Exhibitions. In 1867 the World Exposition of Paris opened its doors and the Shogunate, already on the verge of collapse, saw this as an opportunity to represent Japan towards the outside world and to strengthen its badly damaged reputation at home. With this in mind, a mission led by Tokugawa Akitake (1853–1910), the younger brother of the Shogun, Tokugawa Yoshinobu (1837–1913). Much to the dismay of the Tokugawa mission, yet another delegation from Japan had already arrived in Paris, sent there by the anti-Shogunal lord of Satsuma. None of the two parties enjoyed the authority to claim an exclusive right of representing their country, and thus Japan was present with two delegations at the exposition.

After the World Exhibition in Paris, the Tokugawa mission left France for Switzerland crossing the border at Basle on September 3. In the diary kept by Shibusawa Eiichi (1840–1931)[1], a member of the delegation, we can read that the party enjoyed the fresh evening breeze above the bank of the Rhine river. After their arrival the Japanese visited the "place of prayer and sermons".

[1] During the journey he came to the conclusion that the base of national power was rooted in economic potential; after his return he became an entrepreneur and founded the Tokyo Chamber of Commerce, the first such institution in Japan (Ueda 1990: 615).

The following day the mission boarded a train which took them to Berne where they attended a reception given in their honour by the President of the Swiss Confederation, Mr. Constant Fornerod.

On September 6, 1867, the Japanese delegation was invited to observe a military exercise in the vicinity of Thun. Being members of a proud warrior class at home, the Japanese seemed to have been very impressed by the skills of the Swiss militia soldiers. Shibusawa described Switzerland's militia system:

> "This system relies on conscripted men from the peasantry; the drafted men are employed according to their capabilities. Within a short time, an army of two hundred thousand men can thus be mobilised."
>
> (Plutschow 1978: 516)

Overall, Shibusawa's report did not go into details, recording mainly the daily schedule and the persons whom the members of the delegation met. There was, however, a peculiarity in the generally dry report that catches the eye of the reader; whenever the subject of his observations turned to a view of Swiss landscapes, Shibusawa's restrained tone became emotional, even poetic. Apparently he was very fond of what he saw. The Swiss hosts seemed to have been eager provide their guests with as many opportunities as possible to enjoy breathtaking views – a task not too difficult to fulfil around Berne. The effect of the Swiss endeavour found a clear response in Shibusawa's diary. The views around Berne and Thun are described by him as "heavenly beautiful" (Plutschow 1978: 517).

On September 8, the delegation arrived in Geneva, the "watchmakers' capital" as the report remarks; Geneva struck Shibusawa as a very rich city, also called the 'little Paris', an appropriate expression according to him. The next stop on their journey was Neuchâtel where they met with Aimé Humbert the head of the Swiss mission to Japan in 1863/64.

Back in Berne, the Tokugawa mission was joined by Kurimoto Joun (1822–1897), the Shogunate's representative in Paris. On September 13, 1867, the Japanese left Switzerland continuing their journey northwards to the Netherlands.

Kurimoto himself remained behind and spent some time in Switzerland before he returned to Japan. During his stay he undertook excursions into the Alps around Berne – the first Japanese alpinist in Switzerland.[2] In his autobiography, he remembered Switzerland as a country of extraordinary beauty with landscapes dominated by waterfalls and snow-covered mountain peaks. He also noticed masses of foreign tourists trying to escape the summer heat in the plains (Yamasaki 1986: 285).

While the representatives of the feudal government tried to shore up its reputation abroad, things back home were spinning out of control. The Shogun and his allies had lost any support among the Japanese population and the Shogunal troops were routed by the Imperial forces. On October 14, 1867, the last Shogun, Tokugawa Yoshinobu, offered his resignation to the Emperor who promptly accepted (Inoue 1993: 316, 318).

The Swiss press was not in a position to describe and analyse the intricate political situation in Japan. The public could however get some information from a report released by Kurimoto's office in Paris and published in the Federal Bulletin, the official information platform of the Swiss Government (Bundesblatt 1868/I: 198–203). The report began with a brief survey of the history of the Tokugawa Shogunate and went on to describe some peculiarities of that political system. The note ended with the conclusion that this system brought Japan 250 years of internal peace and order. Trying to dispel foreign worries with regard to Japan's international relations, the note gave assurances that the new government would continue to respect the existing treaties concluded by the

[2] Kurimoto apparently loved nature and adventure. During his career as an official of the Shogunate he visited the islands of Etorofu and Kunashiri north of Hokkaido in 1862. He also travelled to Sakhalin and went as far as the 40th parallel on that island, which was heavily disputed between Japan and Russia (Yamasaki 1986: 286).

Shogunate. It was probably this point which prompted the Swiss Government to publish this diplomatic report in order to assure the business community about Japan's future course.

The Iwakura mission of 1873

The new Imperial Government following the Shogunate was crucial for Japan's transition from a feudal agrarian society to a modern nation-state. This era is known in Japanese history under the name of "Meiji" (Enlightened Rule).

The new Imperial Government was dominated by lower ranking but erudite and rather young (average age 33 years) samurai from the southern feudal domains of Satsuma, Chōshū, Tosa and Hizen. Their biggest worries concerned the unity and independence of Japan in an age of fierce imperialistic competition between the great powers. They came to the conclusion that the best way to face these challenges and to modernize Japan was to learn more about the outside world and to adapt to the new realities.

Leading members of the Iwakura mission; in traditional clothing: count Iwakura.

As a consequence, the Japanese Government of the Meiji embarked on a highly ambitious and unusual strategy. In 1871, a large and very high-ranking delegation headed by the court noble count Iwakura Tomomi (1825–1883) left Japan for the countries with which Japan already had established formal relations. The mission was to last nearly two years!

Among the members of the delegation were several ministers, who were to play key roles in shaping Meiji-Japan's policy.

Leading members of the Meiji Government in the Iwakura mission:

Origin	Name/First Name	From/To
Imperial court	Iwakura Tomomi	1825–1883
Imperial court	Sanjō Sanetomo	1837–1891
Satsuma	Ōkubo Toshimichi	1830–1878
Satsuma	Saigō Takamori	1828–1877
Satsuma	Matsukata Masayoshi	1837–1924
Satsuma	Terashima Munenori	1833–1893
Satsuma	Godai Tomoatsu	1835–1885
Satsuma	Kuroda Kiyotaka	1840–1900
Chōshū	Itō Hirobumi	1841–1909
Chōshū	Inoue Kaoru	1835–1915
Chōshū	Ōmura Masujirō	1841–1869
Chōshū	Kido Takayoshi	1833–1877
Chōshū	Yamagata Aritomo	1838–1922
Tosa	Itagaki Taisuke	1837–1919
Tosa	Gotō Shōjirō	1837–1897
Hizen	Etō Shimpei	1834–1874
Hizen	Ōkuma Shigenobu	1838–1922
Hizen	Soejima Taneomi	1832–1899

The mission pursued two objectives: the first one consisted in the attempt to re-negotiate the existing treaties which were actually discriminating against Japan; the second, and more realistic goal, was to gather as much information as possible about all relevant aspects of modernization and nation-building.

In order to increase the efficiency of this intelligence-gathering endeavour, the delegation was divided into three groups, the first one focussed on legal aspects of a host country, the second one was concerned with questions of economy, taxation and finance. The third group was to look at education in general and business and science training in particular (Beasley 1972: 367–368).

Given the weak position of Japan at the time, the attempt to re-negotiate the unequal treaties was doomed to failure and the members of the Iwakura mission were not given to illusions about the difficulties of their task.

The Government of the United States, their first stop, even refused to discuss a possible revision of the existing treaties between the two countries. Under these circumstances, the intelligence-gathering aspect of the journey became the first priority. With nearly fifty persons, the delegation was huge, comprising a large number of young students, among them five girls aged between six and fifteen years. These young people were placed at host families and learning institutions in order to get a thoroughly Western-style education.

The mass of information collected during the trip was later edited by the mission's secretary, Kume Kunitake (1839–1931), and published in five volumes as a reference book for a wider public. Its style is a mixture of travel guidebook and illustrated encyclopedia. This was the first truly comprehensive Japanese report on Switzerland as well, providing a wealth of data and many pictures of the different places they visited. The majority of the pictures show views of towns and villages.

On January 5, 1873, the 'Neue Zürcher Zeitung' ran a headline about the mission expected to arrive in the summer. The newspaper reported that the

purpose of the visit was a possible revision of the existing Swiss-Japanese treaty of Friendship and Commerce concluded in 1864. Article 17 of the treaty foresaw the possibility of such a revision as early as June 1, 1873, only with mutual consent, however.

The Iwakura mission entered Switzerland on June 19, 1873, at Romanshorn aboard a ferry arriving from Lindau on the German side of Lake Constance; the Japanese delegation was coming from Vienna where they visited the World Exposition. Because the ferry was delayed the guests missed their train and had to wait for more than three hours before boarding the next train to Frauenfeld, Winterthur and Zurich (Pantzer 2002: 363).

The Iwakura report starts with the exact geographic location of Switzerland, a summary of Swiss history, the political structure and a wealth of demographic as well as geographic and economic data (going as far as giving the total number of cows, sheep and pigs). This report provides a stark contrast to the cursory account given by the former Tokugawa delegation. In the Iwakura report the

The University of Zurich.

Japanese reader was confronted with a wealth of detailed information. The style was oscillating between dry descriptions of facts and personal impressions gained during the journey. In the case of Switzerland for example, the reader was informed about the different regions and cantons, their population's characteristics (size, confession, languages) as well as particular customs and traditions. No detail seemed to have been too trivial to be mentioned; with regard to the President of the Swiss Confederation, the report did even mention his yearly salary (2,400 Mexican silverdollars, Kume 1982: 55). Detail, however, does not compensate for some mistakes in the report mainly in connection with the names of some places.

The report pays special attention to the religious divide between the Protestant and Catholic regions in the country with a clear bias towards the Protestant cause (Pantzer 2002: 353-355); little wonder if one keeps in mind that the Swiss Government of that time was predominantly Protestant and the mission's official guides both came from Protestant areas: Hermann Siber from Zurich and Aimé Humbert from Neuchâtel. Siber, Vice-Consul in Yokohama, who spoke fluently Japanese acted as an interpreter for the mission.

Another eye-catching feature of the reporting are the numerous descriptions of sceneries in a way of near euphoria as if describing paradise (for example Pantzer 2002: 358, 384, 406).

Without any prejudice or intent of commenting or judging their subject, the Japanese guests did not shy away from topics that might be potentially troublesome at home. Being brought up in a feudal society and belonging to a privileged aristocracy, the members of the mission did nevertheless describe the Swiss system of direct democracy in great detail. The Swiss constitution, the report went on to explain, was adopted in 1848 and committed to a "confederal policy", that is, the country is divided into 25 cantons, each one with its own constitution. In three of them, Uri, Unterwalden and Appenzell, all men aged twenty or older assemble under the blue sky in order to decide the laws and elect the Government (Pantzer 2002: 354).

The foreign-policy vision of Switzerland, according to the report, rests on three pillars: the defence of national independence, no infringement on the rights of other nations and protection against foreign intervention into domestic politics (Pantzer 2002: 356–357). In order to achieve these objectives Switzerland possesses strong military capabilities. Military matters were another focal point of interest for the Japanese. With regard to the Swiss army the Iwakura report explained its role in the concept of armed neutrality as repelling an invading enemy without pursuing him across the border. The militia system was compared with the functioning of a fire brigade: "Each man has his equipment and rifle ready at home and in case of an attack the ordinary citizen becomes a soldier immediately. Despite being a small country, so goes the conclusion, the Swiss army enjoys a high reputation and every attack will be met with determined resistance" (Pantzer 2002: 357).

Switzerland's economy was equally thoroughly scrutinized and presented something of a riddle to the Japanese. The report concludes:

View of the Federal Parliament Building in Berne.

> "With nearly half of the Swiss population being farmers, the country must be seen as agrarian despite the worldwide reputation of Switzerland's technical products" (Pantzer 2002: 358–360).

The reason for Switzerland's early industrialization is attributed to the poor soil and the difficult traffic conditions due to the topography. As a result, the Swiss economy specialized early on in technical products of a high value typified by the world-famous watches. Another feature caught the mission's attention. According to the report wealth seemed to be distributed rather equally as there were "only very few poor families" (Pantzer 2002: 362). After this general introduction, the tone of the report changed and assumed the form of a travel diary describing in every detail what caught their eyes.

As mentioned above, the mission took the train from Romanshorn to Zurich on the first day of arrival. In the report a detailed description of the landscape of the Protestant (sic) canton of Thurgau unfolds: hilly, agrarian economy, wooden houses – quite like in Japan.

The following day (June 20, 1873) was mainly spent in Zurich and started with several visits to schools, the University and the Polytechnikum; in their report Zurich was not only described as an economic hub, with industries producing textiles, machinery and musical instruments among others. Zurich, according to the Japanese visitors, is also a place of education and formation. The report mentions that boys and girls carrying books under their arms can be seen everywhere in the city. After a statistical survey the reader is provided with an outline of the school system of Zurich including the whole curriculum of the different schools starting with elementary school and ending with the university.

In the afternoon the mission took the train to Berne stopping on the way in Baden and Aarau. Again, the report describes in every possible detail what they saw during their trip. The canton of Berne figured, like Zurich, prominently in their account, with a host of data.

On June 21, Paul Ceresole (1832–1905), the President of the Swiss Confederation, and four other members of the Government gave a reception for Count Iwakura and his delegation. During the audience, the different positions of the two countries became evident: the Swiss side wanted a treaty revision that would lead to increased bilateral trade whereas Iwakura advocated a more balanced treaty based on equal rights (Pantzer 2002: 490–491).

As none of the two countries was in a position to impose its will on the other, the negotiations turned out to be rather symbolic and a revision of the existing treaty was not a topic anymore. Despite the diplomatic failure, Iwakura and his delegates seemed to enjoy their stay in the Swiss capital very much because they stayed longer than planned. Again, the schedule of the mission was packed with visits to a hydroelectric power station on the Aare river and a school.

On June 22 the delegation left Berne for Thun where they witnessed a military exercise before continuing to Interlaken. Travelling through the Oberland the report gives a nearly euphoric description of the scenery dominated by snow-

View of Lucerne.

covered peaks and green lakes. After crossing the Brünig pass the delegation arrived late at night in Sarnen warmly welcomed by the population ringing bells and holding torches and lanterns. Here at a place of historic importance, the report tells the saga of William Tell and the Rütli Oath.

Another tourist highlight of the mission's journey took place between July 23 and 24, 1873. In Lucerne the delegation was joined by the President of the Swiss Confederation, Ceresole. Together they boarded a steamboat to Vitznau where the newly constructed rack railway up to the Rigi Kulm was inaugurated with the Japanese envoys as honorary guests. The report describes in detail the revolutionary technology of the railway system developed by Niklaus Riggenbach (1817–1899) as well as the panorama visible from the Rigi Kulm.

From July 24 to 29 the mission was back in Berne and busy with official talks visiting schools, museums and some sightseeing before they left for Geneva on July 29 with a stopover in Fribourg and Lausanne.

In Lausanne the mission boarded a steamboat and sailed along the coast of Lake Geneva. After their long journey around the world the members of the Iwakura mission seemed to enjoy the last part of their tour as a relaxing time. The Japanese guests stayed for nearly two weeks in Geneva, at that time the largest Swiss city. Days of leisure alternated with days of frantic activities like July 1 when the mission visited the watchmakers' ateliers of Patek & Philippe. The process of watchmaking was minutely described including particularities of the working environment:

> "... The whole process requires utmost precision and in order to ensure a bright light the number of windows is equally important. No political or religious talk is allowed inside the atelier because both lead to noisy disputes. After completion of a watch, those costing more than 700 francs undergo further testing in order to make sure that differences in temperature are not causing time differences. The method consists in placing the watch during 24 hours between ice cubes and afterwards for

> another 24 hours in a cabinet with a temperature of 120 degrees Celsius. The production process is complete only if this method does not result in the slightest difference." (Pantzer 2002: 430).

This example gives us an impression about the style in the Iwakura report when it is dealing with factual reporting from visits of institutions like factories, schools or government agencies. With regard to the latter a visit of the Geneva Cantonal Government administration yielded the following insight:

> "If a lot of easy tasks need to be done and not enough secretaries are available, then those of other departments are called upon when they are not busy. *Because if a bureaucrat has nothing to do, he will get bored and bad habits like this might spread to others in the office.*" (This passage is highlighted in the original report as well, Pantzer 2002: 435).

On July 9, 1873, a telegram from the Meiji Government reached its mission in Geneva urging Iwakura and his fellow delegates to cut short their journey and to return to Tokyo as quickly as possible.[3] Despite this telegram, the delegation took its time to prepare for leave. They attended a series of invitations and went on excursions on and around Lake Geneva enjoying the last and relaxing days of their political journey.

It was only a week later, on July 15, when they left Switzerland on a train to Marseille from where they returned back home to Japan.

With the departure of the Iwakura mission ended the first and official phase of Swiss-Japanese encounter.

[3] The planned visit to Spain and Portugal, their next destinations, had to be cancelled due to domestic unrest in the two countries. A foreign-policy dispute amongst the other members of the Government in Tokyo was the other reason why they were called back.

With regard to Switzerland no report as comprehensive as the Iwakura report was to be published in Japanese during the Meiji era (1868–1912). The Alpine Republic merely became a metaphor in the political discussion of Meiji-Japan (see Morita and Meyer in this book).

On the Swiss side, the best report on Japan during that time was doubtless Aimé Humbert's work published in Paris. Despite the quality of his work, however, Japan became not a topic of mainstream academic research in Switzerland (see Dallais in this book).

Swiss interests with regard to Japan were primarily commercial and reporting was mostly of an anecdotal nature. To speak with Jean-Jacques Rousseau (1712–1778) from Geneva: "… they (the European traders) are more interested in filling their purses than their heads" (cited in: Kapitza 1990 vol. 2: 492). This need not to be true anymore and there is still a lot of rewarding research to be done.

The rack railway to the Rigi Kulm at Vitznau.

Roger Mottini, born 1959 in St. Moritz GR. Graduation from the University of St. Gallen in 1984 with a Master's degree in international relations. 1987–1988 postgraduate studies at the Universty of Geneva (IUHEI) with a focus on international security policy. From 1990 to 1992, research fellow at the University of Tokyo (Tōdai) on a grant from the Ministry of Education of Japan (Monbushō). 1998 PhD from the University of St. Gallen. Dissertation about Swiss-Japanese relations during the Meiji era (1868–1912).

Selected Bibliography

Beasley William G.
1972 "The Meiji Restoration", Stanford: Stanford University.

Bundesblatt der Schweizerischen Eidgenossenschaft
1868 Band I. Bern: EDMZ.

Inoue Kiyoshi
1993 "Geschichte Japans", Frankfurt a.M.: Campus.

Kapitza Peter (ed.)
1990 "Japan in Europa: Texte und Bilddokumente zur europäischen Japankenntnis von Marco Polo bis Wilhelm v. Humboldt", 2 vols., München.

Kume Kunitake, Tanaka Akira (ed.)
1982 "Tokumei zenken taishi Bei-Ō kairan jikki 5" (authentic report of the extraordinary official mission to America and Europe, vol. 5), Tokyo: Iwanami shoten.

Pantzer Peter (ed.)
2002 "Die Iwakura-Mission: das Logbuch des Kume Kunitake über den Besuch der japanischen Sondergesandtschaft in Deutschland, Österreich und der Schweiz im Jahre 1873", München: Iudicium.

Plutschow Herbert E.
1978 "Bericht über den ersten japanischen Besuch in der Schweiz 1867", in: *Schweizer Zeitschrift für Geschichte,* Jg. 28, Zürich 1978.

Ueda Seishō et al. (eds.)
1990 "Konsaisu nihonjin jinmei jiten" (Concise – biographical reference manual to Japanese names), 2nd rev. edition, Tokyo.

Yamasaki Yasuji
1986 "Nihon tozanshi" (History of Japanese Alpinism), Tokyo.

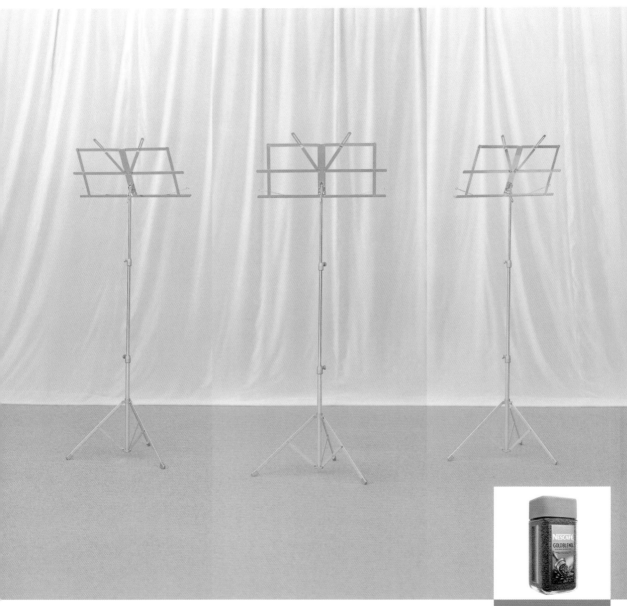

TŌHAKU'S "PINE TREES" – JAPAN'S FOREMOST NATIONAL TREASURE IN ZURICH

By Dr. Katharina Epprecht

Hasegawa Tōhaku (1539–1610) is to the Japanese what Rembrandt is to the Dutch. Although hardly known in the West, Hasegawa Tōhaku's work regularly comes in on top of any inquiry among the Japanese asked to name the most significant work of traditional painting in Japan. So it had to be regarded as a miracle when in 2001 Japan allowed that a considerable part of Tōhaku's finest paintings leave the country in order to be displayed abroad, that is in Zurich – and only there –, because these treasures are far too precious to let them travel around and too sensitive to be exposed to light for more than a few weeks a year. The show in the Museum Rietberg was the world's first ever comprehensive exhibition dedicated to Tōhaku.

The exhibition turned out to be a huge success with more than eight hundred people visiting it on an average day (in a town of about 365,000 inhabitants). Although not many Swiss knew anything about Tōhaku and his work, the visitors probably felt immediately upon entering the exhibition room that they were looking at the works of a genius. Tōhaku's paintings struck a chord with the hearts of modern-day people longing for peace of mind and spiritual balance in a fast changing world. The paintings overwhelm the visitor with an atmosphere of peacefulness and calm serenity; all worldly concerns seem to fade away.

Tōhaku's ink compositions of his maturity are exemplified to perfection by the "Pine Trees". It is the most important and celebrated painting in ink to be created in the country's history. My biggest concern was, that western people could probably not understand why this rather unspectacular painting was praised as Japan's soul and paramount among its National Treasures. However, contrary to my fears, that this unique painting might not be understood, the atmosphere in the room displaying the "Pine Trees" was always one of solemn silence even during the busiest hours. The visitors were visibly struck by the painting and they intuitively grasped the essence of this masterpiece. This work consists of two screens showing several groups of pine trees rising from a sea of mist. By painting the pine trees with only a few brush strokes, Tōhaku succeeded in a unique way to give emptiness in relation to form a higher importance and as such directing every human's perception towards transcendency. This way of percep-

tion found its way into the headlines of the newspapers covering the exhibition: "Nature as a metapher of the spiritual", "Master of the void", "Reduction to the essence", "The perfection of simplicity" and "Happy who lives in the Pine Forest". Whatever our interpretations, they are culturally relative and of minor importance in the face of eternity as the touching words of an old lady spoken without pathos in front of the "Pine Trees" do symbolize, "now I am able to die peacefully".

The religion scientist Yamaori Tetsuo considers the "Pine Trees" to be the ultimate expression of Japanese religious and aesthetic sensitivity. This sensitivity, according to his view, is formed by Buddhist and animistic ideas to consider the void space between the pine trees as the true essence of the picture: "Here the features of the landscape seem to melt into the void behind them. It is almost as if nature itself was being obliterated by some greater power … The pine forest is annihilating itself in a phenomenon suggestive of the Buddha's final nirvana …" Yamaori, however, does not only interpret the "Pine Trees" as a metaphor for Buddhahood, he recognizes elements of Shintō as well: "… the heavenly gods appear suddenly, perform various heavenly acts, and eventually disappear, retiring to another realm. … they vanish from this world and dwell hidden in the invisible background of the cosmos. … Hasegawa Tōhaku's pine forest is the most radical expression of the aesthetic ideal that runs through this religion – feeling of harmony and oneness with nature. In the achievement of this

Pine Trees, National Treasure, Hasegawa Tōhaku (1539–1610)
Pair of six-fold screens, Ink on paper, 155 x 345 cm each
(© National Museum, Tokyo).

ideal, the boundaries between nature, gods and humanity dissolve, giving rise to a sense of impermanence and of beauty of nothingness – in other words, a momentary nirvana."[1]

Tōhaku's life

Not much is known about Tōhaku's life, he remains largely hidden behind several different names he assumed during his career.

Of modest origin, Tōhaku was born 1539 in Nanao, a village on the Noto peninsula in Western Japan at a time, when the Renaissance period in Europe was drawing towards an end. Michelangelo Buonarroti (1475–1564) was already in his sixties and had his work on the Sixtine Chapel completed years ago.

In Japan, Tōhaku left his native village probably around 1571 and moved to Kyōto, seat of the Emperor and Japan's capital of the arts. It is assumed that he was recommended by the monks of his native village to their brethren in Kyōto; there Tōhaku lived in a temple of the Nichiren school of Buddhism, presumed to be the Honpōji. The abbot of the temple, Nittsū Shōnin (1549–1608), became his personal friend and mentor. Both men shared an interest in painting,

[1] Yamaori Tetsuo, *Nature and Religion*, in: Japan Echo, Vol. 32, No. 4, August 2005, p. 50–55.

which they regularly discussed. The fruits of these discussions are recorded for posterity in Nittsū's "Tōhaku's View on Painting" of 1592. Besides proving Tōhaku with intellectual stimulation, Nittsū also introduced the artist to the legendary master of tea ceremony, Sen Rikyū (1522–1591), who like Nittsū, also came from a merchant family from Sakai, a harbor town about sixty kilometres south of Kyōto. As the most important gateway for the trade with China, the merchants of Sakai had become extremely rich and were eager to commission works of fine art.

The tea aesthetic as expounded by Rikyū emphasised the perfection of simplicity and was to assume ever greater importance for Tōhaku. Exponents of this aesthetic saw beauty in the natural, the unfinished and the modest. As far as painting was concerned, this ideal was fulfilled by Chinese ink paintings of the 13th and 14th centuries from Song and Yuan periods, as well as some Japanese monk painters of the 15th century who had been inspired by this deliberately non-academic style.

In the following years, Tōhaku spent most of his life in Kyōto, where he got prestigious commissions among others by the Zen monasteries, Daitokuji and Myōshinji. Tōhaku died 1610, probably in Kyōto, however his grave is unknown as well as the circumstances of his death.

Historical Background

Tōhaku's life fell into a period of great political upheaval. A profound power shift was taking place with the court nobility (kuge) losing most of their political power to the upcoming warrior class (buke); the latter, fragmented and locked into a merciless struggle for dominance, ravaged the country during the Muromachi period (1333–1568). Three powerful warlords eventually ended this internecine warfare and dominated the political landscape of what was to be called the Momoyama period (1568–1615). The expression "momoyama" (peach mountain) is derived from a hill south of Kyōto where the warlord Toyotomi Hideyoshi (1535–1598) built his castle which was destroyed in 1622 by his enemies; at its place peach trees were planted and the resulting landscape came to symbolize

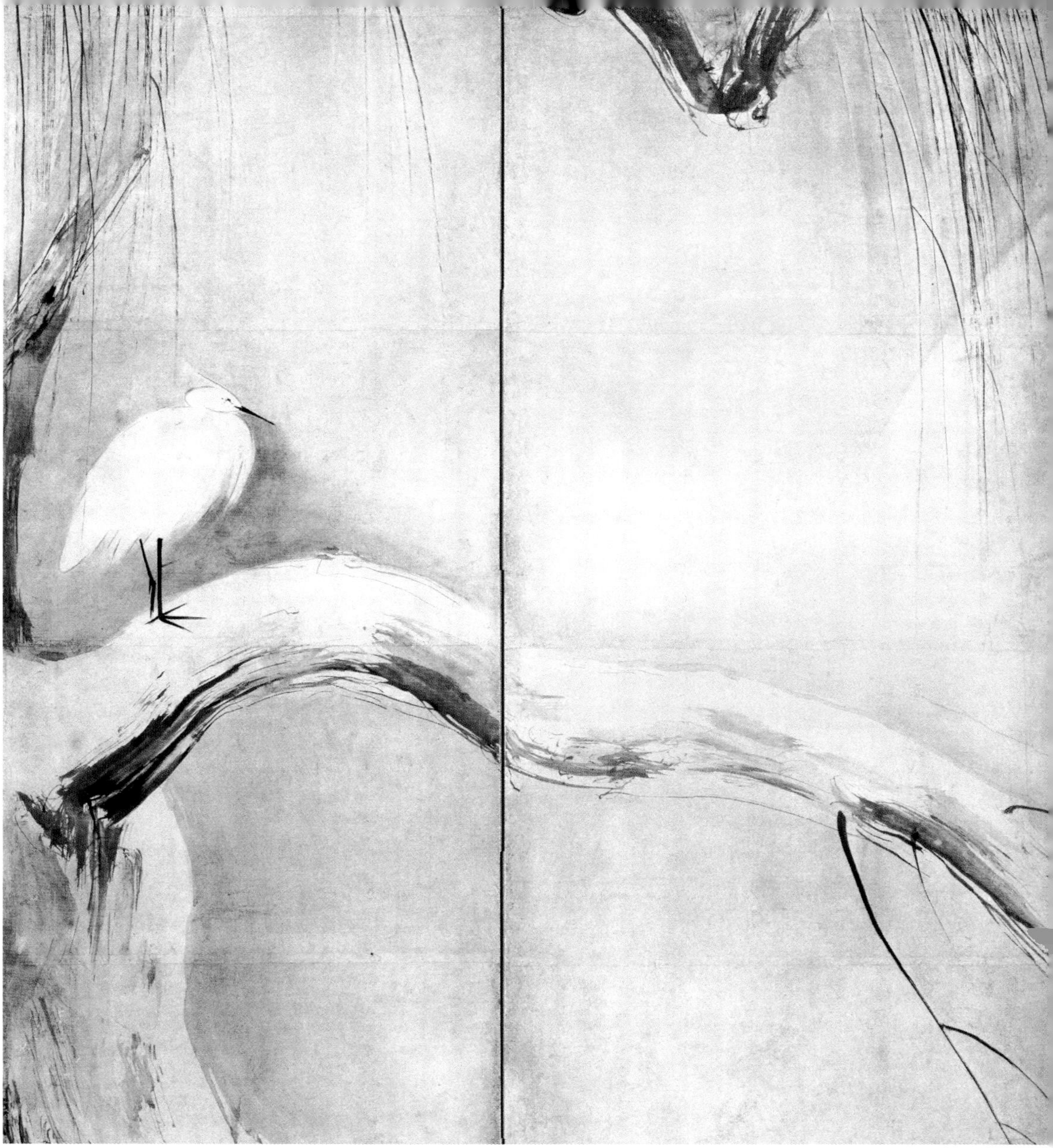

the spirit of the Momoyama period: a hill gleaming with peach trees in full blossom – albeit only for a short time.

The period began with Oda Nobunaga (1534–1584), a general from Owari who occupied Kyōto in 1568 and ending the grip on power of the Ashikaga family in 1573. After the assassination of Nobunaga and his son in 1582, his

Eagret on a Willow Tree, Hasegawa Tōhaku (1539–1610)
Detail of a six-fold screen, Ink on paper, 152 x 370 cm
(© Idemitsu Museum, Tokyo).

lieutenant Hideyoshi took the reins. Nobunaga and Hideyoshi were both of humble origin and they tried to compensate for that with a display of extraordinary luxury and art. Hideyoshi's hubris led him to invade Korea in 1592 and 1597 in an attempt to conquer China; both military expeditions ended in failure. After Hideyoshi's death in 1598, Tokugawa Ieyasu (1542–1616), the scion of an old and noble family, defeated his adversaries in the decisive battle of Sekigahara (1600); in 1603 he declared himself Shōgun (Generalissimus) and founded the Tokugawa shogunate which was to last until 1868. With the violent death of Hideyori (1593–1615), Hideyoshi's son, the Momoyama period ended giving way to the "Edo" period under Tokugawa rule.

Another important event during Tōhaku's lifetime was the arrival of the first Europeans in 1543; they were Portuguese merchants shipwrecked on the shores of Tanegashima, a small Japanese island south of Kyūshū. In their footsteps followed Catholic missionaries from Portugal and Spain who eagerly and successfully spread the gospel among the population in Southern Japan. This "Christian century" (1549–1639) was terminated by the Tokugawa shogunate with military force, fearing that the new faith might become a threat to the established social and political order.

Under Tokugawa rule Japan pursued a policy of near absolute isolation from the rest of the world. This policy of closure, called "sakoku", resulted in more than two centuries of internal peace and cultural

Sparrows in a Tree, Hasegawa Tōhaku (1539–1610)
Hanging scroll, Colors on silk, 92 x 36 cm
(© Private collection Shimane Prefecture).

bloom, however at the expense of technological and economic progress as well as social mobility.

Evolution of the Momoyama style

The Momoyama period (1568–1615) is considered as the epoch marking Japan's passage from the medieval to the early modern era. During that time of political transformation and relative openness an extraordinary efflorescence of the arts took place. The painting of that period can be characterized as spacious and decorative; the new rulers asked for large wall paintings that were conceived as fitting expressions of their wealth and influence.

The contrast between Tōhaku's brilliantly simple ink compositions and the fashionable artistic taste of the time as represented by the Kano School and loved by the powerful of the land could not have been greater. Tōhaku's contemporary, Kano Eitoku (1543–1590), was particularly successful. Thanks to a well-trained team of painters he received most of the major commissions. His large-format pictures appealed particularly to the military rulers Oda Nobunaga and Toyotomi Hideyoshi, who were important patrons. Eitoku's colourful scenes painted onto lavishly guilded wall and door panels decorated their imposing fortified palaces for fifty years. Other powerful personages were anxious to follow the fashion set by Nobunaga and Hideyoshi, and also commissioned large wall paintings. Unfortunately, many of Kano Eitoku's works disappeared together with the castles destroyed during the endless struggles for power among the different warlords. By the time Tōhaku was able to build up his own well-organised workshop, and when Kano Eitoku unexpectedly died at a much too young age, Tōhaku caught the chance to seize more and more prestigious commissions.

The works of Eitoku and Tōhaku can be regarded as the opposing poles of Momoyama painting, clearly visible when looking at Eitoku's "Lions" and Tōhaku's "Pine Trees". The two works testify to the enormous range of styles during that period with regard to the use of colour and gold and also when considering the atmosphere of the two paintings. On one side, the "Lions" exudes a lively, even noisy and boastful atmosphere, while the "Pine Trees" is in a quiet, self-content, even detached mood. Eitoku's "Lions" give an impression of energy, power and supreme self-confidence, reflecting the spirit of the newly emerging military elite of that time. His paintings were probably closer to the 'zeitgeist' of that era. On the other side, Tōhaku's paintings of nature are oscillating between a mysterious detachment and a hilarious and lively lightness.

If one looks at Tōhaku's early pictures, with their minutely painted details, in comparison with the bold ink compositions of his mature later work, it is easy understandable why there had been so many persistent doubts whether all these works had been by the same person. Recent research has dispelled all doubts and the contrasts can be recognised as proofs of his exceptional genius and his faculty of rising to the requirements of the most diverse tasks. The high quality of Tōhaku's art manifests itself in all manners and styles of his painting. He may immortalize the face of a contemporary, he may observe young and hungry sparrows, he may try to search out the mystery of a quiet forest, or he may depict the writhing bodies of dragons on the ceiling of a sacred building – he is always a visionary.

What are the criteria of Tōhaku's style? What are the features equally common to a small silk scroll painted meticulously in colours such as "Sparrows in a Tree" and to "Eagret on a Willow Tree" painted in monochrome ink on a large folding screen? The first picture shows a minutely and carefully descriptive view of nature, the second is a summarily suggestive and rather abstract delineation. These observations are external, technical and stylistic differences. Yet with regard to the artist's own vision, the two pictures are very similar. Both of them reflect the same attitude of the artist towards nature and atmosphere. He respects the essence of the subject of his painting, he keeps his distance from it and does not degrade it to a mere object lying before his eyes. Tōhaku seems to be always endeavouring to get at the core of his motif. The subjects of his pictures are never stereotypes. Tōhaku is always in search of their innermost essence, and in the end we find in his entire work the same harmonious and lyrical tone.

Katharina Epprecht, 1961, studied European and East Asian Art History at the Universities of Zurich and Kyōto. Several scholarships from the Japanese Government enabled her to focus her research on Japanese Art. Hasegawa Tōhaku's oeuvre was the subject of her Ph.D. dissertation. Since 1997 she works as curator of Japanese Art at the Museum Rietberg Zurich. In 2001 she was responsible for the concept and realization of the exhibition "Tōhaku – Highlights of Japanese Painting of the 16th century". At present she prepares an exhibition with precious loans from Japan on "Kannon Bosatsu", the Bodhisattva of Compassion, for the new annex building of the Museum Rietberg, opening in February 2007.

Sannomaru-Shozokan (© The Museum of the Imperial Collections).

A SWISS-JAPANESE HIGH-TECH PARTNERSHIP AS A STEPPING-STONE FOR THE ASIAN MARKET

By Dr. Erich Stuhlträger, BRAINFORCE AG, Zurich

1. Introduction

A widespread prejudice in the West regarding Asian competitors alleges that they are just copying Western technology. This stereotype view can also be found in Switzerland, saying that Swiss products are copied by Asian competitors who sell them in large volumes and at low prices with the objective of squeezing the Swiss companies out of the market. In the past, cases like this truly happened, no doubt. Nowadays, however, in areas of high technology like electronics, pharmaceuticals and precision machinery only a pooling of know-how in production and marketing leads to success for all the partners involved.

There are no standard recipes with regard to the question of what the key factors are, which lead to a sustainable success. Only experience can give some clues to the answer of such questions. In this essay I want to describe how a Swiss-Japanese partnership on a joint high-tech project evolved from difficult beginnings to become an unfettered success story. This example serves also as an illustration to highlight the pitfalls of such a partnership and how to overcome them in order to establish a smooth communication between Swiss and Japanese partners.

2. First Stage: The settings

Back in 1972, Compaan and Kramer produced the first color prototype of a new compact-disc (CD) technology. But it wasn't until 1978 at the "Digital Audio Disc Convention", held in Tokyo and attended by 35 different manufacturers, when Philips put forward the idea of establishing a worldwide standard for CDs. Polygram, a division of Philips, advocated the use of polycarbonate as the material of choice for the CD. In 1979, Sony started to collaborate on this matter with Philips. One year later they agreed on a CD standard adopted by Matsushita as well in 1980. In contrast to the fierce battling over a common video standard, the "Big Four" of the Japanese consumer electronics industry agreed on the same CD standard, and the business took off quickly.

A saying in Japan goes like this: first, we jointly build the sumo rink and the surrounding arena in order to attract many paying spectators, and then we start to fight each other fiercely for the price money.

These were the circumstances under which a Swiss high-tech company specializing in production systems for semiconductors and optical products joined the fray. The company had a longstanding partnership with Philips and quickly recognized the large potential of the CD business. The company developed a so-called "in-line"-production system for the manufacturing of CDs with a capacity of 600 discs/hour (see picture above). This "in-line" concept was the most advanced system worldwide at that time, even for Japanese standards. The unit size of the basic and the handling system measured about 6 m · 10 m · 3 m (length · width · height) and it came with a price tag of about 6 million Swiss Francs. The setting up of the whole system was a daunting task even at the site of a customer close to the company's home base in Switzerland. Despite the difficulties the production process could finally be managed albeit only on a satisfactory level. It was the Japanese market, however, where demand for such a system was highest; maintenance and service around the clock for such systems on the other side of the globe was a huge challenge for the Swiss company.

3. Second Stage: Fateful trial and error in Japan

The Swiss machine-building company already had a longstanding business relationship with a Japanese sales agency dating back to 1948. In order to enter the Japanese CD-manufacturing market, the Swiss sought closer ties with the sales agency in Japan. At that time the agency was selling the products of several different European and US manufacturers trying to sell whatever they could to the big Japanese high-tech companies as the main customers. This strategy was not in the interest of the Swiss manufacturer, however, the CD-production system required a focused sales and service team. After tough and long negotiations with the agency, the latter formed a special sales and service team dedicated entirely to the CD business. The team's objective was to get orders from the "Big Four" electronics giants and their affiliated second brand companies.

The CD manufacturing in Japan was mainly in the hands of the "Big Four" consumer electronics conglomerates with two of them running CD production at their second brand companies as well. Small and medium-sized companies did not have the resources to enter the costly business of CD manufacturing. The "Big Four" and their affiliated companies suffered from the "Not Invented Here" syndrome, and despite a lot of interest for the Swiss system, no orders could be placed with them.

By contrast, the second brand companies were eager to compete with the giants and they ordered the Swiss CD-production system. Two units were shipped to Japan and installed in a huge effort. The service engineers of the sales agency and the customers received a thorough training; thanks to this and together with strong support from Switzerland production was finally up and running smoothly. However, due to low up-time and the high need for spare parts to replace the many moving parts, the production was run at a heavy financial loss. Together with the two Japanese customers the Swiss company tried to attain a better up-time. But despite a good cooperation and a lot of patience shown by the Japanese customers in the face of mounting financial losses, the problem could not be resolved in time. Under these circumstances, there was no hope to ever sell the system to the "Big Four".

Back home meanwhile, the Swiss company had already developed a new-generation machine measuring only 3 m · 3 m · 2 m (l · w · h) and with much less moving parts. This revolutionary "disc-by-disc" concept ensured a simpler handling and increased production to 800 discs/hour costing about 2 million francs. Overall, the new system was an eightfold improvement compared to the former one.

When the new system was introduced into the Japanese market it attracted much interest and stirred up the competitors, an independent one and the "Big Four"-affiliated production system manufacturers. However, because of the bad reputation of the old Swiss system, the new revolutionary concept was considered to be as unreliable as the old one. As a consequence, the Swiss focused their efforts on perfecting the new model and on increasing the up-time of their older systems.

One of the disappointed Japanese second brand manufacturers working with the old system demanded from the Swiss two new systems given for free as a compensation for the losses he incurred with the old system. When this request was turned down, the Japanese company switched to the older but more reliable Japanese systems still being in use. The Swiss company was about to loose its foothold in Japan and threatened by financial compensation claims as well, a truly dangerous situation!

4. Third Stage: Swiss-Japanese cooperation, partnership and take-off

A lucky coincidence took place when just at this critical time the newly appointed Japanese manager of the CD-production division of the other second brand manufacturer returned from the UK. He knew the strengths and weaknesses of the Swiss manufacturer's products and recognized the high potential of the revolutionary new system. He proposed a two-way deal combining the Swiss innovation with Japanese CD-system integration and production know-how. In such an arrangement both sides would gain. His plan contained four main points:

- Delivery of a new system for free as a replacement and compensation for the old one.

- A supplementary system should be delivered in order to attain a high up-time, a low parts consumption and high reliability in a joint effort. If a certain level of up-time could be reached together within a certain time frame, the supplementary system would become the property of the Japanese partner free of charge. On the other hand, the Swiss partner would be allowed to use the production improvement know-how gained during the joint cooperation for free as well.
- The partners agreed on a ban to sell this system in the Asia-Pacific region for six months after production acceptance of the system.
- Both parties keep the project strictly secret, even towards the mother company of the Japanese partner.

There were no guarantees of follow-up sales. The Swiss and Japanese teams, including the one of the sales agency, started to work on the project and quickly developed a sense of mutual trust. Within half a year, the two delivered systems ran at an up-time even unknown to the old-generation Japanese CD-production systems. After three months, an order of six systems was placed, with additional options for the following year. Rumors about the successful systems spread. They reached the Japanese "Big Four" as well as the Korean "Big Two" and their affiliated CD-system manufacturers through their customers, the big American and Asian music labels.

The Japanese second brand company and the European CD manufacturers using the new system beat the other Asian competitors on quality and price. Subsequently the Japanese second brand company became the number one CD brand in the world.

5. Fourth Stage: The unbeatable Swiss-Japanese tandem

The Japanese CD-system manufacturers affiliated to the "Big Four" tried to find out the secrets of the new system. Therefore each one ordered such a system through back channels and had it copied. With the CD market now booming, the efficient and reliable Swiss-Japanese system attracted worldwide interest. The production system was now relatively cheap and very reliable; large orders were placed by manufacturers in the USA, Taiwan and throughout Southeast Asia. The CD-production system became a kind of standard mass product. In addition, the Swiss-Japanese cooperation went on to continuously improve the CD-production system up to a production speed of 1,200 discs/hour and material consumption reduced to ⅔. These improvements allowed the Swiss manufacturer to lower the unit price so much that the Japanese competitors were unable to sell their systems outside Japan. They became dependent on orders from the "Big Four", that is their mother companies. The CD-market share of the Big Four fell to less than 25% whereas the Taiwanese, Korean and Southeast Asian share rose to more than 50%.

6. Fifth Stage: Expanding further in Asia

Meanwhile the jointly achieved success convinced the Swiss system manufacturer and his Japanese partner to broaden and intensify their cooperation. Mutual trust had become so strong that the partners decided to go as far as sharing strategic plans and know-how.

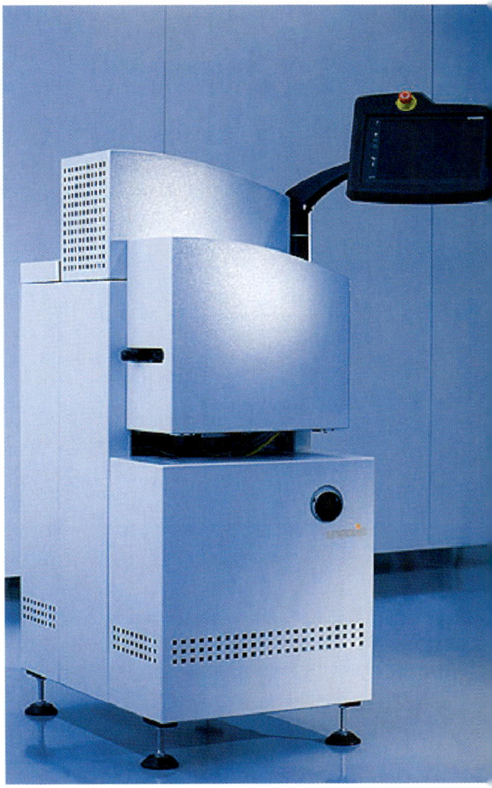

The Swiss side invited the Japanese partners to discuss the blueprints for the next-generation system. Ambitious targets were formulated, calling for a twelve-fold improvement on existing systems. The result was again revolutionary; the new system had a size of only 0.6 m · 0.6 m · 1 m (l · w · h), a production speed of up to 2,580 CDs/hour and the price of a unit was less than one million Swiss Francs (see picture). Material consumption had been reduced by ⅔ and the number of moving parts had been considerably lowered. The whole design was geared towards low-cost production as well as easy and fast service and maintenance. According to the original agreement, the first system was delivered for free under the condition that certain targets with regard to production and up-time were met. A sales ban remained effective for six months after system acceptance by the Japanese partner. As a result of the revolutionary technology a new niche market sprang up, the "production line integrater", companies specialized in integrating this system into existing production lines. For an investment of less than 2 million Swiss Francs anyone could now start a CD production without specific know-how. At that time the return on investment of such a production line was about nine months (in China three months).

During this "Golden Age" of CD production a Thai businessman owning a canned food business was introduced to the Swiss CD-production machine manufacturer. He became so enthusiastic about the system that he bought several units on the spot after some brief calculations. By the way, after the conclusion of the deal he spent an amount equal to the price of one system on Swiss luxury watches as gifts for his extended family.

With the CD-manufacturing business now booming in China and India as well, the price for a CD-R (recordable) tumbled from 10 Swiss Francs to less than one franc. Under this pressure, three of the "Big Four" electronic companies in Japan ditched their Japanese systems and switched to the Swiss system because of the huge performance gap. This step increased the Swiss market share for CD-production systems to about 70%. The Koreans and the last of the Japanese "Big Four" started to outsource their CD production to specialized small and medium-size companies. The Swiss manufacturer now sold more than 4,000 production systems worldwide and dominated the whole industry.

7. Sixth Stage: Further market expansion and termination of partnership

The booming CD market led to overproduction and subsequently to a very cyclical business for the Swiss manufacturer of CD-production systems. Each innovation was followed by a short investment boom, quick market saturation and ending in a downturn. Prices and margins (relative and absolute) for the standard systems eroded quickly.

The Swiss manufacturer tried to counter this boom-and-bust cycle by expanding its product range towards fully integrated production systems counting on the know-how acquired from the Japanese partner. Following this new strategy, the partnership was terminated and the Swiss manufacturer became now a competitor in the business of "line integration" to its former partner. Nevertheless the "line integrator" customers and the Japanese partner remained good customers regarding the core CD-production units offered by the Swiss. Now, however, the cooperation ended at the factory gate in Japan.

The decision to move into the business of production line integration turned out to be a mixed blessing for the Swiss manufacturer. There was still a considerable know-how gap between producing single units and the setting up of fully integrated production lines; problems of maintenance and service for integrated production lines remained formidable. Questions of supply chain management and how to attain a high up-time turned out to be more complex than previously assumed.

Ever since, the Swiss manufacturer's business has been a mixed success.

Erich Stuhlträger, 1953, from Berne; 1984 PhD as mechanical engineer from the Swiss Federal Institute of Technology Zurich. From 1985 till 1990 research in computational fluid dynamics at Tokyo Institute of Technology and as associate professor at Saga National University, Japan. From 1990 to 1995 with Balzers AG, Liechtenstein, as product manager and responsible for marketing & sales Asia-Pacific; he founded and managed the Japanese subsidiary Hakuto-Balzers K.K. (now Unaxis Japan K.K.) till 2000. Co-Founder of BridgeCo AG, a company for plug-and-play high-speed, wireless HW/SW-connections. Since 2004, key-account manager at BRAINFORCE AG Switzerland.

You're looking to reach new heights in Asia.
We're also offering local expertise.

JAPANESE COMPANIES REDISCOVER SWITZERLAND
By Martin Herb

Switzerland is an attractive location, from which Japanese companies can run their international business. An increasing number of companies are beginning to choose Switzerland.

In the early 1960s, Japanese companies began to discover Switzerland as a business location. Sony and Nikon are among the best-known of these early companies. Switzerland, together with the United States, was one of the first countries chosen as an international base for their emerging international activities, which serves as an indicator of the high importance of Switzerland at that time. Today, Switzerland still serves Japanese businesses as a base for the import and distribution of their products for the Swiss market. Of highest economic value is the import of automobiles into Switzerland, which tops the list, followed by machinery and electronics, and with chemicals in third place. Besides the import of goods, the financial sector also represents a strong Japanese business presence in Switzerland. After a phase of consolidation in the banking sector in Japan, seven Japanese financial institutions are now active in Switzerland, which represents an increase after their number had previously dropped to four. Notable among these firms is Mitsubishi Tokyo Wealth Management, established in 2002 in Geneva, which focuses on private banking in Switzerland.

It is worth noting that Japanese companies are increasingly interested in taking over the direct distribution of their products in Switzerland, either by setting up their own distribution network or by taking over their Swiss general distributor. This trend is particularly evident with regard to products requiring specific customer solutions. However, it also applies to the distribution of mass consumer products, as is the case, for example, with Honda, which increased its stake in Honda Switzerland from 50% to 90%. Despite this trend, Swiss importers of Japanese goods remain very successful, as evidenced by the general importer Toyota Switzerland, which belongs to the Emil Frey group.

Among other factors, the high Swiss purchasing power makes Switzerland an interesting market for Japanese companies. According to Nabuyuki Yanai, manager of Honda Switzerland, the neutral Swiss automobile market, with no national automobile manufacturer, also serves to develop the European market.

Another trend has become evident in the previous few years: Japanese companies are beginning to discover Switzerland as a base for their European and even global activities. Among these companies are the tobacco group JT International in Geneva, the refrigeration compressor maker Mayekawa Holding in Zug, and Sunstar, a company in the dental hygiene sector, in the canton of Vaud. As Japanese companies increasingly decide to manage their international business from a foreign location, the trend for choosing Switzerland as an international base is likely to continue. Japanese companies, however, do not view Switzerland as an attractive production location. This is because of the prevailing perception among Japanese businesses that Switzerland is a high-cost country for production and, as a non-EU country, it is less attractive economically. Correcting this distorted image is the task of Switzerland's economic development offices.

Japanese companies are also increasingly entering into cooperation with foreign companies. Examples include Fujitsu Siemens Computers and iSe International Sports and Entertainment Inc. based in Zurich, a less well-known sports marketing joint venture between the giant Japanese and French advertising agencies Dentsu and Publicis. The automobile manufacturer Nissan should also be mentioned at this juncture; taken over and brought back to prosperity by the French automobile manufacturer Renault, the company now operates in Switzerland as Renault Nissan.

As a location, Switzerland has a high potential for attracting Japanese companies, especially with regard to hosting their global or European headquarters. The number of Japanese firm owners settling in Switzerland in order to run their businesses is also set to increase. As a production location, Switzerland can also offer much more than is commonly believed in Japan to be the case. With competence and perseverance, this potential could be tapped by the

Swiss economic development offices. The past decade can be characterized as one of missed opportunities. According to available information, almost one hundred Japanese companies are currently based in Switzerland. In the state of North Rhine-Westphalia alone, where 10,000 Japanese citizens are living, the largest Japanese community in continental Europe, Japanese companies number 480.

Trade Balance

In Switzerland, Japanese companies are associated with their internationally successful and high-quality products: Sony, Toyota, Canon, Nikon, Pentax, Brother, Fujifilm, Honda, Subaru – who does not recognize these brands? But what significance does Switzerland hold for Japan's economy?

Japan represents, with a gross domestic product (GDP) of USD 4,500 billion, the second-largest economic power in world. In the year 2004, Switzerland's imports from Japan amounted to CHF 2.9 billion, with exports to Japan of CHF 5.7 billion (total Swiss foreign trade CHF 139/147 billion). This results in a trade surplus of CHF 2.8 billion in favor of Switzerland. Japan's share of Swiss external trade was 2.1% of all Swiss imports and 3.9% of its exports (Switzerland's share of Japanese external trade was only 0.43% of all Japanese exports and 1% of its imports in 2003). The development of the bilateral trade between Switzerland and Japan over the last few years is "scissors shaped": the Swiss trade balance deficit in favor of Japan turned from 1990 into a trade balance surplus. It is also striking that from 1990 Swiss imports from Japan started to decline, whereas Swiss exports to Japan have shown a steady increase.

An explanation for the steady decline of Japanese imports to Switzerland can be found in the growing international integration of Japanese companies; companies which in the past established a large number of production facilities in locations outside of Japan, such as in Europe (however, not in Switzerland). An example of this can be shown in the case of the automobile industry. 80% of Toyota automobiles sold in Switzerland are now manufactured in Europe. For Honda, this share is 30%.

Total exports/imports (in bn CHF)

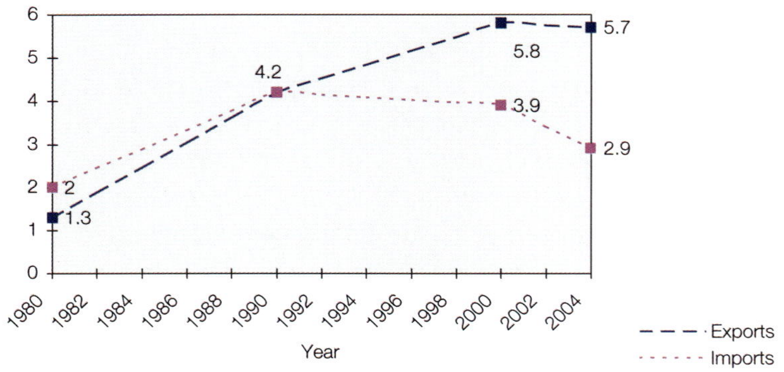

Imports automobiles/machinery + electronics (in bn CHF)

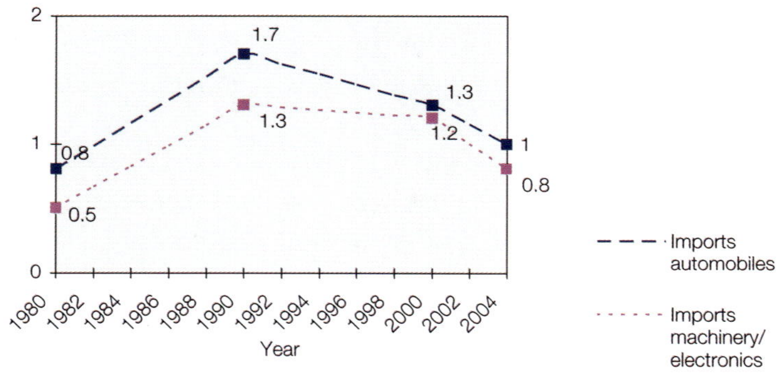

(Based on an article published by the author in the *NZZ* of March 22, 2005)

Martin Herb, Attorney-at-Law, Herb Takata Attorneys at Law, Zurich; Managing Director SJCC Swiss-Japanese Chamber of Commerce.

JAPAN AND SWITZERLAND AT THE BEGINNING OF THE 21ST CENTURY

Interview with His Excellency Mr. Nobuyasu Abe, Ambassador of Japan to Switzerland Questions by Roger Mottini

Q: Japanese people who are not familiar with Switzerland seem to connect four basic images with our country, namely: mountains, watches, neutrality and wealth/banks; is there anything else that could or should be added?

A: The Japanese perception of Switzerland has always been very positive and this has not changed over time. With regard to tourism, the younger generation in Japan has developed a taste for "exotic" destinations in Africa, South America and the Middle East. For obvious reasons, Switzerland's image does not respond to this kind of expectations. Nevertheless its image could be broader; as an example I am thinking here of Sweden which is also well known for its social care and welfare.

Q: How about democracy and federalism – is this a topic in Japan with regard to Switzerland?

A: Japanese pupils learn about direct democracy at school; in Japanese school texts the functioning of popular referendum and initiative is explained and Switzerland is mentioned as a practical example. Swiss federalism, however, may not be so well known.

Q: In the Swiss perception, Japan still suffers from an image of being a very expensive country, what do you think about this?

A: Ten years of deflationary pressure in Japan have certainly changed this; price sensitivity has greatly increased in Japan. Besides, there are many things in Switzerland that are more expensive than in Japan.

Q: For example?

A: For example electronic appliances, public transportation and food.

Q: Despite the longstanding economic relations between the two countries, their mutual FDIs (Foreign Direct Investments) are rather modest – are cultural barriers to blame for this?

A: Not necessarily, there are many examples of foreign companies which are very successful in Japan. There are many Swiss firms that have been very successful and well established in Japan. There are also cases when foreign firms succeeded in the Japanese market with successful tie-ups with Japanese partners. Sometimes, simply introducing foreign ways of production and management may not succeed. Once in the Japanese market, the quality of service is decisive because the Japanese consumers expect high quality of products and services.

Q: The Swiss endeavour to conclude a free-trade agreement with the USA has recently ended in failure; do you think there are chances of such an agreement between Switzerland and Japan?

A: If we look at the structure of bilateral trade between the two countries, the abolishment of the already low custom duties may not do much to increase trade. More significant than free trade would be the negotiation of a broadly defined "economic partnership" covering such wider issues as the issue of mutual certifications as well.

Q: From a Japanese perspective do you think an EU membership of Switzerland would be an advantage with regard to the establishment of European headquarters by Japanese companies?

A: No, I think costs are the most important factor for such a decision; as a manufacturing base Switzerland is not an obvious choice. For 'specialties' like pharmaceuticals, financial services, banking and insurance, however, Switzerland is very attractive.

Q: With regard to Japan's future, do you think Prime Minister Koizumi will step down in September or will he find a reason to continue?

A: Mr. Koizumi is seen as a man who stubbornly sticks to his own words. Therefore, I think he will stick to his word and retire.

Q: What were the main achievements of Prime Minister Koizumi's reform policy?

A: His major accomplishment has been to put the Japanese economy on a firm recovery track having carried out a number of economic reforms. In doing so he dismantled the power base of the vested interests that kept Japan from reforming and adapting to a changed global environment, namely the interests connected with construction, telecommunication and the postal system.

Q: What are the next reform steps if Japan is to continue its course – with or without Mr. Koizumi?

A: In the light of an ageing society, immigration and pension policy will be the most important issues. Japan's economy will face a labour shortage, thus the country has to become more open towards qualified foreign workers. A sensitive and properly managed immigration policy has to address the needs of the economy as well as the problem of social integration. Such a policy will also contribute to ease the pressure on the public and private pension programmes.

Mr. Ambassador, thank you very much.

LOST MEMORIES:
THE SEARCH FOR THE FIRST SWISS IN JAPAN
By Philippe Dallais

The aim of this article is to introduce and question some aspects of the early Swiss encounters with Japan and to evaluate their impact on the representation of Japan in Switzerland. I would like to argue that these experiences have gradually shaped or produced images of Japan during the 19th and early 20th century in Switzerland and to attempt to analyse this topic from an anthropological perspective in the light of some new information and documents discovered recently. The anthropological perspective I would like to emphasize here, is a focus on the importance of reconstructing and reconsidering the various human dimensions and experiences resulting from the contact with Japan and the remaining traces, heritage and transmission of knowledge observable after the return to Switzerland of these men who travelled to Japan, and to propose a preliminary analysis by using not only archives and publications, but also the Japanese materials which are, in Switzerland, mostly kept in Swiss ethnographic museums. Today, we must consider these Japanese collections as an important field of investigation that opens new doors to measure the intensity of the Swiss people's interest in Japan, thus providing new insight and biographic links on many unknown travellers who have apparently not left any written testimony of their travels to the country of the rising sun.

In 2004, the commemoration of the 140th anniversary of the conclusion of the Treaty of Amity and Trade between Switzerland and Japan in 1864, signed by Aimé Humbert from Neuchâtel Canton, was also an opportunity to celebrate another jubilee, being the first well-documented visit to Japan by a Swiss 200 years ago, in 1804. Two unexpected discoveries made during the summer of 2004 will add some more challenging evidence on the mechanisms of memory concerning Japan in Switzerland. Finally, we will examine the role of the earliest Swiss orientalist and a few cases covering the time corresponding to the Meiji period that will be helpful in reconsidering the status of the actors who played a role in translating Japan in Switzerland.

The earliest Swiss sources on Japan and research trends on bilateral relations

The book on Japan in the German language by the Jesuit Renward Cysat (1586) from Solothurn, printed in Fribourg more than 400 years ago, can be considered as the landmark of the earliest Swiss manifestation of interest in Japan. Cysat could gather his information from documents sent to Rome by Jesuits based in Japan (Beckmann 1939; Odori 2004). Between 1586 and the Humbert Mission in 1864 it is usually believed that no Swiss person could have reached Japan, with the exception of Johann Caspar Horner in Nagasaki in 1804–1805 (see infra). Nevertheless, we should today slightly revise this assumption and the case of Cysat teaches us the extraordinary potential of information circulation at such an early date, available to Swiss scholars through different networks and channels hard to reconstruct today. In Swiss libraries, we find nowadays several ancient books from the Netherlands, Germany, England, and France including descriptions of Japan and it seems clear that several people had some interest in East Asia and Japan during the 17th and 18th centuries, before and during the Edo period, the so-called seclusion period (*sakoku*), when only the Dutch and Chinese were allowed to trade in the restricted area of Nagasaki after 1639.

The connection between the Netherlands and the East India Company (V.O.C.) seems to have been underestimated as well as the Swiss people's mobility and participation in extended networks within Europe, as merchants, scientists or

Krusenstern's vessel, the Nadeshda, sailing in the Nagasaki Bay. Horner Collection, 1805, watercolour, 10 x 16 cm, Inv. No. 820.1.04, © Völkerkundemuseum der Universität Zürich.

mercenaries. One of the reasons to explain such ties is of confessional nature; both were protestant territories where some wealthy and influential converted protestant families did find refuge during the 16th century after the Reformation. The V.O.C. and the sea also offered a unique window on remote and exotic destinations and an opportunity for adventure, possible profit, and social status improvement.

It is possible to ascertain today that there were at least two Swiss who landed in Japan, in Nagasaki, during the 17th-century Edo period. The first Swiss we know to have visited Japan left a manuscript in French to be considered as the earliest first-hand written testimony of Japan in Switzerland; it was discovered in 1865, in the attic of a house located in the city of Bulle, and then reached the Fribourg city's Canton and University library (L 509). His name is Élie or Héli Ripon and he originated from the region of Lausanne. Born in the last decade of the 16th century, he embarked in 1617 in the protestant port of Delft and sailed to hunt whales in Greenland. But he soon returned and was hired by the V.O.C. as a soldier and reached Java on November 4, 1618. He helped to construct and defend forts, for example the first V.O.C. settlement in Taiwan, he captured Chinese or Spanish ships, and sailed all around the Indian Ocean and Southeast Asia.

In the V.O.C.'s archives Ripon is quoted five times and we learn that he received the grade of captain. According to Ripon, we count at least three other Swiss with him, from Zurich, Basel and Lausanne, but it is not clear if they went together to Japan. Our knowledge on Ripon ends in 1627 when he came back to Europe and even the last part of his manuscript is missing. On the 370 remaining pages, only a few concern the description of Japan (Ripon 1997: 99–102). It is not the place here to make a long commentary on Ripon, but it seems surprising that he has not become an emblem of the first Swiss view on Japan. It is true that captain Ripon was a professional warrior, a successful specialist of guerilla warfare and that his main preoccupation was war. Nevertheless, he was educated and, if he wrote a vivid and honest account of his travels as a logbook with blood and his sword in mind, he offers a vast amount of fascinating observations of the places and people he visited or fought (see Giraud in: Ripon 1997: 7–25). Ripon must have spent less than three weeks in Japan in 1623 and visited two cities, Languesaqui (Nagasaki) and Corsac (not identified). The shortness of his pre-sakoku period stay can be explained by the fact that the commercial relationship with Japan was peaceful and that his mission was to secure the V.O.C. business in more turbulent East Asian areas. His cultural reference points in order to understand Japan were Switzerland and his knowledge about China. He praises the long Japanese sword which he compares to the "Swiss sword" as both were handled with the two hands. We can understand that he really appreciated Japan from his very positive remarks on Japanese food, expeditious justice system, architecture, and crafts.

The second Swiss was identified by Sigerist (2001: 228) from a rather short passage in a written source as Hans Heinrich Stäger from Glarus who died in 1666, perhaps in Japan, after having spent 17 years as surgeon on board the Dutch fleet.

Japanese material culture, collected between the 17th and the 20th centuries, can also reveal some very complementary information, even though the research is often very difficult for sources preceding the 19th century. Items ranging from art to daily life are found in collections that reached the Swiss ethnographic museums, mostly founded at the end of the 19th and early 20th century. The earliest example of such possible contacts unveiled by an object collection is found in the ethnographic collection of the "Naturwissenschaftliche Sammlung der Stadt Winterthur" (Commission des musées 1984: 346–347), a small lacquered box and a pair of shoes. An old inventory record shows that these items were registered in 1676, an extremely rare testimony, and that they were incorporated into the "Raritätensammlung" (collection of rarities) of the citizens' library (Bürgerbibliothek) founded in 1660. They were brought back by Ulrich Meyer, who spent several years in Banda as surgeon for the East India Company and who perhaps also landed in Nagasaki. In Winterthur, the next recorded Japanese objects entered the collection only in 1878.

Another interesting case can be found in Berne, in the ethnographic collection of the Berne historical museum, which has in its collection a short Japanese sword brought back to Berne in 1668 by Albrecht Herport (1641–1730). Herport was an artist hired by the East India Company who travelled to India, Ceylon, Indonesia, and Taiwan, where Herport acquired this sword, without going directly in Japan. But this is not surprising as many Japanese vessels are attested to come to Taiwan for trade, especially during the main period of the V.O.C. establishment between 1624 and 1661 (Andrade 2005), Taiwan was then invaded by the Chinese Qing forces. Again, it is only in the 19th century that we find the next trace of an early Japanese collection in Bern, when the family Manuel, in business with the Netherlands, offered their Japonica collection to the city museum in 1829 and in 1842 (Psota 2003: 49–50).

Of course, these collections don't necessarily reflect much of the reality concerning the amount of Japanese goods circulating or that reliable knowledge was available on Japan in Switzerland, and it is hard to understand today the degree of exoticism and prestige they represented for their owners. Unlike in the rest of Europe where rich noble people were fond of Japanese objects, porcelains, lacquered items, furniture, and food, mostly soy sauce, we don't find today many traces of such material in the Swiss public or private collections. Even when some items are identified, they still haven't been researched. One exception, for example, is the lacquered Japanese cabinet from the Geneva library (Eracle 1985). This 17th-century cabinet was donated to the library in 1707 by a Geneva patrician named Guillaume Franconis, again actively involved in business relations with the Dutch East India Company. If this explains its origin, we can also assume that Franconis was possibly the first owner after the arrival of the cabinet on a Dutch ship, but we don't know its exact value or how it reached Switzerland. It was registered as "cabinet from the East Indies" and served to keep a medal collection.

At this stage of the research, it is worth noting that traces of Japan in Switzerland are scarcer during the 18th century. In 1727, the Swiss doctor J. G. Scheuchzer based in London translated into English the book "History of Japan" written by Engelbert Kaempfer (1651–1716) who had reached Nagasaki through the V.O.C. and spent two years in Japan in 1690–1692. Kaempfer was a key source on Japan and inspired several 18th-century writings on Japan. Though Scheuchzer's translation is seen today as imperfect, we had to wait until the end of the 20th century to see an almost complete English translation (Kaempfer 1999).

All these early links with Japan lead to the V.O.C. and the business relationship between Swiss entrepreneurs and the Netherlands which paved the way to "East India" for many adventurous Swiss men who unfortunately did not leave many records of their activities. We may presume that much remains to be discovered in some hidden archives and correspondences. The three cases of Ripon, Stäger, and Meyer still need to be investigated in detail. The picture is still not very clear, but we can assume that at least three Swiss did visit Nagasaki on Dutch ships during the 17th century, that it may also have been the case during the 18th century, even if this remains to be verified. In this context, we can still consider Horner as the first Swiss personality who left, as we will see, some concrete firsthand traces of his Nagasaki visit.

At this point, it is important to point out that the study of the early connections of Switzerland with Japan is not very well developed in Switzerland and that Japanese studies is quite a young discipline in the Swiss academic arena. Even if Japanese studies did not make their appearance in Swiss universities, mainly Zurich and Geneva, before the late 1960s, it can be said that the interest in Japan was most developed during the second half of the 19th century on an individual level, influenced by France and Germany, with a focus on establishing commercial ties and on a low-intensity diplomatic activity, as Switzerland was not a maritime and colonial power. From 1859 and 1864, many individuals, entrepreneurs, scientists, and travellers came back from Japan with many Japanese goods which they often donated or sold to the local learned societies and then to ethnographic museums. Proportionally, not many of them wrote about their experience in Japan. There is no museum specialising in Japanese or East Asian arts and culture, except the recent Rietberg and Baur museums,

in Zurich and Geneva respectively, and, historically, none of the museums had ever employed a well-renowned specialist in Japanese culture. Only during the first half of the 20th century, especially in the case of Berne, very few curators encouraging the building of Japanese collections are attested, but without continuity.

The interest in early Swiss-Japanese bilateral connections was at a pioneer investigation stage, always initiated by non Swiss scholars, like the great French orientalist Cordier who presented, at the 10th International Congress of Orientalists held in Geneva in September 1894, a very detailed review of all Swiss people involved in East Asia. Cordier (1894) clearly showed that Swiss, whether Jesuits, members of Protestant missions or laic, were more involved in China than in Japan. He wonders about the lack of study on the rich materials and studies they left and quotes Humbert as the first Swiss in Japan; I will come back to this matter later on. We can feel that Cordier somehow reproaches the local general disinterest in the work and life of these Swiss pioneers in East Asia. Did Cordier touch here a general scholarly trend or pattern or a Swiss attitude toward East Asia and Japan?

In my opinion, it was not until the celebration of the centennial of the Humbert Mission that a new consciousness led to investigating the relations between Switzerland and Japan, with the publication of *Helvetia – Nippon 1864–1964*

This painting is perhaps an illustration project for the Krusenstern Atlas. On the left, the Nadeshda, and the Dutch factory Deshima on the right. Horner Collection, 1805, watercolour, 37 x 53.9 cm, Inv. No. 820.1.12, © Völkerkundemuseum der Universität Zürich.

(Comité du centenaire 1964). Then came the important thesis of Professor Nakai (1967) which was followed by the historiography-oriented publications by Hürlimann (1975), Immoos (1982), Jequier (1990), Mottini (1998) and to some extent Sigerist (2001).

But the future of research on Swiss-Japanese bilateral relations and mutual influences seems now secured, and to have entered a new dynamic. Scholarly exchanges and meetings, including specialists from both countries, as the seminar held at the East Asian Institute, University of Zurich, in August 2003, entitled “Perceptions of Switzerland in 20th-Century Japan: Images, Ideas, Cultural Transfer, Scholarship”, will lead to some new promising considerations. On the museum research side, a newly created network of curators and scholars of Japanese art and applied arts from European museums, galleries, and research institutions, called ENJAC, has already organized two fruitful conferences since 2003 (Kreiner 2005). This recent pan-European collaboration, which includes five Swiss museums, is very helpful for studying the most ancient or more recent traces of Japan left in museums, still keeping a huge amount of unexploited materials, which will enlighten our understanding of bilateral relations in several new directions.

Horner and Rossier – two Swiss in Japan before Humbert

The Swiss physicist, astronomer, circumnavigator, and counsellor to the tsar’s court Johann Caspar Horner (1774–1834) was born in Zurich. Because of his fragile health, his father, a Zurich baker who was captain and belonged to the Zurich city council, decided to send Horner to the gymnasium in order to educate him as a Protestant minister. But Horner soon became interested in mathematics and natural sciences. He started to develop a passion for astronomy, and he pursued his scientific studies in Germany, where he received his doctoral diploma from the University of Jena in 1799.

In 1803, he was hired as an astronomer for a cruise around the world organized by the Tsar Alexander I, under the command of Adam Johann von Krusenstern (1770–1846) from Estonia. Horner got on board Krusenstern’s vessel, the Nadeshda ("Hope"), which was followed by another ship, the Neva. The expedition, which lasted three years (1803–1806), comprised 139 people, crew members and officers, scientists, and the tsar's official envoy Nikolai Petrovich Rezanov (1764–1807).

After a stop in Brazil, passing Cape Horn and sailing through the Pacific Ocean, with sporadic landings on some islands, especially in Nukuhiwa, the largest of the Marquesas Islands, the Nadeshda reached the Russian Peter-Paul's harbour (Petropavlovsk) in Kamchatka. From there the vessel departed for Nagasaki, sailing along the southeast coast of Japan. The Nadeshda arrived in Nagasaki Bay on October 8, 1804 (ill. 1) and left six months later, on April 5, 1805. The Neva did not always follow the same route as the Nadeshda and did not go to Japan. Krusenstern then sailed back north through the Sea of Japan, landing in the northern part of Hokkaido and on Sakhalin Island, where the expedition members met Ainu and Nivkh people. After their exploration, passing also through the Kuril Islands, they came back to Kamchatka and returned to St Petersburg via China (where they stopped at Canton), the Southeast Asian seas, and the Atlantic Ocean. The atlas published by Krusenstern (1813, 1814) provides all the maps needed in order to understand the voyage and offered for this time an extraordinarily interesting and new first-hand realist visual account of Japanese, Ainu, and other peoples. During their long travel, Krusenstern gave Horner's name to a Japanese mountain in Kyushu (Pic Horner, called Kaimondake in Japanese, 922/924 m), at the western entrance to Kagoshima Bay, and to a cape on the northwest coast of Sakhalin Island.

Paravicini (1943: 131–132) quotes Horner as the third Swiss avant la lettre "ethnographer", because he is one of the earliest Swiss travellers around the world, being able to observe unknown remote peoples, after John Webber (1751–1793) from Berne, the expedition artist during captain James Cook's third voyage in the years 1776–1780 (see Hauptman 1996). Traditionally, Horner is considered to be the first Swiss personality to have visited Japan, exactly two hundred years ago. Nevertheless, as we could see, he is certainly not the first Swiss who landed in Nagasaki, but he is clearly the first who did not arrive on a

Dutch vessel and the first to leave some documents to posterity. In July 2004, I had the chance to rediscover at the Ethnographic Museum of Zurich University (Völkerkundemuseum der Universität Zürich) the drawings, paintings and maps he produced during the travel. Several pieces from this collection were shown for the first time during the 2004 symposium in Tokyo on the occasion of the 140th anniversary of the relationship between Japan and Switzerland.

The purposes of this circumnavigation expedition were to explore the northern coasts of America and Japan, and to attempt to establish diplomatic and commercial relations with Japan, as well as scientific researches and the upgrading of maps in order to improve the sea route for the shipping of fur freight all the way to China. The tsar imposed on Krusenstern to take on board Rezanov, who was the son-in-law of the Russian-America Co. (RAC) founder Shelikhov and a majority stockholder in the RAC. Rezanov believed, Japan would become the supplier to Russian outposts engaged in fur trade on the Kurils, Aleutian Islands and in Alaska. As an official ambassador, he thought that he would be successful thanks to the letter obtained in 1793 by the Russian army lieutenant Adam Laksman, who had been dispatched, by the Empress Catherine II, to establish diplomatic relations with Japan. Laksman sailed to Hokkaido and obtained in Matsumae, from two Edo shogunate officials Bugyo Ishikawa Shogen and Murakami Daigaku, only a letter of recommendation for further negotiations in Nagasaki. Nevertheless, Rezanov misinterpreted this letter as allowing trade with Japan. Like Laksman, Rezanov had the idea to return Japanese castaways who were brought to St Petersburg and became the first Japanese to have travelled around the globe. A detailed account is found in Ōtsuki Gentaku's work "Kankai ibun", issued in 1807. Unfortunately, after months of negotiations, Rezanov failed to reach an agreement with the Japanese authorities. He felt personally insulted by the Japanese rebuttal and left Krusenstern's vessel in Kamchatka. Several months later he instigated an aggressive policy against Japanese outposts in the Kuril Islands.

During almost six months spent in Nagasaki, Horner had much time to work on his astronomical observations, to draw maps, and to sketch the surrounding Nagasaki landscape, boats, and people, together with the German physician and naturalist Wilhelm Gottlieb Tilesius von Tilenau (1769–1857), the official painter of the expedition. A careful study of the Krusenstern (1810, 1811, 1812), Langsdorff (1993), and Löwenstern (2003) travel accounts enable us to reconstruct chronologically and in detail what happened during this Japanese episode. These authors witnessed and reported all kind of events and described all they could see and learn about the Japanese people. We find out, for example, that the tsar had prepared a series of gifts for the ruler of Japan who he believed was the emperor. Langsdorff described the best of these gifts among them pocket watches made of gold and silver; however, these gifts were not accepted by the Japanese officials. Nevertheless, each Japanese castaway was offered a silver watch (1993: 171), it is very likely that they were Swiss made and therefore some of the earliest Swiss watches to enter Japan. The narrative atmosphere and the status of the upper-level crew, officers, and scientists prefigure a new way of travelling and a rupture with the 18th-century expeditions.

Unlike people in the other parts of the world they visited, the Japanese were very curious about the Russian ship, its crew, and especially about the ambassador Rezanov. Some came closer to the Nadeshda or even on board and executed many drawings documenting these foreigners who were different from the Dutch. Such documents, as the *Roshia shisetsu rezanofu raikō emaki* (Picture scroll showing the arrival of the Russian envoy Rezanov) of 1804 must be today compared as a mirror image to the several drawings and paintings, 35 years before the invention of photography, which were left by the Krusenstern expedition members. The Dutch officials from the Deshima factory (ill. 5) and the translators were a kind of third party, between the Japanese and these Russian newcomers. It took several weeks before Krusenstern could come closer to the city and anchor in Nagasaki harbour (ills. 2, 4). Rezanov was then allowed to stay in an isolated residence and the Russians could spend some time on land under close Japanese guard. In March 1805, for example, Löwenstern (2003: 261) wrote: "Horner is now on land every day and is undertaking experiments with a pendulum."

Though Horner was a close friend of Krusenstern and among the top personalities on the vessel, he never became a famous figure of the expedition. One of the reasons can be explained by the fact that, unlike Langsdorff (1993) and Löwenstern (2003), he never published a personal account of his travel experience and stay in Nagasaki. Nevertheless, he wrote three scientific dissertations in the third volume dedicated to the expedition, dealing with physical and astronomical observations (Krusenstern 1812) which were not reproduced in the French, English, and later translations. He left several letters sent to his family in which he related some of his travel impressions. In the few passages concerning Nagasaki, he deplored that there were many restrictions from the Japanese authorities and a permanent suspicion of the foreigners. His memories of different episodes of the travel in Japan also appear in his later correspondences.

After returning in 1806, Horner spent some time in St Petersburg and at Krusenstern's home in Tallinn (Reval), of which he made a sketch found in the Zurich collection. He refused a position as professor at the St Petersburg University and would have preferred to organize a new expedition to South America for more detailed astronomical observations of the Southern Hemisphere, but the first war with Napoleon brought some financial constraints in Russia. He returned to Zurich in 1809 and became professor of mathematics, logic, and rhetoric at the Humanities College. He joined the city council in 1816, remaining a member until 1830, and was president of the Zurich Society of Natural Sciences from 1831 until his death in 1834. From people who used to know Horner, we learn that Horner had been really impressed by the travel and that he talked about it to his guests, also showing them his collection of objects from Japan and China, which remain to be discovered.

After his death, Horner's belongings and archives were donated to the Zurich Antiquarian Society and to other Zurich institutions. His ethnographic collection and drawings were then given to the Zurich Ethnographic Museum founded in 1889, and they became therefore our museum's oldest collection. But unlike the object collection, the iconographic documents remained unexploited and were even forgotten like a buried treasure in the museum basement. Though my interest in Japanese collections in Swiss museums started in 1997, with the study of Aimé Humbert and other collections, I became involved from 2002 in a project of making a catalogue raisonné of all Ainu collections kept in Switzerland, including the seven largest Swiss ethnographic museums (Dallais, Tahara 2003; Dallais, Tahara forthcoming). This research offered also a unique opportunity to undertake in-depth investigations on many Swiss travellers who went to Japan at the end of the 19th and the first half of the 20th century. One of the most challenging issues was to find some more information on Horner, as he is also the first Swiss who saw and met Ainu people. Until then, Horner was especially studied in the field of history of science (Mumenthaler 1996).

In April 2004, I was elected as a new staff member at the Zurich Ethnographic Museum, and a large oil painting portrait of Horner, made by David Sulzer from Winterthur, displayed in the museum corridor, reminded me constantly of the possibility that some more Horner documents could exist. By a lucky circumstance, after much research, and thanks to the help of the curator Martin Brauen (Dept. Tibet, Himalaya and Far East) the discovery took place in July 2004 (Arata 2004; Satō 2004). Two hundred years after Horner's voyage, we found a large portfolio containing 132 sketches, drawings, watercolours, and maps; 103 pieces were made during the Krusenstern voyage (20 of them concern Nagasaki), and 29 related to Europe and Switzerland.

The collection even includes a caricature of Rezanov, holding in his hand a small letter certainly suggesting with humour the Laksman letter. We can find many different types of views of Nagasaki Bay and city, or the very precisely drawn scene of the first launch in Japan, on February 6, 1805, of a hot air balloon made of Japanese paper, 22 years after the French brothers Montgolfier had invented the first aerostat (ill. 3). This balloon, made at the residence of Rezanov at Umegasaki, by the scientist Georg Heinrich von Langsdorff (1774–1852), flew in direction of the city, crashed and burned, thus provoking a mini-incident as the Japanese believed at first that it was a fire machine (Langsdorff 1993: 202–203). Each of Horner's drawings is full of precious information and can be related to some textual information, to some other drawings made by Tilesius

or the engravings in the magnificent atlas of the expedition published in 1813 and 1814.

But this Horner collection raises several new questions that will lead to a complete reinvestigation of all the original drawings and paintings made during the expedition. It seems that several officers did produce artwork during the expedition, that they maybe copied or even exchanged each other's drawings. For example, one Nagasaki watercolour depicting Deshima is signed by the lieutenant Fedor Romberg, including a legend in French. Still much promising research has to be conducted on Horner, especially to discover the objects he brought back from Japan, certainly still hidden amongst our collections. All of the Krusenstern expedition's iconographic materials collection of Pacific islands, Kamchatka, Japan, China, and other places will be researched in a comparative approach with others scattered in Europe and Russia (Sondermann 2004).

An artistic reproduction of Horner watercolours was offered to the Emperor of Japan (ill. 4) and to the Prime Minister Mr. Koizumi by Joseph Deiss, then President of the Swiss Confederation, during his official working visit to Japan

"Some interpreters and several Japanese happened to be visiting us on the 6th [February 1805, at the Rezanov's residence in Umegasaki] when I sent up the first balloon in Japan. It climbed to a considerable height, developed a little tear on the top end and fell into the city of Nagasaki. The balloon began to burn after landing because of the burning spirits hanging from it. [...]. (...) I was asked in the future if I wanted to send a balloon up to choose a time when the wind was blowing out to sea and not toward land". (Langsdorff 1993: 202–203). Horner Collection, 1805, ink on paper, 22.5 x 29.5 cm, Inv. No. 820.1.16, © Völkerkundemuseum der Universität Zürich.

in October 2004 (Nagi 2004). Horner's oil portrait and some reproductions of his Japanese images were on display in the Swiss pavilion of the Aichi 2005 World Exhibition. I am also pleased to announce here that our museum director, Michael Oppitz, has decided to organize a special exhibition in 2008 on the Krusenstern expedition, a project that will enable an in-depth analysis of the Japan episode. Since the project has started and thanks to the efficient collaboration of Zurich libraries and different institutions, a lot of new information came to light recently.

A second discovery of importance was made in August 2004 by the British writer and researcher on 19th-century East Asian photography Terence Bennett. Bennett finally succeeded in identifying a person sometimes called the "ghost photographer" in the history of Japanese photography. It was already known that Pierre Joseph Rossier (1829–?), hired and sent to the Far East by the London firm Negretti and Zambra, was the photographer who took the first commercial photographs of Japan from 1859 to 1864. Furthermore, he played an important role in the development of photography in Japan as he taught wet-collodion photography technique to Ueno Hikoma, a pioneer of the first generation of photographers. Rossier was believed to be a Frenchman, and very little information was available on his life and work. Bennett (2004) showed that Rossier was in fact Swiss, born in the village of Grandsivaz in the Fribourg Canton.

Rossier who from now on can be considered as the next Swiss to reach Japan after Horner, in 1859, possibly died in Paris between 1883 and 1894 and is almost completely forgotten in Switzerland. None of his photographs taken in Japan are found in Swiss collections or in the Negretti and Zambra's building in London, as it was destroyed during the Second World War. In 1860, the journal *The Times* of October 3 announced the following sensational news:

"Photographs From Japan – A case of rare and curious photographs of the scenery of this interesting country, and illustrative of the manners and customs of the Japanese tribes (sic)*, which have been executed by a special artist sent*

out for the purpose by the enterprising firm of Negretti and Zambra of London, are expected by the Peninsular and Oriental Company's steamship Ceylon, which will probably arrive at Southampton on Wednesday." (Quoted from Bennett 2004).

Bennett considers that Rossier's very rare Negretti and Zambra photograph series on Japan perhaps consisted of about 25 to 30 images, issued in England in 1861, surprisingly one year after the announcement of their arrival in London; and after that 8 engravings made out of photographs from the series were first published (Smith 1861, Tilley 1861). It seems that no memory of Rossier remains in Switzerland. The only testimony he left of Japan are his photographs, which Bennett will soon publish in his forthcoming book.

If the earliest Swiss travellers left some Japanese objects behind and were at the service of the East India Company, the 19th century saw Horner and Rossier who experienced Japan in a new way: Horner still depending on a foreign opportunity, and Rossier as an independent photographer working under contract but also freelance in Japan. Both left only images, revealing a partial translation of their vision of Japan. Horner did only show his materials privately and Rossier had a short but more international impact. We must wait until the return of Humbert at the very end of the Edo period to see an effective and complex description of Japan.

Aimé Humbert, the earliest Swiss orientalist François Turrettini, and his friend Léon Metchnikoff

In 1859, the Prussian Rudolf Lindau (Hürlimann 1975: 35–36) was sent to Japan by Aimé Humbert (1819–1900) and the *Union Horlogère*. His first attempt to negotiate a trade agreement on behalf of Switzerland and the reports he sent to Switzerland helped to organize the Aimé Humbert Mission to Japan (1863–1864). I will not touch upon the Mission's organisation and history (see Barrelet 1986, Kleinschmidt 2004, Mottini in this volume), but would rather examine the often underestimated role of Humbert as a pioneer in disseminating a new image of Japan through his major publication (1870), his collection, and indirectly his encouraging several entrepreneurs from the French part of Switzerland to leave for Japan. It is interesting to note that Humbert, on a boat returning from Japan to Switzerland, was aware of the Pic Horner on which he made some remarks in one of his letters. Swiss contact with the Netherlands was still a reality at that time and can be seen as a continuum as Dutch personalities helped Humbert first in organising his Mission, but also in persuading the Japanese authorities to sign Humbert's famous first treaty between the Swiss and Japan on February 6, 1864.

After the Mission left Japan, we can witness a new era in Swiss-Japanese relations. There was a rush to Japan of Swiss watchmakers or importers, textile traders, and travellers from industrialized Swiss areas, as well as the beginning of diplomatic activity. Unfortunately, the documentation on Swiss presence in Japan during the late Edo and early Meiji period is not abundant or detailed, and most of the people did not leave many archives behind, like James Favre-Brandt (1841–1923) who came with the Humbert Mission (Mottini 1998: 84–91), or the first Swiss vice-consul in Hakodate (1864–1868), Henri Pierre Veuve. Interestingly, both were born, like Humbert, in the Neuchâtel Canton, famous as a watchmaking region, and died in Japan. Veuve is certainly the first Swiss to have passed away in Japan (1870) during the 19th century; his tomb is located in the Yokohama foreign cemetery. Takeuchi (1983) regards Veuve as a Frenchman, but this misunderstanding can be explained as he had close links with the French expatriates' community and that he had to find some complementary occupation because of the low consular activity required from Switzerland.

Mainly business interests attracted the Swiss to Japan and the current research on this period in Switzerland is mostly made by Swiss German scholars with a strong orientation in the field of economic and commercial development. The question is how the anthropologist can find significant materials in order to try to analyze the complex phenomena of the progressive construction of an image of Japan in Switzerland.

First of all we should distinguish four main contributing dynamics and sources, the image and representations transported by first-hand information or knowledge brought back from Japan at an individual level and spread among a limited circle of relatives and friends. Then the published accounts, by the travelers, thirdly the information from the written media, and finally all kind of influences, fashions, and perceptions from the countries surrounding Switzerland. We should also distinguish popular images from economic or scholarly images. At this point, I would say that the book published in 1964 (Comité du centenaire) offers a good deal of information and helps in understanding the diachronic development of Swiss involvement in Japan. Hürlimann (1975: 63–82) also published an important bibliography in chronological order of the literature on Japan by Swiss authors or published in Switzerland, which reflects different trends in the development of interest in Japan.

The first official visit to Switzerland of a Japanese delegation, led by the shogun's younger brother Akitake Tokugawa (Nakai 1967: 135–145) in 1867, and later the Iwakura mission in 1873 (Mottini 1998: 59–81) did not particularly improve the Swiss public interest in Japan. Swiss people interested in Japan had to rely much on foreign sources and influence or go to neighbouring countries in order to find some attention to their work or to learn the Japanese language. Humbert did publish his book in Paris. Though Japan exerted a constant fascination at a more individual than collective level from the 1870s on, we must wait for the 1930s to attest a real, more intense public attention to Japan, the development of private Japanese art collections, and the first significant exhibitions. This is late compared to European trends. The intensity of private and business experiences always found a weak echo in the public and a low support from authorities.

In my research, being interested in investigating what was left in Switzerland by Humbert, his mission fellows and followers, I could find out that in the Neuchâtel Canton, the Japanese collections in the Neuchâtel Museum of ethnography are not numerous (less than 600 pieces; the most important concentrations are Berne with over 6,000 and Basle with 7,000 objects). I could identify a local pattern to keep and treasure materials from Japan in the families during 3 or 4 generations; it is therefore difficult to judge the roles played by all the watch traders who came back from Japan. Even Humbert has not left much behind on Japan in Neuchâtel and he is rather remembered for his political career and role in the Neuchâtel University (at that time called Academy) than for being a key influential personality who promoted the bilateral relations. No commemorative event was organized in 2004 to celebrate the 140th anniversary of the mission; it instead took place in Zurich (Swiss-Japanese Chamber of Commerce 2004). The most striking issue was Humbert's sudden disinterest in Japan after he published his Japan travel impressions, at first in the journal *Le Tour du Monde* from 1866 to 1869, and then in two volumes in 1870. If his book seems to have served as a kind of reference manual to discover Japanese culture up until the end of the 19th century, Humbert also missed the opportunity to encourage and promote academic "Japanese Studies" in Switzerland which could have served to train future traders intent on going to Japan. But this idea came into fashion only later, in the 1880s, with the development of geographical societies in Switzerland, mostly thought of as a preparation for the European colonies.

Humbert's strategy in 1863–1864 to learn more about Japan through visual documents was described and discussed recently by Balemi (2003: 68–81). He himself explained how he acquired and gathered a huge amount of Japanese prints and photographs taken by Felice Beato in order to illustrate and translate Japan through iconography. This early ethnographic approach resulted in a large collection of over 3,600 images of Japan which were used by Paris artists to create the 476 illustrations for his book. Instead of keeping them for himself or donating this collection to the Neuchâtel city, Humbert donated or sold it around 1871 to the first Swiss sinologist and "japonist", François Turrettini (1845–1908) from a rich Geneva family (Perrot 1996).

Turrettini did not travel to Japan, but he started to learn Chinese and Japanese exactly at the same time Humbert was undertaking his diplomatic mission in Japan. He first began to learn Chinese with the missionary Joseph Guriel in Rome from 1865 to 1866 and then spent about five years in Paris to study Chinese, Manchu, and Japanese under Stanislas Julien and Léon de Rosny. He came back to Geneva in 1871. Against the will of his father, who would have preferred him to follow the traditional classical studies, and facing a global disinterest from the other scholars, he set up a printing shop being able to print Chinese and Japanese characters. He created two collections, "Atsume Gusa" (8 vols., 1873–1881) and "Ban-zaï-sau" (5 vols., 1873–1894), diffused in Geneva, Paris, and London, in which he published his own works and those of famous orientalists, principally translations accompanied with the original Japanese or Chinese text. His predilection was ancient history and he translated, for example, a chapter of the "Heike monogatari", certainly the first time in a European language, the "Nihon gaishi" of the historian Rai Sanyō (1780–1832), or a historical novel of Ryūtei Tanehiko (1783–1842). Turrettini could also get some help for his translations from Japanese people staying in Geneva, on whom we have hardly any information. From 1872, Turrettini hired a Chinese man in order to help him to edit and print his series. He became the first Chinese to receive Geneva citizenship around 1876 (Perrot 1996). Surely the same year, Turrettini met the second companion who will follow his editorial adventure, Léon Metchnikoff (Knapp 1889, Jud 1995) who is also to be placed among the first "Japonists" in Europe.

Born in Russia, Metchnikoff (1838–1888 – his name means "the bearer of the sword") arrived in Geneva in 1864; he started to learn Japanese with Turrettini from 1872. He met by chance Ōyama Iwao, future Minister of the Army, who asked Metchnikoff to teach him French. Metchnikoff then debarked in Japan in 1874 where he taught Russian, mathematics, and history at the Tokyo School of Foreign Languages. Because of illness, he came back to Geneva in 1876 and in the same year started to publish about Japan in Turrettini's series. In 1877, both elaborated the project to issue a review entitled "L'Extrême Orient: recueil de linguistique, d'ethnographie et d'histoire", thirteen years before Gustave Schlegel and Henry Cordier founded the review "T'oung pao", published by Brill in Leiden from 1890. But only one issue came out and Metchnikoff began the redaction of his book entitled "L'Empire japonais" which was printed twice by Turrettini in 1878 and 1881. Surprisingly, Cordier (1894: 22–23), who founded

in 1882 a journal entitled similarly "Revue de l'Extrême-Orient", emphasized that "the two most interesting books ever written on Japan are from two Swiss authors: Humbert and Metchnikoff; the later although a Russian was professor in Neuchâtel".

This late recognition should not hide the fact that to be a "Japonist" in Switzerland was not that easy and therefore we find Metchnikoff going to France with the aim of following the trends in Japanese studies, for example in Lyon at the 1878 third Provincial Orientalists' Congress. From 1882, he became the secretary of the famous French geographer Elisée Reclus, settled in Clarens near Montreux, and contributed some chapters on Japan and Asia in Reclus's "Nouvelle Géographie Universelle". Very interestingly, he was hired at the Neuchâtel Academy as professor of comparative geography in 1883, in my opinion possibly with the support of Humbert, where he certainly taught his students about Japan, although it was never a central topic in his courses. He was among the founders of the Neuchâtel Geographical Society in 1885, but he died in 1888 at the age of 50, from tuberculosis. Thus, the only able person in an academic position who would have had the opportunity to bring some dynamism into Japanese studies at academic level disappeared too early.

Watercolour painted by Horner on board of the Nadeshda, showing a Japanese military outpost guarding the entrance of Nagasaki Bay; an artistic reproduction of this art work was offered to the Emperor of Japan by Mr. Joseph Deiss, then President of the Swiss Confederation, during his official working visit to Japan in October 2004; 1805, 23 x 37.6 cm, Horner Collection, Inv. No. 820.1.01, © Völkerkundemuseum der Universität Zürich.

Turrettini was a visionary man, slightly advanced for his time, and although many people interested in Japan came to him, it is nevertheless hard to estimate the print run and the influence of his publications. It is also still a mystery what Turrettini did with the Humbert materials in his possession from 1871, until the year 1894, which is a very culminating moment. Turrettini took part in the 10th International Congress of Orientalists held in Geneva on September 3 to 12, during which we know that he advertised his publications (but also that he paradoxically interrupted them for good the same year). From Cordier (1894: 21) and other authors who reviewed the Congress (see also Hürlimann 1975: 41) we learn that Turrettini undoubtedly organized the first significant exhibition of Japanese art in Switzerland, as a side event of the Congress from September 2 to 17. Interestingly, two exhibitions of Japanese bamboo craft and bamboo-related objects were organized in Zurich in 1893 and in 1894. The collection was gathered 1890 by Hans Spörry (Brauen 2003: 12–28), employee of a Swiss silk trading company, and though the 1894 exhibition was running from June 15 to October 15, it was not mentioned during the Congress.

Turrettini exhibited a part of his Humbert collection in a famous Geneva building called "Athénée", in the room reserved for the Geographical Society. A friend of Turrettini and president of the society, Arthur de Claparède, who himself visited and wrote about Japan in 1889, stated that the Humbert collection exhibition was absolutely remarkable and that the collection contained a large amount of "inestimable treasures" of Japanese masterpieces. Claparède also regretted that this collection was not celebrated as it would have deserved it. Moreover he noted with essential precision, that the collection consisted of 3,668 pieces, divided into 21 folios and 362 sections.

After the death of Turrettini in 1908, instead of donating or selling to the Geneva library the large collection of Chinese and Japanese books he bought at great expense, his family organized an auction in Paris held in 1914. The dispersion of the largest Swiss Asian library certainly did not favour the rise of Chinese and Japanese studies in Geneva. The Humbert collection could have been lost, but it resurfaced in 1932 in Marseille, more or less complete, in the Louis Lafitte bookseller's catalogue, a note quotes "Collection Aimé Humbert": approximately 3,500 pieces, 808 paintings, 2,515 Japanese prints, 180 chromolithographs, maps, etc., contained in 21 folios. As far as I know, the buyer is not yet clearly identified, but it was asserted that a family member did acquire the whole (Weihe 1992). According to the record kept by Jean Gabus, director of the Neuchâtel Ethnographic Museum, the collection seems to reappear around 1947 at a Neuchâtel antiques dealer. Gabus bought when the museum was offered the Humbert collection in 1949. In his museum report of 1950, he roughly described the collection as divided into 16 folios. Roland Kaehr, who was the first curator to take care of the collection in the 1970s, remembers that it was stored in bad conditions and that some pieces may have been stolen within the museum. For example, the absence of ukiyo-e, erotic woodblock prints, seems suspect. Though it should be once more carefully verified, Balemi (2003: 77) counted 2,631 pieces. Consequently, we can so far conclude that 5 folios and approximately 1,037 pieces are missing.

Weihe (1992) had the chance to identify some pieces from the collection during an auction in Zurich. The former owner was the granddaughter of Aimé Humbert. This helps us to formulate two different hypotheses. Maybe Humbert privately kept a few Japanese prints before Turrettini obtained the collection, or Humbert's descendents kept a selection of pieces between the Marseille acquisition and the final destination in the Neuchâtel museum of ethnography where the collection was never studied or fully registered. Until today, only thirteen pieces by Kawanabe Kyōsai (1831–1889) were seriously identified (Weihe 1992) and one was published in Kyōsai's collected works in Japan. The collection contains documentary materials reflecting what was available on the market, in bookstores around Tokyo at the end of the Edo period, woodblock prints, parts of printed books, and watercolour drawings. The works from foreigners like Wirgman, and photographs from Felice Beato were obtained directly from their authors.

From an art history point of view, this collection was not gathered by a connoisseur as we find later on, but Humbert had a project to write an account of

Japanese society and he was not aware of the artistic value of what he gathered. He organized the images according to their intrinsic thematic representation and managed to obtain as much information as he could from the scenes depicted when he was in Japan. Personally, I am convinced that the Humbert collection is of great interest on several levels and that it should be studied carefully in a multidisciplinary way. The strong aspect is that the engravings from his book were compiled and interpreted from these original documents which played an important indirect role in shaping the construction of a less but still quite imaginary image of Japan in a large public in Switzerland and in Europe.

The fact that Humbert entrusted Turrettini with his collection is certainly a sign that he was concerned about its future. Although the Humbert collection was completely ignored for 110 years, between the first noteworthy exhibition of Japanese art in Switzerland in 1894 and 2004, when a small exhibition on Humbert was organized at the OAG in Japan. The time has come to study this collection in detail. So to say, the French-speaking Canton of Neuchâtel reflects in itself the complex relationship between Switzerland and Japan and provides several examples of missed opportunities to deepen institutional ties with Japan and the curious destiny of several Japanese collections.

Later encounters: the Mayor story and Conrad Meili

In order to investigate very briefly the transition between the 19th and 20th century I would like to quote two further examples. We did review several cases exemplifying how personalities who have had a direct early experience with Japan or who tried to build a bridge between Japan and Switzerland were ignored or not very well remembered in Switzerland. Paradoxically, most of the Swiss who visited Japan after the 1870s seem to have literally fallen in love with Japan, but they had to keep their passion for themselves or to share it with a limited circle of other amateurs. As Cordier pointed it out, the heritage they left was not particularly celebrated or exploited. Of course Swiss people have travelled extensively all over the world for centuries but it seems to me that there is a particular symptomatic and general disinterest in Swiss experiences in East Asia, especially until the 1930s.

Almost every traveller brought back many Japanese goods, craft or art pieces that they often sold or donated to one or several Swiss ethnographic museums from the late 19th century on. Listing Japanese collections in Swiss ethnographic museums is therefore the best way to discover the hidden history of many encounters with Japan in order to reconstruct the puzzle of the early Japanese image-building process in Switzerland. The general pattern can be summarized as follows: The items or ensemble of items reached the museums during the collector's lifetime, at their death, or from the heirs of one or more generations. Private travellers, businessmen, diplomats or their heirs wished to enrich their local museum's collection, to leave their name to posterity or to disencumber their home. Recently, the heirs of the second to the fourth generation feel reluctant to donate their collection to museums because of sentimental feeling or market price awareness, but some exceptional cases arise, when these heirs have no descendants, they themselves then turn to museums in order to give a secure home to their family heritage.

In 1999, André Mayor from Neuchâtel, in his 80s and having no direct heirs, suddenly wished to deposit some Japan-related materials at the Neuchâtel Ethnographic Museum. We received more that 200 glass slides, photographs, and many documents, for example on the Russo-Japanese war (1904–1905). Going together with the slides, four notebooks testified that the father of André Mayor, Robert Mayor (1874–1970), had given more than forty public conferences on Japan all over the Neuchâtel region between 1905 and 1911. Moreover they contained the list of slides used during these lectures, the place they were read, and the money he received for it, but most interestingly also the text of these speeches on Japan. He started at the Neuchâtel Geographical Society but did not speak at the newly founded Ethnographic Museum (1904). He then lectured on Japan for different local societies. This is the first attested and documented attempt to introduce Japan with slides in Switzerland which bears witness to an increasing popular interest in Japanese civilisation.

Looking back to the museum archives, it became clear that Robert Mayor donated Japanese objects at several occasions during his lifetime. After several interviews with André Mayor, I could learn that his father was a great collector and storyteller, and that his fascination for Japan lasted until his death. However, before long there appeared a much more complex story, a business venture in Japan started in 1864, ended in a complete failure and was kept as a family secret.

André Mayor entrusted me with a family document written by his father Robert in 1949, which unveiled an unknown episode of the watchmaking and export history. The story told by Robert started in 1857 with the foundation of the watch company Hormann & Borel, in which his grandfather was involved. His father Georges Mayor (1843–1912) started to be an apprentice there in 1861. In 1864, the company Charles Hormann & Co. was founded and started to export to Japan. Georges became Hormann's associate in 1866 and Robert joined as an apprentice in 1894. Hormann retired in 1898 and the business was taken over by George and his son Robert, the company was renamed Mayor & Co., exporting watches at least to Penang, Bangkok, Shanghai, and Yokohama. The new firm was promised a brilliant future, but the Mayors inherited an important debt contracted by their Yokohama import company, the Colomb & Co. (see Sigerist 2001: 240).

According to Jean de Rham (Comité du centenaire 1964: 77), former Swiss ambassador to Japan, there were about eight Swiss businessmen already in Yokohama before the arrival of Aimé Humbert in 1863. Among them Jules and Paul Colomb, who already were importing watches from Hormann & Borel, perhaps as early as 1860. During decades, the Colomb brothers accumulated unpaid bills and the Mayors were forced to continue their business relations with them in the hope to obtain the money. In 1898, the amount was incredibly high, about 780,000 Swiss francs. In Robert's testimony, we find that in 1898 the business archives going back to the 1860s were already destroyed; this explains the difficulty when attempting to study the early watch trade with Japan. One of the Colomb brothers came to Switzerland every four years and, in 1898, they invited Robert to come to Japan in order to analyse their business situation.

He left for Japan in 1899 and returned very disappointed as the Colombs kept all information from him. Nevertheless, he became very impressed with the country. The business with the Colomb brothers deteriorated further as they did not repay their debts, therefore Robert returned to Japan in 1903 to 1905. Facing unsuccessful negotiations with the Colombs, he spent much time to discover Japan, its culture and collecting Japonica. The sudden death of Paul Colomb in 1912 and the huge debt to Mayor & Co. provoked the bankruptcy of both companies as Robert went back to Yokohama in 1913 and hired a lawyer to force Colomb to pay the due money. All Colomb's belongings were sold at an auction. There we learn that the Colombs had a shop in Geneva where they exported Japanese goods.

The financial struggle with the Colombs, described as fabulous swindlers living very comfortably in Yokohama, ended tragically and the son of Robert Mayor is the last witness of a Neuchâtel watch company's misfortune in Japan. This case is an affair strictly between two Swiss companies, but we could at least learn that the Colombs also sent some Japanese goods to Switzerland and that Robert became a frontier runner, introducing visually and orally his vision and understanding of Japan at a popular level.

The second and concluding case concerns the Zurich-born artist Conrad Meili (1895–1969), one of the last students of Ferdinand Hodler (1853–1918). Unlike his notorious predecessor Félix Régamey, Meili rather belongs to a generation of artists influenced by artists who had already integrated some Japanese art influence in their work, such as Félix Vallotton (1865–1925). He settled in Neuchâtel where he produced several woodblock print series of cubist inspiration and met Kikou Yamata (Yamada Kikuko – 1897–1975) who came for a conference in 1928. They married in 1932.

Kikou was the daughter of Yamada Tadazumi, consul of Japan in Lyon, who was married to a French lady. Around 1923, Kikou became famous in Paris and started a literary career, with a strong focus on Japan, developing a new image of this country thanks to her double identity. From 1930, she introduced *ikebana* in France and in Switzerland, and the couple became mostly active in Paris where Meili was successful. In 1939, they left for Japan where they had to stay ten years because of the war and financial hardship. Meili did teach art in Japan and produced over 600 works which he brought back to Europe in 1949. Meili is certainly the first Swiss artist to have lived and painted in Japan for such a long period.

After their return, they lived in a village near Geneva. This emblematic couple symbolizing Japan nevertheless found it very difficult to gain recognition in Switzerland and they had to travel frequently to Paris. Meili's work always remained quite classical and mainly in the line of impressionism, but his Japan-related works can also be qualified as neo-orientalism. Though he had a fascinating career and life, Meili is one of the lesser-known Swiss painters and his works, especially the paintings executed in Japan, are still completely ignored by the art market and art historians. Even his tomb was destroyed in the 1990s, because the village authorities did not even realize that Meili could become famous in the 21st century.

Conclusion and perspectives

In this preliminary and fragmentary report I tried to propose a diachronic review of a small selection of case studies and new findings. The aim was to investigate some aspects of the Switzerland-Japan relationship and connections in order to analyse the image-building process of Japan in Switzerland, as an exotic, distant, mysterious, and attracting cultural entity. This is of course a unilateral approach, not touching upon the role Japanese people played visiting or living for some time or permanently in Switzerland during the late 19th and 20th centuries. My evaluation attempted to be centred on the human dimension and diversity of Swiss contacts with Japan. Hopefully I won't be accused of chauvinism; I believe in the necessity of a reappraisal of the history of bilateral commercial, diplomatic, intellectual, technical, and tourist relations with Japan, and in the importance of a multidisciplinary approach. The famous, forgotten or until recently unknown Swiss travellers to Japan during the Meiji period and later still need much investigation in order to reconstruct their experience and gather all kinds of information they have left behind.

An interesting hypothesis for the anthropologist is that the early and later images of Japan in Switzerland must be understood as a construct elaborated from early written accounts and the different Swiss and foreign testimonies. However, the difficulty in studying Swiss perceptions of Japan through time is of course a question of the availability of sources or archives, but more specifically to link the Swiss experiences to the different dynamics going on simultaneously in the neighbouring countries, first the Netherlands and then principally France and Germany, and to a lesser extent England and the USA. Multilingual Switzerland was therefore strongly influenced by both French and German patterns of interest in Japan during the 19th and 20th centuries, corresponding to the two dominant languages in Switzerland.

The challenge is to measure the intellectual, popular reception and integration of different images and stereotypes of Japan transmitted through different fields, like various kind of literature (travel, novel, drama), art (Japonisme), Japonica and Japanese art collecting, World Exhibitions, exotic travel, commerce, and diplomacy. As we could see, the introduction of knowledge of Japan and Japanese culture has been quite irregular and difficult to analyse from 1586 to 1804. Sixty years after Horner visited Nagasaki, the Humbert mission started to consolidate the Swiss presence in Japan, although some Swiss like the photographer Rossier or businessmen had arrived already in Japan from 1859.

Nevertheless, research shows today that we can formulate the suggestion that many of these travellers have little or no place in the Swiss memory and that a structured interest in Japan is a recent trend. We should ask ourselves why we can observe a constant fascination with Japan, systematically characterized by individual experience mostly linked to commercial projects but also travels of tourist nature. One strong stable trend is the everlasting attraction for Japanese material culture, crafts and arts, especially from the 17th century. During a long period material culture was the only concrete medium from which most Swiss were able to imagine Japan. The first import channel was the Dutch East India Company, then the Swiss visitors acquired important amount of pieces or even exported Japonica or *"hamamono"* – goods for export from the port of Yokohama

– as the Colombs did. From the time Rossier came to Japan, the rise of commercial photography also played a key role in shaping a new perception of Japan.

In Switzerland, the fact that Japanese collections are found almost exclusively in ethnographic museums is a significant indication. This can be easily explained from the fact that Japan is a remote place on the globe and it was and still is perceived as exotic. By the turn of the 20th century, especially after the Russo-Japanese war (1904–1905), Japan appeared as a rapidly modernizing and industrializing country, therefore the collections gathered were also perceived as part of the "authentic" and traditional Japan on the verge of disappearance. The investigation of museum collections and archives is a recent approach (Kreiner 1981, 2005) and proves to be a rewarding research method in order to obtain significant new or complementary information, as in the cases of Horner or Mayor. It helps to reconstruct the life history of travellers to Japan, to learn about what was available on the market, the taste of the collector, and it can lead to some private collection or documentation. We are still very far from having investigated all materials from Swiss ethnographic museums, and the quantity of collections or archives still in private possession seems to be enormous in Switzerland.

The Swiss image of Japan as a global topic was unfortunately only superficially analysed, since this paper rather introduced new elements and proposals, and showed the importance of anthropology in obtaining new and complementary conclusions to the traditional historic approaches. Historical materials should be revisited and the progressive construction of the image and stereotypes of Japan in Switzerland should also be analysed in a comparative perspective with the perception of China and Korea. The local disinterest in the work and life of the Swiss pioneers in East Asia can be seen as a general trend, pattern or a Swiss attitude. The complex interwoven figure characterized with fascination versus chronic disinterest was also influenced by trade fluctuations (Jequier 1990) and geopolitical events.

Just let's imagine how Horner would have felt if he had known that he would have come back to Japan 200 years later. As a matter of fact, his oil portrait was exhibited in the Swiss pavilion at the 2005 World Exposition in Aichi and more than one million visitors could see it. Furthermore, an exhibition on Horner and the Krusenstern expedition scheduled to be held in 2008 at the Zurich Ethnographic Museum will put particular focus on Japan. The year 2005 also saw the publication of a reprint of the Humbert book (1870), and the official launching of a project by the Neuchâtel Ethnographic Museum in order to study, publish, and exhibit the Humbert Japanese art and photography collection, a major event should occur during the future celebration of the 150th anniversary of the first bilateral treaty between Switzerland and Japan. But life is going on and many projects between our two countries will continue to develop, it is now the responsibility of the different Swiss state departments and institutions to decide if they will encourage and support unambiguously the diversity of bilateral projects or only focus on business-related and applied science projects. The reorganisation of the Swiss university system, also occurring all over Europe in accordance with the Bologna convention, is now endangering the small disciplines, and Japanese studies unfortunately fit this category. To be slightly utopian, I strongly hope that we will assist towards a significant increase of Japanese studies and multidisciplinary projects in the fields of history, art history, anthropology, museums research, political science, and history of science, in order to better understand the mutual influence of both our countries within the European context during the 19th and 20th centuries.

Philippe Dallais, born 1969 in Geneva; made his cursus at Neuchâtel University in anthropology, archaeology and art history; works as Curator assistant at the Ethnographic Museum of Zurich University. His main research interests are the anthropology of contemporary Japan, museology, heritage studies and visual anthropology.

References

Andrade Tonio
2005 "Pirates, pelts, and promises: the Sino-Dutch colony of Seventeenth-century Taiwan and the aboriginal village of Favorolang". *Journal of Asian studies* (Ann Arbor) 64 (2), pp. 295–321.

Arata Shigeo
2004 "Suisu ni ni hyaku nen mae no nihon" (Japan 200 Years Ago Found in Switzerland). *Asahi Shimbun* (Tokyo), July 20, p. 4.

Balemi Silke Karina
2003 *Reisephotographie in Ostasien und europäische Reisebilder in Wissenschaft, Kunst und Alltag von ca. 1860 bis 1914/18*. Locarno: Ed. Pedrazzini.

Barrelet Jean-Marc
1986 "Diplomatie, commerce et ethnographie: le voyage d'Aimé Humbert au Japon". *Musée neuchâtelois* (Neuchâtel) 4: 145–166.

Beckmann Johann
1939 "Der erste Japandruck in der Schweiz". *Zeitschrift für Buchdruck, Bibliophilie und Presse-Geschichte* (Bern) 3: 149–157.

Bennett Terrence
1996 *Early Japanese Images*. Rutland; Tokyo: Ch. E. Tuttle.
2004 "The search for Rossier: early photographer of China and Japan". [Online, released on August 4], http://www.old-japan.co.uk/articles.html.

Brauen Martin
2003 *Bamboo in Old Japan. Art and Culture on the Threshold to Modernity: The Hans Spörry Collection in the Ethnographic Museum of Zürich University*. Stuttgart: Arnoldsche Art Publishers.

Comité du centenaire (ed.)
1964 *Helvetia – Nippon 1864–1964*. Tokyo: Comité du centenaire.

Commission des musées de la Société suisse d'ethnologie (ed.)
1979 *Ethnographical Collections in Switzerland I*. Berne: Société suisse d'ethnologie.
1984 *Ethnographical Collections in Switzerland II*. Berne: Société suisse d'ethnologie.

Cordier Henri
1894 *La participation des Suisses dans les études relatives à l'Extrême Orient*. Genève: W. Kündig.

Cysat Renward

1586 *Warhafftiger Bericht von den newerfundnen Japponischen Inseln und Königreichen, auch von andren zuvor unbekandten Indianischen Landen* [...]. Freyburg: Abraham Gemperlin. (2nd ed. 1592).

Dallais Philippe

2005 "Horunâ, anbêru, soshite sonogo jinruigakuteki shiten ni okeru suisu jin no nihon zô [Horner, Humbert and thereafter: The Swiss image of Japan in anthropological perspective]", in: Morita Yasukazu (ed.), *Nihon to suisu no kôryû bakumatsu kara meiji e* [The relationship between Japan and Switzerland – from the Edo period to the Meiji Era], pp. 71–118. Tokyo: Yamakawa shuppansha.

Dallais Philippe, Tahara Kaori

2003 *Ainu people and Switzerland: catalogue of the Ainu collections from northern Japan. Geneva and Bern*. (Preprint)

2007 *Ainu people and Switzerland: catalogue of the Ainu collections from northern Japan. Basel, Bern, Burgdorf, St. Gallen, Zurich, Geneva, Neuchâtel, Lugano*. Bern [etc.]: Peter Lang. (In preparation)

Eracle Jean

1985 "Enquête sur un cabinet japonais", in: Musée d'ethnographie (ed.), *Le visage multiplié du monde: quatre siècles d'ethnographie à Genève*, 184–191. Genève: Musée d'ethnographie.

Hauptman William (ed.)

1996 *John Webber, 1751–1793: Landschaftsmaler und Südseefahrer*. Bern: Kunstmuseum; Manchester: Whitworth Art Gallery.

Humbert Aimé

1870 *Le Japon illustré*. Paris: Hachette. 2 vols.

Hürlimann Martin

1975 *Schweiz – Japan: Beiträge zu ihren Beziehungen*. Zürich: Schweizerisch-Japanische Gesellschaft.

Immoos Thomas

1982 *Wie die Eidgenossen Japan entdeckten*. Tokyo: OAG.

Jequier François

1990 "Economic and commercial relations between Switzerland and Japan before World War I", in: Yuzawa Takeshi, Udagawa Masaru (eds.), *Foreign Business in Japan before World War II*, 143–174. Tokyo: University of Tokyo Press.

Jud Peter

1995 *Léon Metchnikoff 1838–1888: ein russischer Geograph in der Schweiz*. Zürich: Oriole-Verlag.

Kaempfer Engelbert

1999 *Kaempfer's Japan: Tokugawa culture observed*. Honolulu: University of Hawai'i Press. (Ed., trad. and ann. by Beatrice M. Bodart-Bailey).

Kleinschmidt Harald, Romberg Claudia

2004 *Ein Schweizer in Japan: Die Humbert Mission 1863/64. In Erinnerung an den Abschluß des Handelsvertrages zwischen Japan und der Schweiz 1864*. Tokyo: OAG (Deutsche Gesellschaft für Natur- und Völkerkunde Ostasiens).
[*Tenjikai. emê anbêru. Suisu tokuhakôshi no mita bakumatsu nihon. nihon-suisu shûkôtsûshô joyaku 140nen kinen*; trad.: Toshiko Tanaka, Tomoko Matsumoto].

Knapp Charles

1889 "Léon Metchnikoff". *Bulletin de la Société neuchâteloise de géographie* (Neuchâtel) 4 (1888): 272–276.

Kreiner Josef (ed.)

1981 "Japan-Sammlungen in Museen Mitteleuropas. Geschichte, Aufbau und gegenwärtige Probleme". *Bonner Zeitschrift für Japanologie* (Bonn) 3.

2005 *Japanese collections in European museums: Reports from the Toyota-Foundation-Symposium, Königswinter 2003; vol. I: General prospects; vol. II: Regional studies*. Bonn: Bier'sche Verlagsanstalt.

Krusenstern Adam Johann von [Ivan Fedorovich Kruzenshtern]

1810 *Reise um die Welt in den Jahren 1803, 1804, 1805 und 1806; auf Befehl seiner kaiserlichen Majestät Alexander des Ersten auf den Schiffen Nadeshda und Newa unter dem Commando des Capitains von der Kaiserlichen Marine A. J. von Krusenstern; erster Theil*. St. Petersburg: Gedruckt in der schnoorschen Buchdruckerey, auf Kosten des Verfassers.

1811 *Reise um die Welt in den Jahren 1803, 1804, 1805 und 1806;* [...]; *zweiter Theil*. St. Petersburg: Gedruckt in der schnoorschen Buchdruckerey, auf Kosten des Verfassers.

1812 *Reise um die Welt in den Jahren 1803, 1804, 1805 und 1806;* [...]; *dritter Theil*. St. Petersburg: Gedruckt in der schnoorschen Buchdruckerey, auf Kosten des Verfassers.

1813 *Voyage round the world, in the years 1803, 1804, 1805, & 1806, by order of His Imperial Majesty Alexander the First, on board the ships Nadeshda and Neva, under the command of Captain A. J. von Krusenstern, of the imperial navy*. 2 vols. & Atlas. London: C. Roworth for J. Murray.

1813 *Atlas k Puteshestviiu vokrug sveta Kapitana Kruzenshterna* [Atlas of Kruzenshtern's Circumnavigation]. Morskaia tipografiia.

1814 *Atlas zur Reise um die Welt: unternommen auf Befehl seiner kaiserlichen Majestaet Alexander des Ersten auf den Schiffen Nadeshda und Neva unter dem Commando des Capitains von Krusenstern*. St. Petersburg.

1968 *Voyage round the world, in the years 1803, 1804, 1805, and 1806*. Amsterdam: N. Israel; New York: Da Capo press. (2 vols., facsimile of the London edition, 1813).

Langsdorff Georg Heinrich von

1993 *Remarks and observations on a voyage around the world from 1803 to 1807*. Kingston; Fairbanks: Limestone press. (1812, translated from German and annotated by Victoria J. Moessner).

Lindau Rodolphe

1864 *Un voyage autour du Japon*. Paris: Librairie de L. Hachette.

Löwenstern Hermann Ludwig von

2003 *The first Russian voyage around the world: the journal of Hermann Ludwig von Löwenstern (1803–1806)*. Fairbanks: University of Alaska Press. (Translated by Victoria Joan Moessner).

Metchnikoff Léon

1878 *L'Empire japonais*. Genève: Imprimerie orientale de «L'Atsume Gusa». (Chapters appeared in the *Atsume Gusa* series from 1877).

Milner Steffen Erik

2004 "Le Japon, premier partenaire commercial de la Suisse en Asie". *La vie économique* (St. Gall) 10: 56–62.

Morita Yasukazu (ed.)

2005 *Nihon to suisu no kôryû bakumatsu kara meiji e*. Tokyo: Yamakawa shuppansha.

Mottini Roger

1998 *Die Schweiz und Japan während der Meiji-Zeit (1868–1912): Begegnung, Berichterstattung und Bilder*. Bamberg: Difo-Druck.

2004 "The Swiss-Japanese treaty of Friendship and Commerce of February 6, 1864". http://www.sjcc.ch/sjcc/FileCabinetEventReports/Rede%20Mottini.htm.

Mumenthaler Rudolf

1996 "Die Weltumsegelung Krusensterns mit Schweizer Beteiligung: J. K. Horner", in: Mumenthaler Rudolf, *Im Paradies der Gelehrten: Schweizer Wissenschaftler im Zarenreich (1725–1917)*, 379–394. Zürich: H. Rohr.

Nagi Laurence

2004 "Visite diplomatique, Joseph Deiss est arrivé hier à Tokyo: une aquarelle pour séduire l'empereur". *Le matin* (Lausanne) October 10: 5.

Nakai Akio Paul

1964 "Die Aufnahme der diplomatischen Beziehungen zwischen der Schweiz und Japan im Jahre 1864", in: *Helvetia – Nippon 1864–1964*, 11–68. Tokyo: Comité du centenaire.

1967 *Das Verhältnis zwischen der Schweiz und Japan: vom Beginn der diplomatischen Beziehungen 1859 bis 1868*. Bern; Stuttgart: Verlag Paul Haupt.

Nojima Atsushi

2004 "Ima kara 200 nen mae ni nihon o otozureta saisho no suisu jin!? Yohan-kasupāru horunā. *Grüezi, Schweizerisch-Japanische Zeitung* (Altdorf) 28: 1. [Le premier Suisse qui a visité le Japon il y a 200 ans!? Johann Caspar Horner]. http://mypage.bluewin.ch/gruezi.

Odori Kyōji

2004 "Shiroihada no ajiajin: renvaruto suizāto no *nihonshi* o yomu". *Musashinodaigaku jinbungakkai zasshi* (Tokyo) 35 (4): 103–151.

Paravicini Eugen

1943 "Der Anteil der Schweiz an der Völkerkundlichen Forschung", in: Staub Walther, Hinderberger Adolf, *Die Schweiz und die Forschung*, vol. 2, 128–160. Bern: Verlag Hans Huber.

Perrot Alain

1996 *François Turrettini «Le Chinois», Tschin-ta-ni «le Genevois»: le sinologue et son collaborateur*. Genève: S. Hurter.

Psota Thomas

2003 "Ostasiatika in der ethnographischen Sammlung am Historischen Museum in Bern". *Ostasiatische Zeitschrift* (Berlin) 6: 49–58.

Ripon Elie

1997 *Voyages et aventures aux Grandes Indes: journal inédit d'un mercenaire 1617–1627*. Paris: Les Editions de Paris. (Presentation and notes by Yves Giraud; a new edition is scheduled to be published by the Editions Chandeigne, under the title *Les aventures du Capitaine Ripon (1617–1662): un mercenaire suisse au service de la VOC*).

Satō Yūmi

2004 "Ni hyaku nen mae ni egakareta suisujin niyoru suisaiga ga hakken sareru" (Discovery of 200 years old watercolours painted by a Swiss). *Swissinfo.org* (Japanese edition). Online (18.7.2004): http://www.swissinfo.org/sja/swissinfo.html?siteSect=105&sid=5078260.

Sigerist Stefan

2001 *Schweizer in Asien: Präsenz der Schweiz bis 1914*. Schaffhausen: S. Sigerist.

Smith George

1861 *Ten Weeks in Japan*. London: Longman, Green.

Sondermann Frieder

2004 "Nagasaki 1804". *OAG Notizen* (Tokyo) 10, pp. 22–27.

Swiss-Japanese Chamber of Commerce (ed.)

2004 *Swiss-Japanese Chamber of Commerce Journal* (Zurich) 1–2: special issue on the 140th anniversary. http://www.sjcc.ch/sjcc/FileCabinetEventReports/140Years.htm.

Takeuchi Hiroshi
1983 "Weuve, Henri W., – 1870", in: Takeuchi Hiroshi, *Rai nichi seiyô-jin meijiten*, 39. Tokyo: Nichi gai asoshietsu kabushiki gaisha.

Tilley Henry Arthur
1861 *Japan, the Amoor, and the Pacific*. London: Smith, Elder & Co.

Weihe Hugo K.
1992 "Some unknown works by Kawanabe Kyōsai". *Artibus Asiae* (Zurich) 52 (1–2), notice II.

This article is a revised version of a paper (Dallais 2005) read during the Symposium *The relationship between Japan and Switzerland in the late 19th century, Symposium on the occasion of the 140th Anniversary of the relationship between Japan and Switzerland*, Japan Women's University, Tokyo, October 9, 2004, and published by Professor Morita (2005).

Acknowledgements

I would like to thank heartily the Faculty of Humanities and the Institute of Literature of Japan Women's University, the Swiss Department of Foreign Affairs, Presence Switzerland, the Embassy of Switzerland in Tokyo, especially Mr. Pierre-Yves Fux. My greatest thanks go to Prof. Yasukazu Morita for his support and to Dr. Roger Mottini.

SWITZERLAND'S WAY TO JAPAN
By Dr. Roger Mottini

Recent research unveiled that the first Swiss who set his foot on Japanese soil nearly 400 years ago was probably Héli Ripon, a mercenary born near Lausanne. The next one arrived 200 years ago in Nagasaki: Johann Caspar Horner (1734–1834), physicist and astronomer from Zurich (see essay Dallais in this volume).

At the beginning of the 19th century, Switzerland was not much more than a geographical denomination. Only after a turbulent period of French occupation and domination (1798–1803, 1812), a brief civil war (1847) and enormous pressure from the European powers did the Swiss cantons finally come together in order to form a federal state based on a common Swiss constitution (1848). Despite its political fragility, Switzerland was rather well developed with regard to its economy; the process of industrialization had already begun at the end of the 18th century making Switzerland, together with Belgium, the second-oldest industrialized country after Great Britain (Biucchi/Basilio 1986: 44). Even before becoming a political unity, Switzerland was already Britain's most formidable competitor on the world market for textiles. In 1837 the British parliament received the report of its special envoy who was sent to that country of barely two million people in order to analyse its success (Bowring 1837).

Compared to its economic activities worldwide, however, Switzerland's foreign policy was on a very modest level; Swiss consulates were established only after 1798 and between 1850 and 1865 the first ones appeared in Asia (Documents Diplomatiques Suisses 1990, vol. 1: XIX). The driving forces behind the increase in worldwide foreign policy activities of the young Swiss Confederation were economic worries about protectionist tendencies in the neighbouring countries.

The US endeavour of gaining access to Japan was attentively observed in Switzerland. In 1854 the United States succeeded in concluding the treaty of Kanagawa, forcing a reluctant Japan to open the ports of Shimoda and Hakodate to foreign trade. Two years later, further privileges were granted by the inexperienced Japanese Shogunate. Under massive threats from the American

Consul General in Japan, Townsend Harris (1804–1878), the treaty of Edo (now Tokyo) was signed. The treaties forced upon the Shogun were hugely biased in favour of the USA, stipulating a tax of only 5% (of value) on imports to Japan without reciprocity; a most-favoured-nation clause ensured that all further potential concessions were to be applied in equal measure to every country having concluded a treaty with Japan. Furthermore, foreign nationals of the treaty countries living in Japan enjoyed extraterritorial status, that is, they were exempted from Japanese justice; legal disputes involving foreigners had to be decided by their own consulates!

Business circles in Switzerland quickly realized how advantageous such a treaty arrangement was. The Watchmakers' Association in La Chaux-de-Fonds and the Textile Business Association in St. Gallen took the lead in persuading the Federal Government to establish formal relations with Japan. Textiles and watches accounted for the bulk of Swiss export earnings at that time. Aimé Humbert (1819–1900), the president of the Watchmakers' Association, became the driving force behind the Swiss effort to enter in contact with Japan.

These two organisations hired a German travel-book author and sent him to Japan in order to conclude a treaty on behalf of Switzerland. His name was

The members of the Humbert mission before their departure. Sitting on the chair in front: Aimé Humbert. Standing behind him probably Brennwald.

 Rudolph Lindau (1830–1910). On September 20, 1859, he arrived in Yokohama on a merchant ship, certainly a serious break of etiquette in the eyes of the proud samurai officials. Humbert had been aware of this potential problem and he tried to persuade the French Government to allow Lindau aboard a French gunboat, but his request had fallen on deaf ears.

Armed with only a letter of recommendation from the Federal Government, Lindau's position in Japan was weak anyway. The Japanese officials seemed to have also considerable difficulties in locating the country he was coming from; their first report referred to it as the "confederate republic of Swedenland" (Nakai 1967: 37–40). Even after this misunderstanding had been resolved, the Shogunate was not eager to conclude other treaties with foreign nations than those already concluded with the USA, Britain, France, Russia and Holland. The feudal Government of Japan was actually in a deep crisis. As a keen observer, Lindau himself had no illusions regarding the difficulties of his task. In his report to the Textile Trading Association of St. Gallen, he described the Shogunate as an unlawful and only tolerated Government whereas the legal ruler of Japan was considered to be the Emperor (Mikado) residing in Kyoto (Lindau 1862: 5).

The Shogunate's political stance was weakened by an economic and social crisis, which followed the opening of the Japanese market to a flood of cheap imports from the industrializing countries. Japan's domestic economy, dominated by agrarian and nonindustrial production faced a deadly competition. High inflation caused by a sharply increased foreign demand for Japanese products like silk, tea and raw materials in combination with foreign-currency speculations led to the impoverishment of large swathes of the population. Lindau, in his report to St. Gallen, described an economy bordering on sheer chaos and blamed foreign greed as well as incompetence of the feudal Government for the bleak situation.

Finally, the negotiations between Lindau and the Shogunate collapsed. He succeeded, however, to obtain a written promise from his Japanese interlocutors

to inform the Swiss Government as soon as an improved situation would allow the conclusion of further treaties.

Despite this failure, Humbert kept trying to convince the rather sceptical Federal Council of the necessity to establish official relations with Japan. The Swiss Government hesitated to spend a considerable amount of tax money on an undertaking with an uncertain outcome. In Switzerland at that time, knowledge about Japan was very poor to say the least.

In April 1861, the Federal Government was informed by the Dutch Ministry of Foreign Affairs that the Shogunate had signalled its willingness to start negotiations with Switzerland. The Swiss Government finally moved and appointed Aimé Humbert to head an official mission to Japan in order to conclude a treaty similar to the existing ones. The preparations began at once and the parliament passed a bill to spend 100,000 Swiss francs on the mission to Japan without any opposition to speak of. In order to balance the federal budget, the money was deducted from the military expenditures!

The more difficult part consisted in asking the cantons to provide gifts of value for the Japanese hosts. It took Humbert more than a year to complete the necessary preparations, he even went as far as learning Dutch, which was the language used by the officials of the Shogun to communicate with foreigners.

The Dutch gunboat "Medusa" in the Bay of Yokohama.

In order to impress their hosts, the Swiss were provided with a passage on a gunboat by the Dutch Government that would take them from Nagasaki to Yokohama.

Another problem did arise. The Federal Government was faced with the dilemma of providing a mission large enough to make an impression on the Japanese without, however, spending too much on it. The solution to that problem was rather creative: Aimé Humbert and his appointed secretary, Caspar Brennwald, were paid by the Government, whereas the four other members were given the status of diplomatic attachés but actually travelling at their own expense.

The Swiss mission to Japan included the following persons:
- Aimé Humbert from Neuchâtel
- Caspar Brennwald from Männedorf ZH
- James Favre-Brandt (1841–1923) from Le Locle
- Edouard Bavier from Chur
- Iwan Kaiser from Zug
- John Bringolf from Unterneuhaus SH.

The Swiss arrived on April 27, 1863, in Yokohama aboard a gunboat named "Medusa" – it was probably the first and only time that a warship was flying the Swiss flag. They could not possibly have chosen a worse timing for their mission. The Government of the Shogun was literally fighting for its survival. Its main rivals were powerful feudal lords from southern Japan who had gained a dominating influence at the imperial court in Kyoto. In the name of the Emperor they were openly challenging the rule of the Shogun based in Edo (Inoue 1993: 304). Domestic unrest and armed clashes had reached a level of civil war. The adversaries of the Shogunate assumed a fiercely xenophobic standpoint under the slogan: Sonnō jōi (Revere the Emperor – Fight the foreigners).

Under these circumstances, even the lives of the Swiss were under threat. Public safety was a big concern for foreigners living in Japan at that time; Lindau wrote that the Europeans or Americans carried a pistol with them when they

went outside in the evening (Lindau 1864: 182). The Shogunate reneged on its original promise and Switzerland's case seemed hopeless. Around the time of Humbert's arrival the young Shogun, Tokugawa Iemochi (1846–1866), was in Kyoto in order to secure imperial approval for his policy. This served as a handy excuse for the interlocutors of the Swiss to abstain from serious negotiations. The Swiss tried to gain favour with the Japanese officials by lavishing gifts on them; to their astonishment, however, the Japanese side returned every little gift with a gift of their own, always keeping the balance.

However, the main concern for the Japanese side was the security of their guests and thus they tried to persuade the Swiss to leave Edo for the relative safety of Yokohama. Humbert only accepted a compromise; during the day he and his secretary would stay in Edo and retire for the night on a ship owned by the Shogunate anchored in the Bay of Edo.

While the Swiss tried to advance their cause, a diplomatic war of nerves between the British and the Shogunate took place. For the assassination of an English trader named Richardson at the hands of warriors from the anti-Shogunal Satsuma Clan, the British demanded a high indemnity from the Shogunate holding them ultimately responsible for the crime.

Members of the Humbert mission in Edo ("Le Japon illustré").

On July 31, 1863, the Shogun returned to Edo from Kyoto with the imperial order of expelling all foreigners from Japanese soil!

Under these conditions there could be no talk of concluding a treaty with Switzerland. Nevertheless, Humbert decided to wait for better times.

The Swiss 'attachés' sought to establish as soon as possible businesses of their own, Humbert and Brennwald started to explore the cities of Edo and Yokohama and to take notes. Brennwald later wrote an extensive report about Japanese silk production intended for the Swiss textile industry. Humbert observed the social life of ordinary Japanese city dwellers, not yet aware that he was witnessing the last moments of a dying era. Years later he published his account in two big and lavishly illustrated books covering every imaginable aspect of daily life in Edo from education to funeral ceremonies (see references).

In the meantime, back in Switzerland, not only grew the Federal Government impatient with the long absence of its mission to Japan, the issue was also taken up by the carnival association in the canton of Schwyz. As a result, the Humbert mission became the laughing stock of their carnival (Immoos 1964).

Impatient, the Federal Council ordered Humbert to return by the end of 1863. Humbert answered obligingly, stating, however, that he would return by the end of the *Japanese* year, thereby gaining another month due to the lunar calendar used in Japan at that time. In vain he tried to enlist the support of the American and the French diplomats in Yokohama, both nations had no interest in helping the Swiss. Only the Dutch took up the Swiss cause and intervened on behalf of Humbert. The Dutch Consul General van Poelsbroek went as far as threatening to recommend to his Government to abstain from inviting Japanese officials for a planned diplomatic visit. Now things began to move.

Finally, on January 26, 1864, serious negotiations started. Taking the treaty with Prussia as a model, the negotiations made quick progress.

On February 6, 1864, the first treaty between Switzerland and Japan was concluded and Switzerland became the first nonmaritime nation to establish relations with Japan.

The Federal Council was very satisfied with the treaty, which granted Switzerland the same privileges enjoyed by all the other nations dealing with Japan. Although Japan was still a rather poor country and the market potential seemed to be very limited, the Swiss Government was optimistic that "the diligent and intelligent character of the Japanese people" will certainly make these relations fruitful and lasting ones (Hardegger 1986: 299).

Let me conclude with a few remarks concerning the destinies of the Swiss mission's members:

Aimé Humbert's books about society in the closing days of feudal Japan became classics; a hundred years later they were translated into Japanese and used as teaching materials for Japanese students in order to bring back to them part of their own heritage.

Kaspar Brennwald, his young secretary, teamed up with another Swiss businessman, Hermann Siber; together they founded 1864 a trading company still doing business in Japan.

James Favre-Brandt, with barely 22 years of age the youngest member of the Swiss mission, did never return to his native country; he married a Japanese woman and founded a successful import company. He also guarded an important secret. In the violent power struggle between the late Shogunate and its opponents from the southern feudal domains of Satsuma and Chōshū he played an important role. A keen and intelligent observer, the young Favre-Brandt quickly realized how shaky the Government of the Shogun really was by the time the Swiss-Japanese treaty of 1864 was concluded. One day the Swiss was approached by young influential samurai from the southern domains of Satsuma and Chōshū who asked him for support. He sold them a large number of modern French infantry rifles increasing the rebels' firepower considerably. After the collapse of the Shogunate at the end of 1867, his connections reached into the highest echelons of the new Imperial Government of the Meiji which was dominated by the same samurai he supported in their quest for power. Like a Swiss banker, however, he kept a lifelong silence about his connections and influential friends. Favre-Brandt is buried on the Foreigner's Cemetery in Yokohama.

Edouard Bavier entered the silk-trading business founding his own trading company which lasted until 1987.

Iwan Kaiser worked from 1864 to 1867 as an independent civil engineer in Yokohama before returning to Switzerland.

John Bringolf accompanied the mission as a journalist and wrote extensively about Japan in the newspaper "Schaffhauser Nachrichten".

Selected References

Biucchi Carlo, Basilio M.
1986 "Die industrielle Revolution in der Schweiz", in: Cipolla C.M./Borchert K. (eds.), Wirtschaftsgeschichte Bd. 4, Stuttgart.

Bowring John
1836 Report on the Commerce and Manufactures of Switzerland, London.
1837 Bericht an das englische Parlament über den Handel, die Fabriken und das Gewerbe der Schweiz, Zürich.

Hardegger et al.
1986 "Das Werden der modernen Schweiz", Luzern.

Humbert Aimé
1870 "Le Japon illustré", 2 vols., Paris.

Immoos, Thomas
1964 "Die Japanesenspiele in Schwyz", in: Helvetia – Nippon, Festschrift zum Abschluss des ersten schweizerisch-japanischen Handels- und Freundschaftsvertrages vor 100 Jahren, Tokyo.

Inoue Kiyoshi
1993 "Geschichte Japans", Frankfurt/M.: Campe.

Lindau Rudolph
1862 "Handelsbericht über Japan, dem Kaufmännischen Directorium in St. Gallen erstattet", St. Gallen.

Nakai Akio P.
1967 Das Verhältnis zwischen der Schweiz und Japan – Vom Beginn der diplomatischen Beziehungen, Diss. Universität Bern.

Nakanishi Michiko
1989 "Suisu tokuhashisetsudan no raihama to shōkan no sōgyō" (Arrival of the 2nd Swiss mission at Yokohama and the founding of trade business), in: Yokohama kyoryūchi no shosō (Aspects of the foreign settlement in Yokohama), Yokohama kaikōshiryōkan (ed.).

Schweizerische Eidgenossenschaft
1990 Documents Diplomatiques Suisses, vol. 1, Berne.

A MODEL STATE: THE IMAGE OF SWITZERLAND IN PREWAR JAPAN

By PD Dr. Harald Meyer

1. Fukuzawa Yukichi and Katō Hiroyuki[1]: First impressions of Switzerland

The first products from Switzerland brought to Japan on a Dutch merchant ship were watches reaching Dejima, the Dutch trading post in Nagasaki, already during the Edo period (1603–1867). After the arrival of the so-called "Black Ships" in 1853 under the command of US Commodore Matthew Calbraith Perry (1794–1858) the opening of Japan started.

Since the conclusion of the first treaty with Japan in 1864, Switzerland has been known there as the land of the watches and the Alps. Fukuzawa Yukichi (1835–1901) mentioned Switzerland in his book *Sekai kunizukushi* ("About all Countries in the World," 1869):

"If you follow the Rhine up to the headwaters, you will have a fine view of the majestic Swiss Alps. The Swiss Federation is a small country highly esteemed for its education system and artistic handicrafts. The capital is Berne, which is famous for its watchmakers. The citizens of this mountainous country are of great modesty, austerity and steadfastness. Though being a small nation, Switzerland is respected all over the world." (1)

From the beginning of the relations between the two countries, Switzerland enjoyed a good reputation in Japan. Already in 1861, Katō Hiroyuki (1836–1916) praised Switzerland in his writing *Tonarigusa* ("Grasses next door") for its federal system. (2) It was, however, not until the late Meiji era (1868 – 1923) that a comprehensive study about Switzerland was written by a Japanese scholar.

2. Abe Isoo's idealization of Switzerland

"This small country of complete freedom! Where else can there be found a nation that exists only for the purpose of granting its people wealth, liberty and equality? How can other countries still be eager for glory and territorial expan-

[1] Regarding Japanese names, they are given according to Japanese custom: family names precede given names.

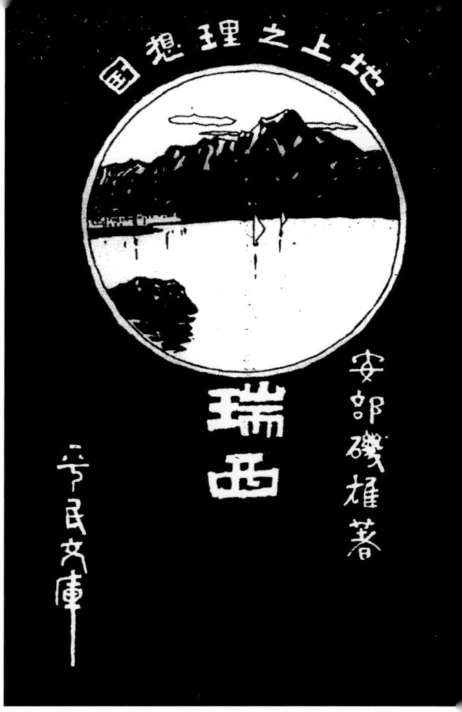

sion? All the other countries in this world should be ashamed and venerate this small and yet ideal nation." (3)

Switzerland appeared as the most ideal country on earth in a book written by Abe Isoo (1865–1949), one of the leaders of the early socialist and democratic movement in Japan. In this 100-page publication of 1904 entitled *Chijō no risōkoku – Suisu* ("Ideal State on Earth – Switzerland") Abe describes the political system and social conditions in Switzerland. Though written more than a hundred years ago, his account of the Swiss political system is basically still quite accurate. Abe's work was republished in 1947. Although his study tried to purvey a sense of objectivity, he partially idealized the Swiss society of that time:

"Those who comprehend Switzerland only as a material paradise are not aware of its true condition. Switzerland is pursuing much more than just material aims. Its towering liberalism appears to be more sublime than the highest peaks of the Alps and its fine social order more pleasant than the Lake of Geneva. However, this book about the most ideal nation in the world is not about Switzerland's high mountains and blue lakes, but about its liberty, equality and peace." (4)

Overall, metaphorical comparisons between Switzerland's liberalism and the Alps or its social order and blue lakes are very rare in Abe's book and serve only to point out clearly the actual objects of his study. While exploring the political institutions of Switzerland, Abe tried to reveal the fundamental ideas of this country, namely "liberty, equality and peace." In Abe's view, those values are of universal truth and should be adopted by all other nations. He describes the political system of Switzerland as the truest form of democracy:

"Politics in Switzerland consists of pure democracy based upon the representation of the people. The governments of the cantons are assemblies of direct

Title of Abe's book.

representatives of the people, and their political measures reflect the general will of a majority of voters. Considering the universal suffrage of the Swiss people and their right to make political decisions by the referendum, one must confess that civil rights and true liberty are realized to the highest degree in Switzerland." (5)

In his study about Switzerland as the most ideal of all democratic nations, Abe Isoo concentrates on the three fields of "politics," "education" and "social conditions." To get a closer view of its structure, it is necessary to present the table of contents as below:

Chapter "1. The Federal States System" starts with the following remark:

"A typical empire with federal organization is Germany. Typical republics with federal organization are the United States of America and Switzerland. In the thirteenth century, three cantons formed a defensive alliance and over time, more and more cantons joined the alliance, the number eventually reaching twenty-five. A centralized government was established in 1848, almost sixty years after the foundation of the United States. Relative to their area and population, those twenty-five cantons are of great variety." (6)

Abe Isoo had come to understand that the special features of Switzerland's political system were the result of an alliance of the cantons evolving into a federal organization. In the same chapter Abe also analyzes the distinctively Swiss phenomena of direct democracy and permanent neutrality. Abe showed great interest in institutions such as the referendum and initiative, which he describes as follows:

"The English expression 'referendum' is usually translated as *chokusetsu rippōken* [direct legislative]. It means that the people is given the possibility to vote on new bills even after they are passed by the national parliament or the council of a canton. If there is opposition against a bill, it will be put to the vote. Since the voters have the power of legislation, it seems to be appropriate to call this system direct legislative. On the other hand, 'initiative' enables the voters to present a petition and have it put to the vote ... For the time being,

I shall translate this system as *kengiken* [the right of presenting a petition]. Even in a very democratic nation like the United States, those two systems of direct voting do only exist on city level. In Switzerland however, they exist on the national as well as on the cantonal level. Clearly enough, this demonstrates the truly democratic spirit of Switzerland." (7)

Abe adopted terms like "referendum" or "initiative" from English sources dealing with Swiss politics. While quoting them in *katakana* syllables, he also added Japanese translations written in *kanji* (Sino-Japanese characters). Due to his statement "the English expression 'referendum' is usually translated as *chokusetsu rippōken* [direct legislative]," we can assume that this translation already existed during the latter half of the Meiji era. On the other hand, Abe writes about the term "initiative": "For the time being, I shall translate this system as *kengiken* [the right of presenting a petition]." This means that he was actually creating his own translation. During Japan's modernization many Western terms which did not yet exist in the Japanese language had to be translated somehow. As the above example demonstrates, foreign words were not only adopted phonetically, but also translated with two or more Sino-Japanese characters. The acceptance of Western terms was one of the key elements for the introduction of democratic ideas in prewar Japan and Abe played also an important role in this translations effort.

3. Abe's idealism

The most interesting question is: why did Abe write this book about Switzerland and what was the purpose of idealizing its political and social system? Looking at his career, Abe Isoo can be characterized as one of the foremost pioneers of the so-called era of Taishō Democracy. Born in Fukuoka, he graduated from Dōshisha University, where he converted to Christian faith under the influence

Ink sketch by Fukuzawa Yukichi.

of Niijima Jō (1843–1890). From 1892 to 1895, he studied in the United States at Hartford School of Theology (Connecticut). There he was drawn to Christian socialism; back in Japan, he devoted himself to social reform. In 1903 he became professor at Waseda University in Tokyo. Together with Katayama Sen (1859–1933) and Kōtoku Shūsui (1871–1911) Abe founded the *Shakaishugi kenkyūkai* ("Society for the Study of Socialism") in 1898. The aim of this organization was to found a socialist movement with an ideology embracing not only Marxist thoughts but democratic ideas and Christian humanitarianism as well. In 1901, members of this organization formed Japan's first socialist party, the *Shakai minshutō* (Socialist Democratic Party). Abe wrote the party's manifesto, a combination of socialist and democratic elements within the legal constraints of the Meiji constitution. However, only two days after its foundation the party was banned by the authorities. Nevertheless, Abe's manifesto had already been published on May 20 in a newspaper called *Hōchi shinbun* (Information Paper).

Abe and his followers denied calling for violent actions or revolution, they were in favor of general elections, universal suffrage and the cutting of military expenditures as well as supporting the trade union movement. The party base was not formed by workers but mainly by progressive intellectuals who were critical of the imperialistic politics and their promoters, the oligarchs of the Meiji government called *genrō* (elder statesmen). (8)

Despite the failure of the first Socialist Democratic Party, this small group of reformers, who were led to socialism through Christianity, succeeded to form the basis of the Japanese socialist, democratic and labor movements. In 1910, the socialist movement was shaken by the so-called "high treason incident" (*taigyaku jiken*). In this incident, Kōtoku Shūsui together with other anarcho-socialists were arrested put on trial and executed for allegedly plotting to assassinate the Emperor Meiji. After this incident socialist groups disappeared completely for almost a decade.

During and after this time, Abe Isoo distanced himself from radical standpoints and always propagated a vision of gradual social reform and change. He was against violent actions to overthrow the government and maintained his stance even towards some of his fellow activists who were becoming more radical. Instead, Abe joined the more moderate elements of the democratic and labor movements. After an extended period of political writing, he was among the founding members of the Socialist People's Party (*Shakai minshūtō*) founded in 1926. Elected as party chairman, he resigned from his post at Waseda University and in 1932 he was elected to the Diet. In the same year, he formed the *Shakai taishūtō* (Socialist Masses Party) and was again elected as chairman. In the late 1930s the *Shakai taishūtō* shifted to the right and Abe felt uncomfortable again. In 1940 he resigned together with other moderate members from the party and helped founding the *Kinrō kokumintō* (National Labor Party) in order to continue the moderate social-democratic tradition; however, this party was outlawed by the government soon after its formation. In 1940 Abe resigned from the Diet. After World War II, he served as an adviser to the newly formed *Nihon shakaitō* (Japan Socialist Party) until his death in 1949. (9)

Abe Isoo's political conviction and his social democratic idealism were the main reasons why he wrote about Switzerland. From his point of view, an ideal state consists of socialistic and democratic elements. Abe made a fine distinction between a socialist government and a combination of socialistic and democratic ideas. Socialism according to Abe Isoo meant mainly working for public welfare, namely support of the workers and the trade unions. With regard to democracy he asked for universal suffrage and political structures supporting party politics and the representation of the voters' will. It can be said that early Japanese socialism was intertwined with democratic ideas and early Japanese democratic thought was also connected with socialistic ideas. Abe writes about Switzerland:

"The Swiss system cannot be called purely socialistic. However it is evident, how much it relies on socialistic ideas. Within the financial sector, for example, a great number of monopoly companies are state-enterprises. [...] Many social problems are solved through governmental measures, which also fulfills socialistic demands. Socialists were standing up for the formation of Labor Exchanges and unemployment insurance, and their voices were heard. The field of welfare work is also based upon socialistic ideas. [...] In Switzerland, there is no big gap between rich and poor because there are not too many people living in extreme wealth or great poverty. Likewise, this corresponds to socialistic thought. As a matter of fact, the Swiss Socialist Party is of course accepted by the authorities, but has hardly any influence. Still this is not regrettable at all. In a society where socialistic policy is already translated into action, there is no need to form socialistic parties or groups." (10)

Amazingly, Abe concluded that important socialist demands like the support of the laborers and public welfare were satisfied in Switzerland to such great extent that a socialist movement was not necessary. That is why Switzerland appeared to him as the most ideal of all nations.

Another question regards the timing of Abe's book; why did he decide to publish such a book in the spring of 1904? The answer can be found in the preface as well as in the conclusion, where he writes about his motivation:

"Actually, I was planning to spend a few years on researching. But then I felt that the book should be published during the Russo-Japanese war, and so I started writing in haste. [...] Today, our country is making great efforts for the war against Russia. In hard times like these, it is my great pleasure to dedicate this little book to my compatriots." (11)

During the cabinet meeting on February 4, 1904, the opening of the hostilities against Russia was decided. Most intellectuals at that time belonged to the warmongers. In June 1903, the *Tōkyō Asahi shinbun* published a so-called "Memorandum of seven Doctors of the Imperial University" calling for drastic measures against Russia's invasion into Manchuria. Intellectual resistance was only offered by socialists like Kōtoku Shūsui and Sakai Toshihiko (1871–1933), or the Christian Uchimura Kanzō (1861–1930). In articles of the newspaper *Yorozu chōhō* ("General Morning Paper"), they protested against the imperialistic policy of the Japanese Government. After the editor, Kuroiwa Shūroku (1862–1920) joined in the war-mongering, they all quit working for the newspaper. In

October 1903, Kōtoku and Sakai founded their own newspaper, the *Heimin shinbun* ("The Common People's Journal"). At first, they were successfull in selling eight thousand copies of the first edition in November. But because of its critical articles against the Russo-Japanese war and its call for socialistic reform, the *Heimin shinbun* was outlawed in January 1905. During the existence of the newspaper, a book series called the *Heimin bunko* ("The Common People's Library") was published, containing Abe's study of Switzerland. Collaborating with the *Heimin shinbun* meant that Abe supported socialistic, democratic and pacifistic ideas. By writing about Swiss democracy, neutrality and welfare, Abe implicitly opposed the Russo-Japanese war.

In August 1903, Abe participated in a seminar organized by socialist societies. His speech was entitled: "Switzerland as an Island of Peace on Earth" (*Sekai no heiwakyō Suisu ni tsuite*). (12) With this lecture, Abe was openly opposing the preparations for the war against Russia and with the publication of his book about Switzerland, he came out against the outbreak and continuation of the war. By idealizing the decentralized form of government in Switzerland, he implicitly criticized the centralization of power in Japan and Japanese imperialism:

"Today the great powers are concentrating completely on foreign policy, so they are not capable of conducting a serious domestic policy. The centralization of power is necessary in order to realize an imperialistic policy. Decentralization of power can be compared to the distribution of money: if there is no fairness, many citizens are deceived. I believe that after the collapse of imperialism the age of decentralization will arrive and the great powers will accept this excellent system of Switzerland." (13)

Abe Isoo's social democratic idealism can finally be interpreted as a longing for "the collapse of imperialism" in the near future. From today's point of view, his hope was premature. The collapse of imperialism did not happen before Abe's death. Nevertheless, the outcome as we know it demonstrates how progressive his idealism was, unfortunately his voice went unheard in prewar Japan.

Abe Isoo's enthusiasm for the Swiss political and social system rested also on his conviction, that Switzerland and Japan had similar geopolitical environments. Switzerland was surrounded by four great powers – Germany, France, Austria and Italy; in Abe's view, Japan was in a similar position, surrounded by Russia, China, the United States and Australia. As natural defense, Japan was protected by the sea in the same way as Switzerland was protected by the Alps. Considering those similarities, Abe believed that Switzerland could serve as a model state for Japan. Instead of being in conflict with its neighboring countries, Japan should concentrate on domestic affairs just like the Swiss Government. (14)

4. Conclusion

Looking back, it is hard to figure out whether or not the Swiss model was transferable to Japan. Only at the end of his book, Abe Isoo delivers a direct comparison between Switzerland and Japan. But he did not offer a blueprint for political and social reforms modeled after the Swiss system. In doing so, he might have incurred the wrath of the censors and, as a consequence, the ban of his book. During times of strict censorship, Abe could express himself only in a metaphorical way. While writing a book about Switzerland during the Russo-Japanese war, he called for peace, democracy and social reform. Abe Isoo was one of the foremost theoretical exponents of a democratic movement, which later was to be known as "Taishō democracy."

The so-called "Taishō democracy" appears almost as a genre within modern historical research in Japan. The term "Taishō Democracy" did emerge only until the end of the First World War, when Japan was on the Allied side and fighting "to make the world safe for democracy."

The Japanese democracy movement was actually launched in 1912 by the "first campaign to protect constitutional government." The first success of the movement was the elevation of Hara Kei (also Takashi, 1856–1921) to the premiership in 1918, for he was the first commoner as a party leader to hold that post. Despite several setbacks, "Party rule" in Japan dates back from that time until the beginning of the Shōwa era in 1926. Most historians date "Taishō democracy" from the end of the Russo-Japanese war in 1905 up to the introduction of universal suffrage in 1925.

Yet, there is still a lack of research in Japan concerning the selection and analysis of sources on "Taishō democracy." Historical materials of great importance like Abe Isoo's *Chijō no risōkoku – Suisu* have not yet been taken into account by Japanese historians. Without analyzing Abe's writing, one cannot fully understand the origins of the democratic movements during the late Meiji and the Taishō era. (15)

Notes

(1) Quoted in Morita Yasukazu, *Suisu: Rekishi kara gendai e* [Switzerland: From its Past to the Present] (Tokyo: Tōsui shobō, 1994 [1980]), 21.
(2) Ibid., 22–29.
(3) Abe Isoo, *Chijō no risōkoku – Suisu* [Ideal State on Earth – Switzerland] (Tokyo: Daiichi shuppan, 1947 [1904]), 33f.
(4) Ibid., 3.
(5) Ibid., 5.
(6) Ibid., 4. Since the formation of the canton of Jura in 1979, Switzerland now consists of 26 cantons.
(7) Ibid., 14.
(8) See Katayama Tetsu, *Abe Isoo den: denki, Abe Isoo* [A Biography of Abe Isoo] (Tokyo: ōzorasha, 1991), 53–56. Also see Takano Zenichi, *Nihon shakaishugi no chichi: Abe Isoo* [Father of Japanese Socialism: Abe Isoo] (Tokyo: Abe Isoo kankôkai, 1970), 410–419.
(9) See Kindai Nihon shakai undōshi jinbutsu daijiten (ed.), *Kindai Nihon shakai undōshi jinbutsu daijiten* [Encyclopedia of Personalities in History of Modern Japanese Social Movements] (Tôkyô: Nichigai associates, 1997), 101.
(10) Abe Isoo, *Chijō no risōkoku – Suisu*, 98–100.
(11) Ibid., 1/100.
(12) See Morita Yasukazu, *Suisu: Rekishi kara gendai e*, 42.
(13) Abe Isoo, *Chijō no risōkoku – Suisu*, 98.
(14) Ibid., 96–98.
(15) For an exhaustive study on the Taishō democracy movement see: Meyer, Harald. *Die "Taishō-Demokratie".* Begriffsgeschichtliche Studien zur Demokratierezeption in Japan von 1900 bis 1920. Bern: Peter Lang, 2005 (Welten Ostasiens, Bd. 4, hrsg. von Robert H. Gassmann, Andrea Riemenschnitter, Pierre-François Souyri und Nicolas Zufferey).
On Abe Isoo see also: Meyer, Harald. "Pioneer of 'Taishō Democracy': Abe Isoo's Social Democratic Idealism and Japanese Concepts of Democracy from 1900 to 1920". *Japanstudien.* Jahrbuch des Deutschen Instituts für Japanstudien, Bd. 14, 2002: 313–327.

A similar version to this paper was first published as follows:
Meyer, Harald/Hashimoto Tetsuya. "Searching for the 'Ideal State': Switzerland as a Model and Social Democratic Thought in the Late Meiji Era (1868–1912)". *Kanazawa daigaku keizai gakubu ronshû [Studies of the Faculty of Economics, Kanazawa University]*, Vol. 22, No. 2, March 2002: 263–279.

Harald Meyer was born in 1972; he attended Zurich University, where he majored in Japanese and Chinese Studies. While receiving his M.A. (Lizentiat) and Ph.D. degrees in Japanology he was working as an Assistant at the same University. From 2000 to 2002: Visiting research scholar at Kanazawa University (Ishikawa Prefecture, Japan) majoring in Modern Japanese History. Since 2002: Chief Assistant (Oberassistent) for Japanology at Zurich University, since 2004 PD (Privatdozent).

SWITZERLAND AND THE SWISS IN JAPANESE TEXTBOOKS

Heinrich Reinfried, University of Zurich

1 Introduction

1.1 The scope of the survey

An investigation of textbook content does not necessarily provide an indication of what students know at the end of their school career. There is no way of knowing how many students read the whole book, how many skipped parts of it and how many virtually ignored it. Textbook content may, however, be regarded as the lowest common denominator of what is regarded as "essential or desirable knowledge" for students. Content and the way it is presented may at times also indicate what is deemed politically feasible or desirable. Where there are a lot of publishing companies competing to sell their products to schools – as is the case in Japan – the choice of what to include in a textbook also mirrors teachers' and parents' expectations.

This investigation sets out to supply answers to the question as to which aspects of Switzerland are generally considered by Japanese textbook authors to be of sufficient importance to be presented to Japanese students. How often and in how much detail is Switzerland mentioned? Where do Japanese textbooks see Switzerland's contribution to world civilization? Does the information in textbooks help students acquire a balanced impression of Switzerland? Information about Switzerland conveyed in or omitted from the textbooks will give us a fair impression of how the image of Switzerland is being shaped and propagated in Japan and may therefore be taken as fairly indicative of the popular perception of Switzerland in Japan.

1.2 How significant are the results?

In order to answer these questions, a sample of 52 textbooks was scanned for references to Switzerland.[1] 18 of them are textbooks for primary schools, 15 for secondary schools, and 17 for high schools. The sample includes two textbooks on Switzerland produced by the Japanese School in Zurich, which are used

[1] The Japanese School in Zurich was kind enough to provide me with all the books in use at their school for the education of Japanese students. I am also very grateful to all my acquaintances and former students in Japan, who sent me the textbooks they had used at school.

only in Switzerland. Also included in the survey were 4 encyclopedias likely to be used for ready reference by pupils at primary and secondary school level. The textbooks surveyed cover the school subjects of National Language (14), Social Studies (13), History (11) and Geography (8). 8 textbooks are readers for ethics, which are used as supplementary reading material *(fukudokuhon)* since ethics is not a school subject in its own right. The survey of Swiss personalities mentioned in Japanese textbooks also covers textbooks in Natural Sciences. The earliest publication dates back to 1986, the latest being published in 2002. 24% of the material surveyed was published in the year 2000 or later. 70% of the surveyed books were published by the major Japanese publishers of textbooks and received official approval for use in schools by the Ministry of Education. Textbooks produced by these publishing houses[2] are regarded as authoritative and are used in schools all over Japan. Valuable additional information about foreign personalities mentioned in Japanese textbooks was provided by the "Learner's Who's Who" *(gakushū jinbutsu jiten)* in the appendix to the various "Encyclopedias for Children" published by Shōgakukan, which are based on surveys of the full range of textbooks in use in Japan.

2 Information on Switzerland in Japanese textbooks

Switzerland is mentioned in 16 out of the 52 textbooks in the sample, most frequently in geography textbooks (total of 7) followed by social-studies textbooks (4), history (4) and ethics (1).

Switzerland's geographical position in Europe is shown on all detailed maps in primary as well as in secondary school textbooks and atlases.[3] Statistical tables regularly list Switzerland among the major nations of the world. Even primary school textbooks feature a section presenting facts and figures for quick reference and comparison such as the capital city of each country, other major cities, population, trade figures, GNP and foreign aid. Here, interested stu-

[2] Tôkyô Shoseki, Teikoku Shoin, Mitsumura Tosho, Kyôiku Shuppan, Shimizu Shoin, Yamakawa Shuppan and Jikkyô Shuppan

[3] cf. TEIKOKU HENSHÛBU (1991: 49–50); GOTÔ Yoshiyuki (1986: 1–2)

dents can learn, for instance, that Berne is the capital of Switzerland[4] and that Switzerland's per capita donations to foreign aid in 1998 amounted to 0.33% of GNP, as against Japanese donations of 0.28% of GNP.[5] Statistics in a 1986 secondary school textbook contain information about total area, population and population density, number of employed in primary, secondary and tertiary sectors, GNP per capita, main products and trade figures with Japan.[6] If only one Swiss town features on the list of the world's major cities, it is Zurich.[7]

The Swiss flag is always shown in its correct square size as specified by Swiss law[8] in lists showing the flags of the world,[9] at least in textbooks approved by the Ministry of Education. The "Geographical Encyclopedia for Children", on the other hand, explains the origins of the Swiss flag in the 14th century, but shows the rectangular version of the flag with a length/width ratio of 2:3, which is allowed only for maritime shipping under the Swiss flag.[10] In another encyclopedia for children, the Red Cross flag is explained as the *"inverse Swiss flag"*.[11] The Swiss flag is at times even shown without any reference to Switzerland at all. Thus, in an illustration to a short reading passage about a sports event, the Swiss flag appears besides the Japanese and the German flags, apparently just to indicate that a highly competitive sports event is taking place.[12]

4 GOTÔ (1986: 121–122)
5 ITÔ (2002: 285)
6 GOTÔ (1986: 121–122)
7 ibid.: 120; GOTÔ (1991: 120)
8 "The Swiss Flag has a white cross in a red field; the cross is the same length on all sides and each arm is one-sixth longer than its width. The actual measurements of the arms of the Swiss cross was officially fixed by the Federal Law of 12 December 1889. The official Swiss Flag (as used in the Army, etc.) is square and not rectangular. Only the flag of Swiss vessels is longer (length/width = 2 : 3), as fixed by a decision of the Federal Government of 9 April 1941, and confirmed by the Federal Law of 23 September 1953 concerning maritime shipping under Swiss Flag." Retrieved 18/03/04 from http://www.eda.admin.ch/tokyo_emb/e/home/polsys.html
9 NAKAMURA, TAKAHASHI (2002: 26); SHIRAHAMA (2001: 30); SHÔGAKUKAN (1992: 151), GOTÔ (1991: 1); GOTÔ (1986: 1)
10 SHÔGAKUKAN (1992: 151)
11 SHÔGAKUKAN (1993: 185)
12 KAIGO (?a: 70)

In history textbooks, Switzerland is often simply mentioned in passing. The name of the city of Locarno turns up on the occasion of the Locarno Treaty of 1925[13] and Geneva frequently appears in history textbooks as host city to the League of Nations.[14] Some textbooks, however, refer to the League of Nations[15] or to the United Nations[16] without specifically naming Geneva.

Detailed presentation in textbooks occurs where textbook authors consider Switzerland to be unique in some way. This epithet appears to apply to the Swiss economy (Alpine dairy farming), to the landscape and scenery (geomorphology, glaciers, Alpine scenery), to social harmony in a multilingual and multiethnic environment (languages and religions) and to the political system (federalism, direct democracy).

Among foreign personalities portrayed in detail or mentioned briefly in Japanese textbooks, 11 Swiss are included, namely Henri Dunant, the spiritus rector of the International Red Cross, the natural scientist Auguste Piccard (together with his twin brother Jean and his son Jacques), the author of "Heidi" Johanna Spyri, the novelist Hermann Hesse, the expert in constitutional and international law Carl Hilty, the painter Paul Klee, the reformers Huldrych Zwingli and Jean Calvin and the mathematician Leonhard Euler.

3 Topoi in the presentation of Switzerland

3.1 "Switzerland is a small country."

Some geography textbooks simply use Switzerland as a metaphor for "a very small country", one that is in fact even smaller than Japan: *"Half the size of Hokkaidō, Switzerland is landlocked and has a total population of 7.4 million".*[17] One textbook asks students to compare the size of the four main Japanese

[13] EGAMI, YAMAMOTO, HAYASHI, NARUSE (2002: 290)

[14] SASAYAMA, ABE, OKUDA (2001: 181); TABE (2002a: 154); HAMASHIMA SHOTEN HENSHÛBU (1992: 147)

[15] MIYAHARA, KUROHA (1991: 277)

[16] NAKAMURA, NISHIWAKI, ÔGUCHI (2002: 154–157)

[17] YAMAMOTO, MASAI (2002: 214)

islands with that of Austria, Switzerland and Germany.[18] On a comparative map in another textbook, Switzerland, the Netherlands and Singapore are all placed in the Pacific Ocean to the southwest of Hokkaidō to make students aware of the fact that *"one tends to believe that Japan is a small country, whereas in fact it belongs to the larger countries in the world"*[19] .

3.2 "Switzerland is an idyllic country."

The information on Switzerland contained in the textbook sample makes Switzerland look rather idyllic. In a collection of colour photographs of various countries around the world, Switzerland is represented by a view of archetypal Swiss mountain scenery with the Matterhorn towering above the picturesque village of Zermatt. The caption here says: *"Switzerland is a country famous for its many mountains. Many people visit it for sightseeing or for skiing."*[20] On a bird's-eye view of a cross section of Europe stretching from Hamburg to the Adriatic, Switzerland is depicted as an idyllic garden. Inserted into the landscape are the icons of a cow grazing on the northern slope of the Alps, tall buildings in Basel, the clocktower in Berne, and a watch. On the basis of this information alone, students would probably describe Switzerland as a pastoral country situated somewhere near the Black Forest to the southeast of the Bavarian castle of Neuschwanstein. Another small photograph on the same page shows cattle grazing on the slopes of the Alps. The caption explains that cattle are driven up and down the Alps according to the season.[21]

Generally speaking, the Swiss landscape appears to be given preferential treatment. Thus, a Swiss map[22] adorns the cover of one high school geography textbook[23] and photographs of the Swiss landscape are frequently used to demonstrate geomorphological features of the Alps, one example being when an aerial

[18] TABE (2002b: 28)
[19] NAKAMURA, TAKAHASHI (2002: 19)
[20] ibid.: 26
[21] SHIRAHAMA (2001: 31–32)
[22] SWISS FEDERAL OFFICE OF TOPOGRAPHY, Landeskarte der Schweiz 1:50,000, Blatt Arolla, Nr. 283.
[23] SATÔ, TANIOKA (2002)

photo of Interlaken is used to illustrate the form of U-shaped glacial troughs.[24] Glacial morphology is explained with other photographs of Swiss landscapes and glaciers[25] and even the consequences of global warming are illustrated by a historical painting of the Rhône glacier juxtaposed with a photograph of the same scene today.[26] Great care is taken, moreover, to explain the connection between glacial geomorphology and Alpine dairy farming: *"In the Swiss Alps, rather than the steep slopes in the U-shaped valleys, the gentle slopes of the region above [the major trough] are used as grazing grounds."*[27]

Ecological problems liable to mar the image of an idyllic small country appear very rarely. On a map showing the extent to which forests are dying in Europe as a result of acid rain, Switzerland is shown to be affected to about the same degree as Germany.[28] One map showing the water pollution of the river Rhine suggests that the situation in Switzerland is rather less severe than in neighbouring Germany and in the Netherlands.[29] Traffic problems are hinted at by a photograph of the proverbial traffic jam on the autobahn leading to the Gotthard tunnel.[30]

3.3 "Switzerland is a peaceful country, uniting different languages, cultures and religions."

In Japanese textbooks, frequent mention is made of the fact that Switzerland is a multilingual and multiethnic country with different religions.

A linguistic map of Europe in a textbook published in 1986 suggests that Switzerland is predominantly inhabited by German-speaking people.[31] Another textbook, published in 1990, explains that there is no such thing as a Swiss

[24] YAMADA, OTÔ, YAMAGA (1990: 29)
[25] e.g. the Aletsch glacier in YAMAMOTO, MASAI (2002: 75)
[26] HAMASHIMA SHOTEN HENSHÛBU (1992: 8)
[27] YAMAMOTO, MASAI (2002: 59)
[28] NAKAMURA, TAKAHASHI (2002: 129)
[29] GOTÔ (1991: 38, map 3); GOTÔ (1986: 38, map 3)
[30] SHIRAHAMA (2001: 33)
[31] GOTÔ (1986: 33, map 3)

language, but that either German, French or Italian *"and other languages"* are spoken, and then goes on to show correctly on a map where the various languages are spoken.[32] Languages in Switzerland are explained at length in one paragraph of a new geography textbook:

"Switzerland is a confederation of 23 Cantons (with an additional 3 half-Cantons). Each of the Cantons has its own language. Every community has the right to decide which of the official languages they want to use. Thus, the peace between the different languages can be relatively well kept."[33]

A graph of ethnic groups in Europe in a recently published textbook shows Switzerland to be more or less equally divided between Germanic and Latin ethnic groups,[34] while another textbook appears to treat German-speaking Switzerland in a preferential way:

"German-speaking Swiss are the most numerous; besides there are French-, Italian- and Romansh-speaking Swiss."[35]

Although it is true that German speakers – with a share of 63.9% of the total population – outnumber speakers of other languages, there are nevertheless as many as 19.5% French speakers and 6.6% Italian speakers, but only 0.5% Romansh speakers.[36]

A map explaining the various annual Christian holidays shows Switzerland to be divided into Protestant and Catholic Cantons.[37] When, as is the case in a recent publication, a map shows Switzerland to be a favorite destination for migrant workers from Turkey and the former Yugoslavia,[38] it would be all the

[32] YAMADA, OTÔ, YAMAGA (1990: 17)
[33] YAMAMOTO, MASAI (2002: 125)
[34] TABE (2002b: 118)
[35] YAMAMOTO, MASAI (2002: 214)
[36] BUNDESAMT FÜR STATISTIK (2002)
[37] NAKAMURA, TAKAHASHI (2002: 126)
[38] TABE (2002b: 117)

more important to mention the 2.2% Muslim residential population in Switzerland today. Instead, a new textbook states that *"the population is almost equally divided between Catholics and Protestants",* thereby disregarding not only the growing Muslim population, but also the 7.4% Jewish residential population in Switzerland.[39]

As a multiethnic nation, Switzerland is usually named alongside such countries as China, Malaysia, Sri Lanka, Israel, Nigeria, former Chechoslovakia, the former Yugoslavia, the former Soviet Union and Canada.[40] A linguistic map of Switzerland shows the regional distribution of the four official languages, but the accompanying text adds Belgium, Canada, Spain, Singapore, Malaysia as well as all African nations to the category of multilingual countries. In another textbook, a linguistic map of Switzerland is illustrated by a Singapore supermarket with a billboard in English, Malay, Chinese and Tamil.[41] A photograph in another chapter shows a Malaysian newsstand with newspapers in a great variety of different languages.[42]

3.4 "Switzerland has a long history."

The chapter on *"The establishment of centralistic states in Western Europe"* mentions the origins of Switzerland in a short paragraph:

"The peasants in the region of Switzerland had since the 13th century started independence movements, defeating several times the ruling power Austria, and reached factual independence by the end of the Middle Ages. This was de facto acknowledged in 1648 (Treaty of Westphalia)."[43]

A small map with the caption *"German and Italian region at the end of the 15th century"* lists a *"free confederation" (jiyū renpō)* on the territory of pres-

39 BUNDESAMT FÜR STATISTIK (1997)
40 YAMAMOTO, MASAI (2002: 126)
41 SATÔ, TANIOKA (2002: 134-35)
42 ibid.: 251
43 EGAMI, YAMAMOTO, HAYASHI, NARUSE (2002: 139)

 ent-day Switzerland.[44] In the chapter dedicated to the Protestant Reformation, historical events in Switzerland are outlined, as well as the basic tenets of the Protestant movement. The exponents of the movement named are Huldrych Zwingli in Zurich and Jean Calvin in Geneva, but explanations focus mainly on Calvin, whose doctrine of predestination *"spread widely among the burghers in the early period of capitalism".*[45]

Another feature of Protestantism mentioned here is the election of elders from the congregation to assist the pastor.[46] A map shows how the Protestant movement emanating from the city state of Geneva later spread to France, England, Scotland and the Netherlands.[47] At the same time, a footnote also mentions the activities of the Anabaptists in Switzerland and the fact that their teaching spread to Germany and the Netherlands, adding that they were persecuted by the Catholic and the Protestant church alike *"because their belief was regarded as a threat to the state".*[48]

In a discussion on the differences between parliamentary and direct democracy, Switzerland is named as one of the places where the rights associated with direct democracy such as referendum, initiative and recall are exercised. These concepts are said to have been *"advocated by Rousseau"*[49] and elaborated by the political philosophers Alexis de Tocqueville and James Bryce.[50] The textbook then goes on to say that even in modern times direct democracy is alive, albeit in *"small-sized communities in the provinces".* Direct democracy is said to be a feature

[44] ibid.: 139
[45] ibid.: 160
[46] ibid.: 160
[47] ibid.: 159–160
[48] EGAMI, YAMAMOTO, HAYASHI, NARUSE (2002: 159, footnote 1)
[49] ITÔ (2002: 133)
[50] ibid.: 60

"... not only of the ancient Greek polis and the towns of the Middle Ages, but also of American Town Meetings and of the Landsgemeinde (jûminshûkai) in each Swiss Canton".[51]

A recently published geography textbook also attaches great importance to the institution of the Landsgemeinde. The two-page article on Switzerland is headed by a photograph of the Landsgemeinde in Sarnen with the caption *"Swiss citizens voting by raising their hand".*[52] After describing the federalistic Swiss political system, in which every Canton has its own constitution and government, the text goes on to explain that in some Cantons in Switzerland *"voters exercise their political rights in the form of direct democracy".*[53] In fact, the Landsgemeinde in Sarnen, Canton of Obwalden, which is shown on the photograph, was abolished in 1998. At present (2003), the Landsgemeinde is held once a year in only two Cantons, namely Glarus and Appenzell Innerrhoden.

3.5 "Switzerland is politically isolated."

Switzerland's political isolation within Europe is implicitly highlighted in the chapter on Germany in a geography textbook, where there is a detailed discussion on the benefits of membership of the European Union (EU).[54] A drawing shows the benefits Germany enjoys as a member of the EU, namely the absence of border controls and tariffs, the free flow of capital and labour, student exchange programs and the standardization of electrical appliances. In contrast, a map of the EU and a photograph of the Swiss-German border in Basel, where cars are queuing up on the autobahn to pay the road tax before entering Switzerland, show Switzerland to be isolated.[55] One textbook, though, hints at possible changes in the near future:

[51] ibid.: 133
[52] YAMAMOTO, MASAI (2002: 214)
[53] ibid.: 214
[54] NAKAMURA , TAKAHASHI (2002: 119–129)
[55] ibid.: 127

"Recently Switzerland has declared its intention to eventually join the EU – a possible turning point for the principle of eternal neutrality."[56]

One such turning point has already arrived as the Swiss electorate voted in favour of joining the United Nations (UN) in a popular referendum on March 3, 2002. Since Switzerland joined the UN officially on September 9, 2002, the following information in a textbook published in 2002 is therefore already out of date: *"Switzerland is not a member of the United Nations, but participates actively in UN organizations such as the ILO or Unicef."*[57]

3.6 "Switzerland is prosperous" – but why?

Descriptions of the Swiss economy are characterised by a strong dichotomy between a romanticised image of Alpine dairy farming and the acknowledgement of the fact that Switzerland has one of the highest per capita GNP in the world.

On the one hand, textbooks explain how cattle are moved from the valleys to the Alps during summer; there is even a chart showing the altitudes at which cattle graze in summer.[58] And in a recently published textbook, Switzerland is highlighted in the appendix to the chapter on Germany with a close-up on the story of "Heidi" by Johanna Spyri. A photograph shows cows lying in a lush meadow with huge snow-covered mountains and a village with lots of chalets as a backdrop. A map then indicates where Maienfeld – *"the model for the Dörfli [village] in the story of Heidi"*[59] – is situated and the well-known literary figures of Heidi and Peter are used to explain how peasants in the Alpine regions drive cattle and goats to the Maiensäss and the Alps in summer, returning them in autumn to their owners, who live in the villages down in the valley.[60]

[56] YAMAMOTO, MASAI (2002: 214)
[57] NAKAMURA, TAKAHASHI (2002: 127)
[58] GOTÔ (1991: 37, map 7); GOTÔ (1986: 37, map 7)
[59] NAKAMURA, TAKAHASHI (2002: 130)
[60] ibid.: 130

On the other hand, textbooks make clear that Switzerland has a positive trade balance with Japan[61] and one of the highest per capita GNP in the world.[62] Swiss export items mentioned are *"watches, pharmaceuticals and gold"*.[63] Not until the year 2002 does a high school geography textbook actually attempt to give a comprehensive explanation for Switzerland's prosperity.[64] In a paragraph entitled *"The wealthiest country on Earth"*[65] the authors point out that the Swiss have achieved one of the highest per capita GNP on earth in spite of the almost total lack of natural resources. The next paragraph, entitled *"Industry on a high technological level"*, gives the following explanation:

"Since there are almost no natural resources, industries with a high added value such as food processing, precision machinery and chemical industry developed in this country."[66]

Dairy farming is said to be widespread, *"but since milk in Switzerland is produced too far away from the consumers, it is therefore processed into cheese or butter or – mixed with cocoa – exported as milk chocolate"*.[67] A passage about the Swiss watch industry hints at economic difficulties in the past:

"For many years, precision machinery industry focussed on the production of watches, but after they had met with fierce competition from the Japanese watch industry, they are now concentrating on luxury watches."[68]

Further Swiss industries include *"electric power generator facilities"* and *"aluminium due to the abundant electricity"* as well as *"the chemical industry center-*

[61] GOTÔ (1986: 121–122); TEIKOKU HENSHÛBU (1991: 64)
[62] EGAMI, YAMAMOTO, HAYASHI, NARUSE (2002: 347)
[63] TABE (2002b: 195)
[64] YAMAMOTO, MASAI (2002: 214–215)
[65] ibid.: 214
[66] ibid.: 214
[67] ibid.: 215
[68] ibid.: 215

ing around the pharmaceutical industry".[69] The article goes on to point out the high technical expertise of small to medium-sized enterprises. Big enterprises are said to outsource production abroad while keeping research and development as well as the financial departments in Switzerland. In the last paragraph, entitled *"Financial Services and Tourism",* the authors write:

"Large amounts of capital flow to Switzerland from all over the world because banks guard their clients' secrets and because Switzerland enjoys a very stable currency. By reinvesting this capital, banks earn a lot of commission."[70]

As to tourism, the textbook goes on to point out that Switzerland is *"blessed with beautiful mountains and lakes and provides very good tourist services with mountain railways and hotels, thus earning large amounts of foreign currency".*[71]

4 The Swiss in Japanese textbooks

Famous personalities are important cornerstones of the self-image of a nation and an important source of national pride. It is therefore in the interest of each nation to count as many famous personalities as possible among its citizens. In Japanese textbooks, Japanese as well as foreign personalities are frequently presented to Japanese students as role models.

Hardly any mention at all is made of Swiss personalities. Henri Dunant (1828–1910), the spiritus rector of the International Committee of the Red Cross, always makes it onto the list[72] as do the reformers Zwingli and Calvin. The Swiss scholar Carl Hilty (1833–1909) was chosen by Japanese textbook authors to praise the "joys of professional work" with an adage which is as redolent of Calvinism as it is of *Sekimon Shingaku* philosophy:[73]

[69] ibid.: 215
[70] ibid.: 215
[71] ibid.: 215
[72] EGAMI, YAMAMOTO, HAYASHI, NARUSE (2002: 236)
[73] cf. BELLAH, Robert N., Tokugawa Religion, The Values of Pre-Industrial Japan. New York/London, 1957: 115

"There is no greater joy in life than when one has found the occupation which is most suited to oneself. Those who seek happiness should above all try to find out what this occupation is."[74]

However, the fact that certain artists are Swiss is not always revealed. A sculpture by Alberto Giacometti (1901–1966) adorns the title page to a section on poems without any reference to the artist's nationality.[75] Indeed, an enumeration of eminent 19th- and 20th-century European personalities in the fields of literature and fine arts does not list any Swiss at all.[76]

Problems arise in those cases where individuals have multiple nationalities. Thus, Nobel Prize winner Hermann Hesse (1877–1962) is correctly introduced in the appendix to a translation of one of his short stories as having been born in Germany and later becoming a naturalized Swiss.[77] Those who, despite having been born in Switzerland, spent most of their life abroad are often claimed by other nations as part of their cultural heritage. Le Corbusier (1867–1965), the Swiss architect, urban planner and painter, was born in La Chaux-de-Fonds but spent almost the whole of his working life in France. The "Who's who for Children" describes him as the *"Swiss-born French architect".*[78]

Then there is the case of Geneva-born philosopher Jean-Jacques Rousseau (1712–1778). His main work, *"Le Contrat Social",* is indispensable to any explanation of the origins of modern democracy and hence of the spirit of the Japanese constitution of 1947. Against the backdrop of impending political reforms in Japan, a recently published textbook even emphasizes Rousseau's strident criticism of parliamentary democracy and the fact that he advocated direct democracy.[79] At the time of Rousseau, Geneva was an independent

[74] KAIGO (?a: 34), quoted from HILTY, *"Glück",* 1891/95, reprinted in 1988)
[75] YAMAMOTO (1991: 93)
[76] EGAMI, YAMAMOTO, HAYASHI, NARUSE (2002: 242, 358)
[77] "Shônen no hi no omoide" in: ISHIMORI (1991: 257) (translated from: Hesse, *Schön ist die Jugend,* 1937)
[78] SHÔGAKUKAN (1993: 56)
[79] ITÔ (2002: 134)

city-state and ally of the Swiss Confederation. Geneva was therefore neither French territory nor did it belong to the Swiss Confederation. Rousseau himself was born in Geneva, but spent nearly half his life in Paris. In a German dictionary he is listed as a *"French-Swiss philosopher and writer".*[80] The passages on Rousseau in Japanese textbooks, however, seldom mention his nationality.[81] When they do so, he is described as a *"Frenchman"*[82] or a *"French author and philosopher"*[83], only rarely as a *"Swiss philosopher".*[84]

The notion of Rousseau being a French philosopher is reinforced in a textbook, which shows a picture of his tomb in the Pantheon in Paris.[85]

5 Switzerland and the Swiss in Japanese Encyclopedias for Children

In the Encyclopedias for Children published by Shōgakukan, we find scattered fragments of information about Switzerland and the Swiss. Facts about Switzerland center on the geography of the rural regions: Under the entry "Snow and Ice", a picture of the Findelen glacier is used to illustrate the term "glacier",[86] the Matterhorn is listed among the highest mountains in the world as *"an Italo-Swiss mountain"*[87], and the Jungfrau mountain railway can be found among the "Famous Trains of the World".[88] Apart from these entries, the emphasis is rather on exotic and quaint aspects of Switzerland. Among the musical instruments of the world, a Swiss alphorn is shown with a caption saying that this instrument can *"produce a few sounds".*[89] In the chapter on domestic animals,

[80] MEYERS GROSSES TASCHENLEXIKON (2001, vol. 9: 73)
[81] EGAMI, YAMAMOTO, HAYASHI, NARUSE (2002: 185); EGAMI, YAMAMOTO, HAYASHI, NARUSE (1998: 167)
[82] INADA (1992: 20); HAMASHIMA SHOTEN HENSHÛBU (1992: 100); KAIGO (?b: 95)
[83] ITÔ (2002: 130) and NAKAMURA, NISHIWAKI, ÔGUCHI (2002: 38)
[84] SHÔGAKUKAN (1993: 386)
[85] INADA (1992: 168)
[86] SHÔGAKUKAN (1991: 463)
[87] SHÔGAKUKAN (1992: 97,145)
[88] ibid.: 106
[89] SHÔGAKUKAN (1991: 92)

cows are shown on a Swiss alp.[90] The "Postage Stamps of the World" include a stamp issued in Switzerland in 1964 which shows a colour drawing of a water lily.[91] Among the "Puppets of the World" we find a wooden puppet of a Swiss alphorn player of the kind one finds on souvenir stalls.[92] Icons on a European map indicating the places of origin of the most popular children's stories show where Heidi lived in the Swiss Alps, just to the southeast of Little Red Riding Hood in Germany.[93]

Yet opportunities to introduce the reader to aspects relating to Swiss industry are often neglected: among the "Chocolates of the World", readers find chocolates from Japan, the USA, the Netherlands and Germany, but not from Switzerland;[94] the picture of a giant Swiss watch on the facade of a Tokyo skyscraper – part of an advertising campaign to launch it onto the Japanese market – is simply a *"giant watch",*[95] not a "Swiss giant watch".

In the *"Who's who for Children",* an encyclopedia containing only biographies of famous Japanese and foreign personalities, published in 1993, Switzerland is depicted as a country where famous people such as Charlie Chaplin spent their *"happy later years".*[96] The entry for Albert Einstein states that he was born in Germany and that *"he worked at the Berne Patent Office",*[97] but omits to mention that he studied and later taught at the Universities of Berne and Zurich and at the Federal Polytechnic in Zurich and that he acquired Swiss citizenship in 1901. Henri Dunant is not granted an entry of his own, but is presented as an insert in the entry for Florence Nightingale.[98] The only Swiss to receive in-depth coverage is Auguste Piccard (1884–1962), whose space and the deep-sea

[90] ibid.: 115
[91] ibid.: 143
[92] ibid.: 365
[93] SHÔGAKUKAN (1992: 125)
[94] SHÔGAKUKAN (1991: 311)
[95] ibid.: 345
[96] SHÔGAKUKAN (1993: 163)
[97] ibid.: 4
[98] ibid.: 185

exploits are presented in detail on two whole pages together with those of his twin brother Jean and his son Jacques.[99]

The *"Geographical Encyclopedia for Children"* also mentions a Swiss "Piccard" as world record holder in deep-sea diving.[100] This, in fact, refers to Jacques Piccard (born in 1922), son of Auguste Piccard, who, in 1960, dived to a depth of 10,916 metres with his bathyscaph "Trieste".

The *"Learner's Who's Who",* which students find in the appendix to the encyclopedias for children, lists all Japanese and foreign personalities mentioned in Japanese textbooks.[101] 55 non-Japanese are listed, but there are no Swiss among them.[102] The enlarged version which was published two years later includes a brief biography of the Swiss mathematician Leonhard Euler (1707–1783).[103] The *"Learner's Who's Who"* in the appendix to the *"Geographical Encyclopedia"* lists the Swiss artist Paul Klee,[104] the author Johanna Spyri[105] and Jean-Jacques Rousseau, who is here referred to as a *"Swiss philosopher".*[106]

[99] ibid.: 214–215
[100] SHÔGAKUKAN (1992: 82)
[101] cf. JINBUTSU GAKUSHÛ JITEN in: SHÔGAKUKAN (1991: 487ff.)
[102] Roald Amundsen, Archimedes, Hans Christian Andersen, Jesus Christ, Aesop, Thomas Edison, Albert Einstein, Eratosthenes, Galileo Galilei, Mahatma Gandhi, Ganjin, Pierre Curie, Marie Curie, Johannes Gutenberg, Coubertin, Jacob Grimm, Wilhelm Grimm, Erich Kästner, Confucius, Robert Koch, Vincent van Gogh, Copernicus, Christopher Columbus, Francisco de Xavier, Ernest T. Seton, Franz von Siebold, Buddha, Albert Schweitzer, Charles Darwin, Walt Disney, Florence Nightingale, Napoleon I, Isaac Newton, Alfred Nobel, Pascal, Townsend Harris, Jean-Henri Favre, Ernest F. Fenollosa, Henry Ford, Khubilai Khan, Ludwig van Beethoven, Matthew G. Perry, Alexander G. Bell, Helen Keller, Mother Teresa, Jules Mazarin, Douglas MacArthur, Marco Polo, Gustav Maeterlink, Amadeus Mozart, Claude Monnet, Wilbur Wright, Orville Wright, Abraham Lincoln, and George Washington (cf. SHÔGAKUKAN 1991: 487–502)
[103] SHÔGAKUKAN (1993: 334). The Swiss mathematician Leonhard Euler was added to the earlier list together with the following 11 non-Japanese personalities: the Egyptian mathematician Ames, Itô Hirobumi's assassin An Jun Gung, the English statistician John Grant, the Greek philosopher Simplikios, the Dutch mathematician Simon Stevin, the Greek philosopher Thales, the Austrian zoologist Karl von Frisch, Giordano Bruno, the English doctor and palaeontologist Gideon Mantel, the French mathematician Louis-Joseph Lagrange, and a "German biologist named Radcliffe (sic)" (cf. SHÔGAKUKAN 1993: 327–388)
[104] ibid.: 341
[105] ibid.: 352
[106] ibid.: 86

6 Conclusions

Although information on Switzerland and the Swiss in Japanese textbooks has increased in the past few years, it is still scarce. In most cases, the information is correct, but brief and disjointed, the result being that only by accessing many different textbooks can students find sufficient information.

Switzerland is presented to Japanese students as a "normal country". Features of Swiss society such as multilingualism, direct democracy and federalism, which constitute an integral part of the traditional Swiss self-image and national pride, are viewed from a global perspective: Switzerland is a multilingual nation, but so are many other countries. The Swiss enjoy basic democratic rights such as initiative and referendum, but so do voters at American town meetings. Modern democracy is said to have originated in France. In the discussion on federalism, the USA, Germany and Canada are often quoted as examples, whereas Switzerland is sometimes even omitted. Only a few Swiss personalities are ever mentioned in Japanese textbooks. Even personalities like Auguste Piccard and Henri Dunant cannot match the popularity of the literary figure of Heidi.

In general, information about Switzerland in Japanese textbooks conveys a positive, albeit somewhat one-sided image. To a certain degree, Switzerland is idealized, a case in point being when "eternal neutrality" is mentioned without reference to the Swiss militia system and to the principle of armed neutrality. The same holds true for the bias towards rural Switzerland and the Alpine economy. The resulting lopsided image of Switzerland as a predominantly agrarian country hardly accounts for Swiss prosperity. Even recent publications focus almost exclusively on Alpine pastoralism in their description of Switzerland, while the urban sprawl between Geneva and St. Gallen, where the majority of Swiss live and work, is ignored. In fact, only 4.6% of the Swiss working population work in agriculture,[107] and of these, only about a third work in the Alpine regions.[108] Swiss export statistics indicate that in 2003, only 1.19% of total exports to

[107] BUNDESAMT FÜR STATISTIK (2003: 9)
[108] BÄTZING, MESSERLI (1991: 151)

Japan were agricultural or forestry products, while the share of chemical products amounted to 44.72%, with 32.8% for instruments, watches and jewelry and 11.86% for machinery and electronics.[109]

There is a considerable gap between the Japanese image of Switzerland and the way Swiss see themselves. The textbook *Watashitachi no suisu (Our Switzerland)* compiled by teachers at the Japanese school in Zurich in 1991 (revised edition 1997) represents an interesting attempt to blend the Japanese image of Switzerland with the Swiss self-image. Based mainly on Japanese-language material published in Japan and in Switzerland, 33 out of 192 pages are devoted to the geography of Switzerland, 40 pages to Swiss industry, 26 pages to Swiss history and 28 pages to the Swiss political system.[110]

With ample space available, Swiss personalities and their achievements receive more coverage.[111] But even this textbook does not mention the existence of any 19th- or 20th-century Swiss literature. The Calvinistic Swiss work ethic, however, is evoked in a statement by an anonymous Swiss woman scientist in pharmaceutical research:

"We have to work very hard – every day, often even on Saturdays and Sundays, sometimes all night long. Of 10,000 experiments, only one is successful!"[112]

[109] EIDGENÖSSISCHE ZOLLVERWALTUNG (2004)

[110] Sources include i) Japanese Government institutions such as the Japanese Embassy in Switzerland, ii) Japanese institutions briefing Japanese expatriates with factual information on foreign countries such as the *nihon kokusai mondai kenkyûjo,* iii) Japanese-language publications by Swiss Government organizations such as OSEC, iv) translations into Japanese of books on Switzerland written by Swiss journalists and v) books written by Japanese historians on Swiss history. Cf. MOTO CHUURIHI NIHONJINGAKKÔ KYÔSHOKUIN (1997)

[111] Besides Johanna Spyri, Heinrich Pestalozzi and "Geneva-born" Jean-Jacques Rousseau, Swiss culture is represented by the artists Arnold Böcklin, Giovanni Segantini, Ferdinand Hodler, Paul Klee, Alberto Giacometti, Max Bill and the architect Le Corbusier. MOTO CHUURIHI NIHONJINGAKKÔ KYÔSHOKUIN (1997: 177–184)

[112] MOTO CHUURIHI NIHONJINGAKKÔ KYÔSHOKUIN (1997: 111)

The principle of armed neutrality *(busō chūritsu)* is mentioned in the context of the Vienna Congress,[113] the Swiss army in the context of World Wars I and II. In a short paragraph about World War II, most of the space is devoted to the Rütli speech by General Henri Guisan, in which he called upon the Swiss population to resist the Axis powers.[114] In the description of the present-day political system, however, neither the army nor the militia system is mentioned. While a graph of the Federal Government offices lists a *"Ministry of Defense"*[115], the explanation in the text mentions among the tasks of the Federal Government only the *"upkeep of law and order within the country".*[116]

With space in Japanese textbooks being limited, it would be unrealistic to expect Japanese textbooks to contain more information on Switzerland in the future. It is therefore all the more important to use what little space is available in such a way as to convey a realistic impression of Switzerland. A shift in the Japanese perspective towards urban Switzerland centering on the economic regions around Zurich, Basel and Geneva would be conducive to creating a more realistic image of Switzerland in 21st-century Europe. The Swiss Government could support this process by offering a Japanese-language version of its comprehensive information on Switzerland on the official website of the Swiss Embassy in Tokyo.[117]

Heinrich Reinfried, 1945, from Zurich; 1975 PhD from London University. Professor for Japanese language and culture at Zurich University, St. Gallen University and different institutions of higher education.

[113] ibid.: 153
[114] ibid.: 155–156
[115] ibid.: 163
[116] ibid.: 161
[117] A list of websites of various foreign embassies in Japan in one of the Japanese textbooks surveyed does not list the English-language website of the Swiss Embassy, but the Japanese-language website of the Swiss Tourist Office in Japan. Cf. NAKAMURA, TAKAHASHI (2002: 217)

Works cited

1 Publications in Japanese

EGAMI Namio, YAMAMOTO Tatsurô, HAYASHI Kentarô, NARUSE Osamu
2002 *Shôsetsu Sekaishi [History of the world].* Yamakawa, 384 pp.
江上波夫，山本達郎，林健太郎，成瀬治（著作）．詳説世界史，改 訂版．山川出版社．文部科学省検定済教科書.

EGAMI Namio, YAMAMOTO Tatsurô, HAYASHI Kentarô, NARUSE Osamu
1998 *Kôkô Sekaishi. Sekaishi B [History of the world for high schools B].* Yamakawa, 352 pp.
江上波夫，山本達郎，林健太郎，成瀬治（著作）．高校世界史, 改 訂版, 世界史B. 山川出版社. 文部科学省検定済教科書.

GOTÔ Yoshiyuki et al.
1991 *Chûgakkô shakaika chizu [Diagrammatic charts for social studies in secondary schools].* Teikoku shoin, 142 pp.
後藤孝之(著作者代表者)．中学校社会科地図, 四訂版. 帝国書 院編集部編, 帝国書院. 文部省検定済教科書.

GOTÔ Yoshiyuki et al.
1986 *Chûgakkô shakaika chizu [Diagrammatic charts for social studies in secondary schools].* Teikoku shoin, 142 pp.
後藤孝之(著作者代表者)．中学校社会科地図, 三訂版, 帝国書 院編集部編. 帝国書院. 文部省検定済教科書.

HAMASHIMA SHOTEN HENSHÛBU, ed.
1992 *Saishin zusetsu. Gensha [Diagrammatic charts for social studies].* Hamashima shoten, 279 pp.
浜島書店編集部．最新図説, 現社. 浜島書店.

INADA Kenichi, ed.
1992 *Kôkôsei no gendai shakai [Society today. Social studies for high school students].* Gakushû kenkyûsha, 224 pp.
稲田献一(監修)．　高校生の現代社会，改訂版．学習研究社．文部　省検定済教科書, 224 頁.

ISHIMORI Nobuo et al.
1991 *Kokugo 1 [National language 1].* Mitsumura shoten, 311 pp.
石森延男ほか30名(著作)．国語 1. 光村書店. 文部省検 定済教科書.

ITÔ Mitsuharu et al.
2002 *Kôkô gendai shakai [Society today. Social studies for high school students].* Jikkyô. 336 pp.
伊東光晴ほか9名(執筆・編集)．高校現代社会. 実教出版. 文 部科学省検定済教科書.

KAIGO Tokiomi, ed.
?a *Atarashii Seikatsu 1 [New Life 1].* Tôkyô Shoseki, 144 pp.
海後宗臣(監修). 新しい生活 1. 東京書籍.

KAIGO Tokiomi, ed.
?b *Atarashii Seikatsu 2 [New Life 2].* Tôkyô Shoseki, 144 pp.
海後宗臣(監修). 新しい生活 2. 東京書籍.

MIYAHARA Takeo, KUROHA Kiyotaka et al.
1991 *Kôkô Nihonshi [History of Japan for high schools].* Jikkyô, 372 pp.
宮原武夫, 黒羽清隆ほか6名(著作). 高校日本史, 三訂版. 実教 出版. 文部省検定済教科書.

MOTO CHUURIHI NIHONJINGAKKÔ KYÔSHOKUIN, eds.
1997 *Watashitachi no suisu [Our Switzerland. Revised edition].* Japanische Schule in Zürich. Uster, 196 pp.
本チュリッヒ日本人学校教職員(編集). わたしたちのスイス, 改訂版. 本チュリッヒ日本人学校, Uster.

MOTO CHUURIHI NIHONJINGAKKÔ KYÔSHOKUIN, eds.
1991 *Watashitachi no suisu [Our Switzerland].* Japanische Schule in Zürich. Uster, 192 pp.
本チュリッヒ日本人学校教職員(編集). わたしたちのスイス。チュリッヒ日本人学校, Uster.

NAKAMURA Kenichi, NISHIWAKI Yasuyuki, ÔGUCHI Yûjirô et al.
2002 *Shin chûgakkô. Kômin – Nihon no shakai to sekai [Japanese society and the world – New civic education for secondary schools].* Shimizu Shoin, 200 pp.
中村研一, 西脇保幸, 大口勇次郎ほか10名 (著作). 新中学校, 公民, 日本の社会と世界. 清水書院. 文部科学省検定済教科書.

NAKAMURA Kazuo, TAKAHASHI Nobuo, eds.
2002 *Shakaika. Chûgakusei no chiri – Sekai no naka no Nihon [Social studies. Geography for secondary school students – Japan in the World].* Teikoku Shoin, 227 pp.
中村和郎, 高橋伸夫(監修). 社会科, 中学生の地理, 世界の中の 日本, 最新版. 帝国書院. 文部科学省検定済教科書.

SASAYAMA Haruo, ABE Kiyo, OKUDA Yoshio, eds.
2001 *Chûgaku shakai. Rekishi. Mirai o mitsumete [Focussing on the future – Social studies for secondary schools: History].* Kyôiku shuppan, 234 pp.
笹山晴生, 阿部斉, 奥田義雄(監修). 中学社会, 歴史, 未来をみ つめて. 教育出版. 文部科学省検定済教科書.

SATÔ Hisashi, TANIOKA Takeo et al.
2002 *Shinshô Chiri B [New and detailed Geography B].* Teikoku shoin, 296 pp.
佐藤久, 谷岡武雄ほか8名. 新詳地理B, 初訂版. 帝国書院. 文 部科学省検定済教科書.

SHIRAHAMA Mutsuo et al.

2001 *Shinpen chûgakkô shakaika chizu. [Diagrammatic charts for social studies in secondary schools].* Teikoku Shoin, 142 pp.
白浜睦男 ほか６名（著作）. 新編中学校社会科地図, 最新版, 帝国書院編集部編, 帝国書院. 文部科学省検定済教科書.

SHÔGAKUKAN, publ.

1993 *Nijûisseiki kodomo jinbutsukan [The 21st-Century Encyclopedia for Children. Who's who].* Shôgakukan, 388 pp.
21世紀こども人物館. 小学館.

SHÔGAKUKAN, publ.

1992 *Nijûisseiki kodomo chizukan [The 21st-Century Encyclopedia for Children, World Watch].* Shôgakukan, 309 pp.
21世紀こども地図館. 小学館.

SHÔGAKUKAN, publ.

1991 *Nijûisseiki kodomo hyakka [The 21st-Century Encyclopedia for Children].* Shôgakukan, 517 pp.
21世紀こども百科. 小学館.

TABE Hiroshi et.al.

2002a *Atarashii shakai, rekishi [New Society: History].* Tôkyô shoseki, 207 pp.
田邉裕ほか３７名（著作）. 新しい社会, 歴史. 東京書籍. 文部科学省検定済教科書.

TABE Hiroshi et al.

2002b *Atarashii shakai, chiri [New Society: Geography].* Tôkyô Shoseki, 201 pp.
田邉裕ほか３７名（著作）. 新しい社会, 地理, 東京書籍. 文部科学省検定済教科書.

YAMADA Akira, OTÔ Masahide, YAMAGA Seiji, eds.

1990 *Atarashii shakai, chiri [New Society: Geography].* Tôkyô Shoseki, 313 pp.
山田侃, 尾藤正英, 山鹿誠次（監修）. 新しい社会, 地理. 東京書籍. 文部省検定済教科書.

YAMAMOTO Kenkichi et al.

1991 *Hyôjun kokugo 1 [Standard national language 1].* Shôgaku tosho, 277 pp.
山本健吉ほか17名（著作）. 標準国語1, 改訂版. 尚学図書. 文部省検定済教科書.

YAMAMOTO Masamitsu, MASAI Yasuo et al.

2002 *Shôsetsu chiri B [Geography B].* Ninomiya shoten, 303 pp.
山本政三, 正井泰夫ほか13名（著作）. 詳説地理B, 最新版. 二宮 書店. 文部科学省検定済教科書.

BÄTZING, Werner und MESSERLI, Paul, eds.
1991 *Die Alpen im Europa der neunziger Jahre.* Geographica Bernensia, Band P22. Geographisches Institut der Universität Bern.

BUNDESAMT FÜR STATISTIK
1997 *Neue Tendenzen im Religionsgefüge der Schweiz.* Pressemitteilung Nr. 63.

BUNDESAMT FÜR STATISTIK
2003 *SAKE 2002 in Kürze. Wichtigste Ergebnisse der Schweizerischen Arbeitskräfteerhebung.* Neuchâtel.

3 Websites

EIDGENÖSSISCHE ZOLLVERWALTUNG
2004 *Ausfuhr nach Japan.*
Retrieved 18/3/2004 from:
www.afd.admin.ch/d/aussen/zahlen/laender/japan_ausfuhr.php

SWISS EMBASSY TOKYO
2004 Retrieved 18/3/2004 from:
www.eda.admin.ch/Tôkyô_emb/e/home.html
www.eda.admin.ch/tokyo_emb/e/home/polsys.html
www.swissworld.org

SWISS TOURIST OFFICE IN JAPAN
2004 Retrieved 18/3/2004 from:
www.myswiss.jp

THE CHANGING IMAGE OF SWITZERLAND AND ITS INFLUENCE ON JAPAN'S SOCIETY

By Prof. Dr. Yasukazu Morita

Summary (R. Mottini)

The first Japanese report mentioning Switzerland was published in 1861 by Katō Hiroyuki[1] (1836–1916), the first dean of Tokyo Imperial University (today Tokyo University), in his book "Neighborly grass" (*tonarigusa*). In his later published book outlining different political systems (*rippō seitairyaku* "Outline of constitutional political systems") he presented Switzerland as an example of a "pure republic" based on political equality; he also explained the Swiss federal structure.

His intellectual rival Fukuzawa Yukichi (1835–1901) noticed Switzerland 1867 in his book "notes about the eleven treaty countries" (jōyaku *jūikkoku ki*). According to him, Switzerland was a country with no king or president, divided into 21 "provinces" each one sending two representatives to an Upper House in the capital named Berne. During the early Meiji era Switzerland appeared in Japanese school texts for geography and European history with a brief outline of its history until the congress of Vienna.

As a political alternative to the imperialistic power policy of Meiji-Japan, Switzerland emerged as a topic in the so-called "Liberty and Civil Rights Movement" (*jiyū minken undō*). In this movement William Tell became a symbolic icon for the struggle for freedom and democracy. Schiller's drama appeared 1880 in a popular Japanese version by Saitō Tetsusaburō under the title "The bow chord of Switzerland's independence and freedom". Two years later, another version, written by Yamada Ikuji, took the title "Tell – pioneer of freedom". In 1887, Ueki Emori (1857–1892), a leading figure in the freedom movement of the Meiji, issued an anthology of freedom songs containing a lofty song under the title "Switzerland's independence" (*Suisu dokuritsu*). Ueki Emori compared Switzerland's struggle against tyranny with the American fight for independence and Tell's deed with Brutus's assassination of Cesar.

[1] For Japanese names, the family name is first; for Western names the given names precede the family names.

In 1904/05, Switzerland was depicted by Abe Isoo in a highly idealized way and served as a rallying point for those opposing the war with Russia (see article Meyer in this book).

Anesaki Masaharu (1873–1949), religion scientist, published 1908 a diary about a journey he undertook six years earlier through central Switzerland under the title *hanatsumi nikki* ("Flowers of Italy, Diaries of a Pilgrimage").

After the Second World War, Switzerland resurfaced as a topic in the political discussion of Japan. In May 1947, Abe's book was republished as part of the series "Standard works on problems of Japan's society" (*Nihon shakai mondai meicho sen*). In 1949 Ōuchi Hyōe, professor at Tokyo University, reminded the public of Abe's fateful predictions and the alternative he depicted using Switzerland as a model. In the same year Kawasaki Sanzō published a book about Switzerland depicting its cultural institutions as genuine strengths which enabled the country to escape the ravages of war. The author was correspondent in Geneva between 1941 and 1945. His book was meant to offer a vision of democracy, prosperity and peace to the people of his destroyed home country. In the postwar discussion about Japan's political future, Switzerland and Swiss neutrality played a prominent role. It started with General Douglas MacArthur's remarks in 1947 stating that Japan should become the Switzerland of Asia. In 1949, a young Nakasone Yasuhiro, he was to become prime minister from 1982 until 1986, came out strongly in favor of Japan becoming neutral like Switzerland. MacArthur himself emphasized his standpoint in an interview with Reader's Digest Magazine in 1950, stating that Japan should become a neutral country like Switzerland. In the same year, Taoka Ryōichi published a book entitled "The permanent neutrality and the guarantee of Japan's security" (*eisei chūritsu to Nippon no anzen hoshō*).

With the cold war unfolding, however, the neutralization of Japan gradually lost its appeal. In 1952 Switzerland's democracy was the topic of two Swiss books in French by André Siegfried and Pierre Béguin translated into Japanese by Yoshizaka Shunzō and Tsuruoka Senjin. Two years later, the laws for the creation of Japan's Defense Agency (*bōeichō*) and the Japanese Self-Defense Forces (*jieitai*) were enacted.

In 1956, a discussion around Japan's schooltexts started to unfold. On this background Watanabe Takeshi published a book explaining the armed character of Switzerland's permanent neutrality (*Suisu kokumin no idai na seishin ni manabō: Jiei no doryoku nakushite dokuritsu nashi* – "Let's learn from the grand spirit of the Swiss people: No independence without efforts towards self-defense). Watanabe's book saw a second edition in 1959 – a year before the renewal of the Japanese-American security treaty. In this edition Switzerland's discussion of acquiring nuclear weapons was mentioned.

In 1961, two comprehensive studies about neutrality were published by the Japanese Research Institute for International Affairs (*Nihon kokusai mondai kenkyūjō*), dwelling upon the evolution of Swiss neutrality and comparing it to Swedish neutrality. In 1962 a study by Kitamura Takajirō focussed on Swiss neutrality during the Second World War: *Dainiji taisen to Suisu no chūritsu* (The Second World War and Switzerland's neutrality); he drew the conclusion that Japan could not follow the Swiss way as the geopolitical positions of the two countries were too different.

In 1968 Miyashita Keizō published his study *Chūritsu o mamoru – Suisu no eikō to kunan* ("Preserving neutrality – Switzerland's honour and trouble"). He highlighted the point of armed self-defense in the Swiss neutrality concept as a "tough reality" rather than an idealistic vision.

The Japanese translation in 1970 of the official Swiss Handbook for Civil Defense (*minkan bōei*) turned out to be a bestseller in Japan. In its comment the necessity of common and individual efforts to contribute to peace was emphasized; Switzerland's long peace, according to the Japanese translators, rested on an efficient combination of military and civil defense. After the devastating earthquake of 1995 around Kōbe, the handbook was re-edited under the title: *Minkan bōei. Shinsōban. Arayuru kiken kara mi o mamoru* (Civil defense. New edition. How to protect oneself from different dangers).

In 1971 Sugita Ichiji and Fujiwara Iwaichi from the Japanese Defense Agency published a study entitled *Suisu kokubō to Nippon* (The Swiss territorial defense and Japan). In their study they discussed MacArthur's vision and the need to see self-defense as part of an overall endeavor for the promotion of peace, democracy and stability in Asia.

During the end of the seventies, the economic promotion association of Kōbe propagated Switzerland as a model for democracy, freedom and peace. During the same time a public discussion between Seki Yoshihiko, professor at Waseda University, and Morishima Michio from London University drew widespread attention. Seki was in favour of strong defence capabilities like the Swiss ones whereas Morishima stated that Switzerland's neutrality was paramount to its security during the Second World War.

In my own book *Suisu: Rekishi kara gendai e* (Switzerland: from past to present) from 1980 I described Switzerland as resting on three pillars: federalism, direct democracy and armed neutrality. This book was directed against a selective perception of Switzerland using it as a metaphor in order to highlight individual preferences without paying attention to Swiss history and the political mechanisms of decision making there. Ever since, Swiss neutrality did not appear as a fixed idea for shaping Japan's security policy anymore.

Yasukazu Morita, born 1940 in Tokyo/Shinjuku; 1970 PhD in humanities from Tokyo University. Professor and Dean of Faculty of Humanities at Japan Women's University. Several publications on Swiss history and geography.

スイス像の変遷とその日本社会への影響
—主として、明治期と維新1945年以降を対象にして—

森田安一

はじめに　—幕末・開国期のスイス像—

日本は1864年にスイスと和親通商条約を締結した。スイスはヨーロッパ中央の山国で、海軍を持たない小国ではあったが、ヨーロッパ列強に互して比較的早く幕末日本にスイス政府代表団を送り、開国後8番目に和親通商条約の締結を果たした。

この和親通商条約締結以前に、スイスの政治制度をかなり正確に紹介した人物は加藤弘之であった。彼は文久元年（1861年）に『隣艸』を著している。*1幕末の尊皇攘夷論者からの攻撃を避けるために、加藤は「隣国のことを論ずる」とカモフラージュして、西洋の立憲政体を詳しく紹介した。その中でスイスの政体を「万民同権」［＝民主共和制］と見なし、もっとも望ましい政体としている。『隣艸』は日本における立憲思想を考察する上で重要な文献であるが、明治32年まで公刊されることはなかった。しかし、『隣艸』の7年後（1868年）に書かれた『立憲政体略』の記述から加藤がスイスを具体的にどのように見ていたかはわかる。「この［万民同権＝万民共治の］政体を立つる各国、多くは元来自主の数邦を合して1国となせるものなるがゆえに、その数邦は上下同治の国の州県のごとき者にはあらず、各邦かならずまた政治ありて邦内の政はすべてこの政府にて施行し、ただ全国に関係することは全国の大政府にて施行す」*2と。スイスのカントンと連邦の関係を簡潔に述べている。

さらに加藤はスイス連邦政府を次のように説明している「スイッツルのごときは7局を立て、いわゆる合議府7人おのおの1局の長となりて、その職務をつかさどり、平常のことはその長これを定決して施行し、ただ少しくつねに異なることは、みな合議府7人相議してこれを定む。ただし7人中首領1人あり、年々改選す」*3と。加藤はその実現を考えていなかったが、スイスをモデル国家化していた。

福澤諭吉も慶応3年(1867年)に『条約十一国記』を書き、スイスの政治のしくみを次のように紹介している。「此国の政事は寄合持にて国王もなく亦大統領といふ者なし。国を2十1郡に分けて1郡より2人づつ評議役を出し、これを上院といひ、又国中の人別2万人の内より1人づつの割合にて評議役を人選して、これを下院といふ。いずれも3年づつ交代なり。斯くして上下2組の評議役を発て『ベルン』という都に寄合て、国の政事を取扱ふことなり」と*4。

加藤と福澤の議論については、すでに拙著において紹介済みなので、明治初期の教科書にスイスがどのように記述されていたかを次に見てみよう。

1、明治初期の小学校歴史・地理教科書に見られるスイス像

明治初期には欧化政策が取られ、欧米の歴史・地理、さらには政治制度に強い関心が寄せられており、スイスはさまざまに取りあげられている。

小学校歴史教科書として、明治5年の小学教則以後に文部省が著作刊行した『史畧』4巻がある。巻3と巻4の2冊に西洋史が割り当てられ、西洋史に大きな比重がかけられている。『史畧』は明治5年に刊行され、およそ5年の間に13万部以上発行され、歴史教科書としては大変普及したものである*5。巻4にスイスの歴史は簡潔に述べられている。シュヴァーベン戦争は次のように書かれている。「1499年獨逸帝マキシミリヤンの時一擧して此國の動亂を平定せんと欲し大軍を以て攻来ると雖も國民1致して激烈の戦争を為し6回の接戦に於いて盡く墺國の兵を破りしかば近隣の州郡益々同盟に加はる者多く其勢彌強盛に及べり」と*6。また、代表的な小学校外国史教科書といわれる明治9年刊の田中義廉『萬国史略』（巻之3）はウィーン会議後のスイスの歴史を次のように書いている。「維也納（ウィーン）ノ大會議ニ於テ再ヒ獨立國トナリ、従来ノ聯邦19部ノ外、猶
日内瓦（ジュネーヴ）牛弗砂徳（ヌシャテル）瓦来斯（ヴァリス）ノ3部ヲ合スルコトヲ得タリ爾来舊時ノ弊習、悉ク去テ、全ク、合衆政治トナリ、國内平穏ニシテ、政令其宜キヲ得、文學藝術日々ニ進ミ、4民各其業ニ安シテ、國家最開明ト稱スルニ至レリ」と*7。スイスは政治が安定し、経済が興隆し、文化が進展した最高の国家と見なしている。岩倉使節団が「相対的に高い関心」をスイスをはじめとする小国に示したといわれるが、『特命全権大使米欧回覧実記』が公刊（明治11年）される以前に、小学校教科書にはスイスをモデル国家化する記述が溢れていたのある。同様のスイスの歴史記述は他の歴史教科書にも見られる。*8

明治初期の地理教科書にもスイスは比較的詳しく紹介されている。黒田行元『萬国地名往来』（1873年【明治6年】刊）は世界各地の地勢風土・人口・文化を紹介しているが、スイスについては次のように記している。「海なき國の瑞士、餘所の軍に取合はず、常に太平無事なるは、西洋中の桃源と、言ふべき程の風氣なり」*9と。また、假名垣魯文『世界都路』(1872年【明治5年】)「沸と日耳曼列国の、中に挟まる瑞西。小國ながら共和政、民の教の道届き、國に報ゆる眞ごころの、怠まで年を経る儘に、小敵と見て侮らず。軽しめざるは大國の、目にも餘れる智仁勇。兼備の徳と知られけり」と*10、歴史教科書同様の論調が見られる。

しかし、歴史・地理教科書で西洋を知ろうとする姿勢は明治13年までであった。外国史書を小学校教科書にすることは明治13年の教育令以後なくなった。歴史は尊皇愛国を教える学科として、日本史だけを小学校では教えることになったからである。

2、自由民権運動期のスイス像

小学校教科書から外国史が消えたが、その頃にシラーの戯曲『ウィリアム・テル』が相次いで翻訳され、スイスの自由・独立の話は日本に広く広がった。それは自由民権運動の展開と無縁ではなかった。

明治13年に斎藤鉄太郎はシラーの戯曲を『瑞正独立自由の弓弦』と題して翻訳している。全訳をした様子はないが、その序において次のような解説が付されている。「此書や一人の義勇を以て長く国家自由独立の基を闢し事を書せし者にして今に至て彼国の之を尊こと猶我4十7の義士の如しといふ・・・・・中古1千3百年の頃瑞正國は墺国の所領にして其知県の苛政に苦み居たりしが国内3郡の人民自由を唱ゑ師を起し知県を退け遂に其国の自由の基を闢し」*11と。序を書いた人物は竜山人と称し、明確な人物像は不明であるが、テルを赤穂浪士と比較し、馬琴風の通俗読本を意識させている。しかし、知県、すなわち代官の横暴に抵抗し、自由を獲得する点が強調されている。明らかにシラーの傑作を日本に紹介することを単に目的としていたのではなく、当時高まっていた自由民権運動を意識した政治小説的な意味合いを持たせていたと考えられる。

明治15年(1882年)には山田郁治訳『哲爾自由譚』が出版されている。その緒言には、この冊子が「勧善懲悪を旨として」書かれていることを謳い、本文の訳には「壓政の岸を船出して、自由の港に達すると思はばさのみ艱難も、之を避るに足らざらん。自由の海の航行のせんどうとなり后の世に名を貽さんも難からず」とあり*12、せんどうに「船頭と先導」をかけて、漢字のルビを振っている。テルを自由の海の船頭＝先導とし、自由民権運動を後押しする文章が読みとれる。

こうしたテルを自由の象徴とし、スイスを自由郷と謳ったのは自由民権運動の中心人物である植木枝盛である。彼は明治20年10月に『自由詞林』を発表し、その中で「瑞西獨立」を書き、熱烈にスイスの自由を歌い上げて行く。その冒頭と結びの部分を示せば、次のようになる*13。
雲に聳ゆる白山や　其の風景も倫なく　いまは春風和みつつ　自由の花の匂ふなる瑞西の國は其むかし　墺地利に併されて　さも苛酷なき暴政の　嵐の斷ゆるひまもなし左れば世の為め民の為め　天下の為めに　師をおもひ起しにし　維廉剔爾のこころざし
・・・・・
墺地利の百萬の　其大軍もいかでかは　敵することのなかるべきぞ　妖氛遂に打ち晴れて山なす屍めで度くも　築き興せり自由郷　河なす血潮めで度くも　染め出しけり自由郷

自由を獲得するためには、死をも覚悟する姿勢を謳い、枝盛は自由民権運動を盛り上げようと努めている。枝盛はテルを中心としたスイス独立闘争を、イギリスの暴虐に抗したアメリカの独立運動と、カエサルの奸計邪謀から「民の自由」を守ったブルータスの行為と並べている。テルが歴史上の人物と思われていた時代では、スイス建国の英雄は自由民権運動に影響を与えたことは間違いないであろう。

テルの自由獲得闘争は明治時代を通じて日本の知識人の心を捉え続けていた。それは姉崎正治(1873ー1949)（嘲風）の日記『花つみ日記』から読みとれる。姉崎は日本における宗教学の確立に大きな功績を残した人物である。1904年（明治37年）より東京帝国大学教授となったが、彼のもう1つの功績には、1923年（大正12年）から1934年（昭和9年）まで東京帝国大学の図書館長を務め、関東大震災で焼失した図書館の復興に尽力したことである。

『花つみ日記』は姉崎の留学中の日記であるが、その冒頭に「ゴットハルトの雪」と題して、明治41年4月5日の朝にチューリヒを出立して、ゲシュネンで1泊するまでの体験が書かれている。
「此の湖水（フィーアヴァルトシュテッテ湖）を見ればテルの芝居を思ひ出す。此の湖水のぐるりに住むだ強い気丈な人民の獨立心がこの自由国スイスの基本をなしたのである。湖水の南につきる處はフリューレンの村、6年の前に船でこの湖を渡り、この村から馬車でテルの村であったといふアルトドルフに泊まった昔しを活き活きと思ひ出される」と*14。

6年前（明治35年）のアルトドルフの体験は『花つみ日記』の外篇第1「我れやいづこの記」に次のように書いている。
「きみはドイツの人とは見えず、さるにても瑞西の国を能く知り、又シルレルがテルの文をも能く誦し給ふ事よ」と*15。

アルトドルフの宿の人とうちとけ、そこで言われたことを自慢げに書いている。姉崎がシラーのテル劇中の句を覚えていたほど、明治の末近くには日本ではテルの話についてはよく知られていた。

また、姉崎は馬橇に乗って悪魔の橋Teufelsbrückeへ行く途中御者の子ども時代の話から次のようなことも書いている。「子供の時から夏は羊を追ふて山の岨に朝から晩まで、冬は雪の中でくらす。身体が丈夫になるのも無理でなく、又人民が自由の精神に富むでをるのも自然であると思はれる」と*16。
この発言からは、スイスには自由の精神が溢れているという認識があったことがわかる。

3、安部磯雄『地上の理想国・瑞西』

嘲風がスイスを自由溢れる国として体験しているときに、スイスを理想国家として高く評価する書籍が刊行された。1904年（明治37年）に出版された安部磯雄の『地上の理想国・瑞西』である。

安部はキリスト教社会主義の立場から1901年（明治34年）に片山潜らと社会民主党創設し、日本の社会民主主義の父と言われる人物である。この書物は

3部構成からなっている。第1篇では「政治」を扱い、スイスは自由民権が発揮され、純粋な民主主義が行われている、とする。第2篇教育では、1国の文明を知るには、教育の状態を見るべきであるとして、教育制度を論じる。第3編「社会問題」ではスイスの制度は社会主義的ではないが、社会主義政策が大胆に行なわれ、社会福祉も充実していると説いている。

安部はスイスを「自由の小天地」で「真性の自由民権」が確立する国として理想化する。まず、総論の最後の部分で次のように述べる*17。

「屹然として立てる自由主義は彼のアルプス山よりも崇高に、整然として乱れざる社会組織はゼネバ湖よりも1層優美である。吾人が茲に紹介せんとする地上の理想国は山高く水清き瑞西にあらじして、自由、平等、平和の横溢せる瑞西である」と。

さらに第1編第1章「連邦組織」の結論部分でもスイスを理想化する*18。

「要するに瑞西の政治は純粋なる民主主義にして其本位は人民である。州政府と雖も全く人民の代表者であって、其政策は多数人民の意志の発言したるものである。瑞西で用いつつある選挙法及び直接立法権なるものを見たらば、何人にても真性の民主主義が瑞西に於て最も多く発揮せられつつあることを認むるであろう」と。

安部がスイスを理想化したもう1つの側面はスイスの社会福祉、社会政策にあった。社会主義者の安部はこの点に強い関心を示し、『地上の理想国・スイス』の第3篇は本書の半分以上を占めている。また、日露戦争勃発の危機を迎え、中立にも強い関心を示し、非戦の立場から「結論」の部分で再度スイスを理想とし、見ならうことを主張する*19。

「瑞西は独墺の如く王侯を以て天下に鳴るの野心を棄てた。然し彼は柔和にして平和の宣傳者たる天使を以て任じて居るのである。想ふに我國の前途も亦瑞西の如くなるではないか。否斯くなさねばならぬのではないか」と。

安部の本書執筆の理由は、本書再販（後述）の解説を書いた権田保之助が安部から聞かされた言葉を書いている。「戦争の悪夢から覚まさせようといふ目的で、私は今『地上の理想國　瑞西』といふ本を書いてゐますが、この世の中に瑞西といふやうな國があって、その國の生活がどんなにうまく営まれてゐるか、そしてどんなに羨ましい状態にあるかを知っただけでも、戦争熱狂に対する反省の念が國民の間に湧き起こることだと思ひ、又、さうなることを希望してゐるのです」と。[*20]

こうした非戦姿勢を裏付けるように、本書刊行の前年1903年（明治36年）9月15日発行の『6合雑誌』の社論で安部は「吾人は露國と戦ふべきか」を書き、非戦を唱えた。翌10月には、みずから創設の先頭に立った社会主義協会が主催した非戦演説会でも非戦を訴えた。8日の第1回演説会は「露國内部の潮流を見よ」、同月20日以前に行われた第2回演説会では「世界の平和境スイスについて」であった。

そこで安部は、「『ヨーロッパの屋根』の高冷の山岳地帯に、『永世中立』と平和の孤高を守って1人わが道を往くことこそ、『神』がわが国に期待せる道なることを説いた」と伝えられている。[*21]この時の安部の気持ちは『地上之理想国・瑞西』の第1篇「政治」の最後の言葉でも表されるであろう。「噫自由の小天地！国民に幸福を与へ自由平等を与ふ、これを外にして国家生存の目的果たして何処にあるか。噫国家の栄誉何物ぞ、領土の拡張何物ぞ。世界の列国は宜しく此1小理想国の前に拝跪して羞死すべきである」と[*22]。

平民新聞によると、『地上之理想国・瑞西』は出版された明治37年に1、932冊が販売されたという[*23]。明治末期に於いてこの販売数は驚異といえる。少なくない影響を与えたのではないだろうか。

4、『地上之理想国　瑞西』の復刊

スイス像が日本社会で再びクローズアップされたのは第2次世界大戦後のことである。安部の『地上之理想国　瑞西』が大原社会問題研究所によって「日本社会問題名著選」の1冊として、昭和22年5月に再刊された。本署の解説を書いている権田は昭和21年9月1日（終戦ほぼ1年後！）の日付のある「

跋」で次のように書いている。[*24]「國土と國民とを窮乏のどん底へ叩き落としてしまった今次事変の後、今にして始めて、デンマルクに學べとか、スイスを知らなくてはならないとか云ふ声が方々に挙がっている。今更らながら何の話だと、少々くすぐったい感じがする。既に4十何年かの昔に、わが安部先生は明かにそれを示してゐるではありませんか」と。

この安部の著作に触れながら、大内兵衛は昭和24年10月11日の『朝日新聞』紙上に「スイスの経済」を書き、スイスのデモクラシーを讃えている。

「いまから50年前、安部磯雄が『理想の国瑞西』を書いたのも、ゼームス・ブライスが、この国の如きをもってデモクラシーの型としたのも、言葉と伝統を異にする多くのカントン（州のこと）が集まって、完全に平等な人種の政治を作り出したことを喜んでいるからである。いまやそのデモクラシーは完全にその果実を収穫している。私には、これがデモクラシー1般の性質なのか、それともスイスに限ってこの特異な現象なのか、よくわからないけれども、スイスは今日そのデモクラシーを大いに誇りとしている。」

大内は東大教授退官後、招かれて昭和24年9月にスイスで開かれた国際統計会議に出席し、その時の旅行体験を帰国後『スイス紀行　世界の問題』と題して刊行した。本書は、2部構成を取り、後篇「世界の問題」にスイス経済の記事は採録されている[*25]。前篇「旅日記」には、ベルン人の生活、スイスの時計、国際都市ジュネーブに触れ、敗戦後の日本の貧しさとスイスの豊かさを比較・論評している。

これより先、昭和24年2月に川崎3蔵が『戦なき國の繁栄　スイス一過去と現在』を書き、その「はしがき」に「スイスの長所や文化的な施設、徹底した民主主義、平和への努力の数々を範とするに十分であると思う」と述べている[*26]。川崎は読売新聞欧州特派員として戦中戦後の4年と半月の間「平和のサンプルともいうべき永世中立国スイス」で暮らし、帰国後直ぐにこの本を書いている。戦禍で疲弊した日本人が「平和に生き、民主政を心から理解し、高度文化を満喫」できるようにと、スイスの歴史・政治・経済について体験をふまえて叙述した。

安部磯雄の本は、彼自身自序において「大部分はヴィンセント氏の『瑞西の政治』及びドウソン氏の『社会的瑞西』より抜粋したもの」と述べているように、スイス滞在経験を踏まえた本としては川崎の本をもって嚆矢とされるが、戦後日本にどの程度影響を与えたかは定かではない。

5、「東洋のスイスたれ」

戦後の混乱期に「平和なスイス」に学べという声に決定的な後押ししたのは日本占領軍総司令官ダグラス・マッカーサーであった。彼は「日本は東洋のスイスたれ」と発言し、戦後の日本の進むべき道を示したと云われる。しかし、この人口に膾炙した言葉がいつどのような機会の述べられ、どうしてこれほどまで広がったかかならずしも定かではない。片山哲がその著『回顧と展望』の中で、マッカーサーの次ぎような言葉を引用している。昭和22年(1947年)5月に片山が首班指名を受け、マッカーサーと会談したときの話である。

　「マッカーサーのファースト・インプレッションは人なつこくって、大変私にはよかった。ことに『君はクリスチャンであると聞いている。ほんとにその精神に依ってやってもらいたい』ということと、『日本は民主主義で進まなければいかん。民主主義発展のためには援助を惜しまぬ。細かい点については自分はあまり言わないけれども、日本はこれから、東洋のスイスたれ』と言った。その点において私は非常に賛成し、後になっても。彼はたびたびこれを繰り返していったことがある。日本は絶対平和国、中立国でありたいと思ったので、私も『東洋のスイスとしてやりたい。もう戦争はこりごりなので、戦争の放棄は私もどこまでも守り通そう』と答え」たと、回想している*27。

これより以前にマッカーサーが「日本は東洋のスイスたれ」と発言したかどうか、また、片山が言うようにマッカーサーがたびたび口に出したか確認できない*28。しかし、この言葉がクローズアップされるのはおよそ2年経った昭和24年3月以降であろう。

同年3月3日付け『朝日新聞』はマッカーサー元帥が「日本の中立を維持」することを言明したと報じている。イギリスの「デイリー・メール」紙の記者に元帥が「戦争が起こった場合、米国は日本が戦うことは欲しない。日本の役割は太平洋のスイスになることである」と述べたとしている。同じ3月3日付け『毎日新聞』は社説において「日本の中立」について書いている。「マッカーサー元帥は、英国の大記者ウォード・ブライス氏との会見で、太平洋における日本の将来の地位に［スイスを］あてはめて語った。これは連合国の責任ある当局者によって、日本の将来あるべき姿が、具体的に語られた最初の言葉である」と。社説は元帥が「日本に望むところは中立の維持以外にない」としているのに対して、「日本人自身の強い決意なくしては、中立の特権は得られないであろう」と結んでいる。

こうした新聞記事をうけて、衆3両院で中立問題が取りあげられて、吉田首相に質問の矢が向けられている。3議院では帆足計（社会党）が4月7日に次のように述べている。「マッカーサー元帥は、『日本の役割は太平洋におけるスエーデンやスイッツルにごときものであるべきだ。』と語ったということであります。［中略］武装を放棄せる国家たることを名誉と考え、［日本は］賢明なるスウェーデン、スイッツルのごとく、1切の国際紛争に超越して、永世局外中立の立場を守り抜くことが必要である」と政府の立場を追求している*29。4月15日の3議院予算委員会でも、帆足は繰り返し次のような発言をしている。「マッカーサー元帥は、日本が太平洋のスイッツルであることを望むと言われたと言いまするが、非常に国民の胸にこの言葉は感銘しておる次第であります」と*30。帆足は同じ1949年の『世界評論』において、マッカーサー元帥の言葉やスイスとスエーデンの中立に再度触れた後に次のように述べている。*31

「しかしながら、平和と中立を守り抜くという仕事は、とおりいっぺんの決意や努力でできることではない。他人のことに干渉せず、同時に他人から干渉されないがためには、キゼンたる不羈独立の精神が必要である。戦いなき國スイスの自立は、ウィリアム・テルの伝説をほこる自由国民のたかい自覚と自尊心によるものであることを忘れてはならぬ」と。

衆議院では4月16日に中曽根康弘が永世中立に疑義を言明した吉田茂を批判して次のように述べている*32。

「われわれは新憲法を制定して、われらの安全と生存を諸国民の公正と信義に託し、戦争放棄を厳粛に宣言したのであります。かくて、絶対平和主義と中立堅持は8千万民族の決意であって、象徴たる天皇も、この民族の意志を明らかに表明されておられるのであります。日本国民は、最近のマッカーサー声明中に、日本をスイスのごとき中立国にいたしたいとの文字を共感を持って読んでおるのであります。しかるに、1国の総理大臣たるものが、軽々にこの国民の総意に対して疑義を表明し、しかも国民代表の質問に対して何らの説明をなさないということは、無責任もはなはだしいといわなければなりません。（中略）憲法に表明された日本国民の平和主義、戦争放棄宣言を冒涜するものとして、まことに遺憾の意を表明する次第であります。」後の中曽根の政治的豹変は想像を絶する発言である。

翌25年1月28日民主党の北村徳太郎は「連合国を代表するところの最高司令官たるマツカーサー元帥は、日本は太平洋のスイスたれということを声明しておるのである。われわれは、どこまでもこの線に沿いながら、日本憲法の明示する、戦争を放棄して、どこまでも平和主義をもつて1貫するという立場において、全面講和でなければならぬという点を主張しておるのであります」と述べている[*33]。中立と全面講和を絡ませた討論が国会では続いていく。

6、小学校社会科教科書に現れるスイス像

国会で「東洋のスイス」を絡ませた議論が行われている頃、『リーダーズダイジェスト』の1950年6月号に、J・P・マッキヴォイによるマッカーサーとの単独会見記が掲載され、再度マッカーサーは「極東のスイス」を語っている[*34]。

「武力をもつことは日本を侵略しようとする国に侵略を思いとどまらせることにはならず、かえつて侵略を誘発することになるだろう。日本は“極東のスイス”となり、スイスが中立であるのと同じ理由で中立であるべきだ」と[*35]。

学会では、昭和25年5月に国際法の権威・田岡良1が『永世中立と日本の安全保障』を出版している。国際法上における永世中立の意味を論じたもので、必ずしもスイスの中立だけを扱ってはいない。しかし、スイスの永世中立は重視し、「日本をめぐる国際情勢は、歴史上永世中立を発生せしめた国際情勢と類似するものをもつている」と述べ[*36]、政治家への期待を示している。

日本の“極東スイス中立論”は大きな反響を呼び起こし、中立国スイスへの熱いまなざしが注がれるようになり、小学校社会科の教科書にスイスに学ぼうという単元が見られるようにもなる。ある小学5年の社会科教科書『小学生の社会』の「工業と日本の将来」に次のような文が見られる。ある生徒が日本の将来は、工業、とくに長い歴史をもつせんい工業に力を入れるべきと主張したことに対して、明君という生徒は立ち上がって次のように述べる。

「せんい工業は、ぼくも大さんせいですが、ぼくはとくにスイスに学んで一時計や、けんびきょうや、写真機や、エンジンや、そういった精密工業に力を入れたいと思います」と述べ、それに対して3吉君が次のように述べる。

「ぼくは、日本を観光国にしたいと思います。その点、明君のまねをするようですが、スイスに学びたいのです。日本はイタリアのように海の風景と、スイスのような山の風景と合わせた美しい國です。そのためには設備において、将来のあらゆるくふうをしなければなりません」と[*37]。

また、小学6年の社会科教科書には、「貿易をおこそう」の単元でスイスを取りあげている。

「その面積は、41,295平方ｋｍで、わが国の9州ぐらいであり、人口は。およそ470万人、そのせまい土地の24.9％は牧場、耕地は、16％となっている。チーズ・バターのほか、小麦・じゃがいもをはじめ、農作物はほとんど輸入している。鉄・石炭などの資源にとぼしく、いずれも外国から買いいれている。このような、小さな国ではありけれども山のおおい国土を利用して、水力で電気をおこし、これで有名な時計をはじめ、機械類・染料・薬品・精密機械・織物などを生産し、これを外国に輸出している。

つまり、食料と、原料とを輸入し、工業をさかんいおこして、その製品を輸出しているのである。

”りんごのまと”の物語にみられるような、まずしい国であったスイスは、アルプスの山の中にありながら、こうして世界の国々とむすびつくことによって、平和でゆたかな生活をきずいてきたのである」と*38。

7、再軍備とスイス像

1950年（昭和25年）1月、マッカーサー元帥は年頭の辞において、日本国憲法は自衛権を否定せず、という声明を出し*39、同年7月に警察予備隊の創設指令を出した。その頃から日本における対スイス観も変化が生まれてくる。中立思想を媒介にして、スイスを単純にモデル国家と見るだけではなく、スイスの国情を正確に知ろうという姿勢である。1952年に岩波書店から2冊の翻訳書が出た。A. シーグフリート、吉阪俊藏訳『スイス　—デモクラシーの証人—』とP. ベガン、鶴岡千仭訳『ヨーロッパのバルコニー　—第2次大戦中のスイス—』である。吉阪はその小序において次のように述べる。「敗戦後の日本は民主的平和国としてスイスを手本としてその独立と繁栄とをはかるべきことが説かれている。・・・日本よりも小国で海に面せず食料は足りず原料は乏しいにも拘わらず世界で最も進んだ工業国となり、その国民は世界でもっとも高い水準の生活を営んでいる。本書はその原因をはっきりと説明する外、将来に対するあり方をも示唆している」と*40。

1954年6月に防衛庁設置法・自衛隊法が公布され、翌月に施行された。翌年1955年（昭和30）日本民主党（当時）が編集刊行した『うれうべき教科書の問題』では、社会科教科書の内容が「偏向教育」として批判され、政治問題化していった。こうした政治状況の中でスイスの中立についてさまざまな書籍・論文が出されている。

こうした政治状況の中で特筆すべきスイス論は、1956年に刊行された渡辺剛『スイス国民の偉大な精神に学ぼう＝自衛の努力なくして独立なし＝』である。渡辺は「ありのままのスイスの姿を探求する」必要を説き、スイスの中立が武装中立であることを強調している*41。ただし、非戦論者・安部磯雄の

『地上之理想国　瑞西』を評価しており、渡辺の立場は不分明である。

渡辺の記述それ自体はおおむね正しいが、ことさらに軍備を強調し、中立の維持の条件は「侵略者には最後の1兵にいたるまで断固として抵抗するという全国民の固い決意と、それに相応する最新の軍備」にあるとする*42。ちょうどこの時期における防衛力強化の風潮の中でのこの発言は、平和国家スイスのイメージを悪用した「軍事国家スイス」モデル論と捉えられる。これまでのスイス観に完全に逆転したスイスモデル国家論が生まれた。1959年（昭和34年)日米安保条約改正の前年にこの本は改訂版が出され、その前年にスイス政府が戦術核兵器を装備する用意のあることを声明した事柄を書き加えさえしている。

昭和36年には、中立に関する2冊の総合的研究、日本国際問題研究所編『中立主義の研究』上下2巻と日本国際連合協会京都本部編『中立及び中立主義』が出版された。その中で前述の田岡が前著では「スイス」の中立を扱い*43、後著では「中立の本来の意味　ースイス及びスェーデンの歴史に照らして」を書いているが*44、これは19~20世紀のスイス中立の歴史が克明に描き、貴重な仕事である。

田岡らの研究や時事評論家たちの見解を吸収しながら、北村孝2郎はもっぱら第2次大戦中におけるスイスの中立に焦点を合わせて、『第2次大戦とスイスの中立』を昭和37年に出版した。その上で、「日本は東洋のスイスになりえない」という結論を導き出す。「もとよりスイスとわが国とは、根本的に諸種の事情を異にする。また伝統や環境も違う。だから、たとえわが国がスイスの亜流を汲んで永世中立を志しても、それは虎を描いて猫となる類に等しく、また、それによってわが国の独立と平和を維持しようとしても、それはおそらく難事中の難事だと断ぜざるをえないのではなかろうか」と*45。

北村は戦時中のドイツ・スイス滞在の経験をも踏まえて、スイスの中立論を展開したが、戦時体験のない若い世代に属するドイツ文学者・宮下啓三は多くの文献を渉猟して、昭和43年(1968年)に『中立を守る　スイスの栄光と苦難』を著した。第2次大戦中におけるスイスの中立の実体をコンパクトに、しかも平明に叙述した。「軍備なき中立の理想をかきみだす」恐れを抱きつつ、「中立という抽象的な言葉の背後にきびしい現実がかくされている」こと、「現実であるからにはもはや理想ではない、という事実」を認識する必要を説いた*46。

8、『民間防衛』の翻訳

宮下が危惧したように、その後昭和46年になると、スイスの厳格な武装中立を評価する著作が刊行された。杉田1次・藤原岩市の共著になる『スイスの国防と日本』である。杉田・藤原は旧陸大の卒業生で、自衛隊の中枢にいた人物で、その立場からスイスの国防を手本にすべきことを説いている。「はしがき」でまず次のように語る。「マックアーサー元帥が『日本は極東のスイスたれ』と言ったからとて、たやすく日本がスイスのようになれるものではないが、スイスの国情に疎いことも手伝って、日本の国民大衆は中立や永世中立を標榜したり、宣言しさえすれば、スイスやスエーデンのような国になれると思っているものもすくなくないようである」と。「結言」では、「マックアーサー元帥の言葉を思い起こすまでもないが、いまこそスイスの精神を学び世界的視野に立って『アジア』の平和地繁栄に貢献することが、1970年代、日本に課せられた大きな問題ではないか？」と述べている*47。スイスの民主主義、自由と平和は全国民の生命を賭けた努力の賜物であることを強調して、当時の軍備増強政策を後押しをした。

この本が出た前年1970年には『民間防衛』Zivilverteidigung　の翻訳が出されている。「地域住民の防災対策にすぐ役立つ必携書」と銘打って、爆発的に売れた。しかし、本書翻訳の意図は訳者あとがきに明瞭である*48。「第2次大戦後しばらくして『太平洋のスイスになれ』という言葉がわが国でもてはやされた時代がある」と書き出し、「われわれが平和愛好國スイスを語る際、どういうわけかスイス国民の平和を守るための努力、国民1人1人の大変な負担とこれを耐え抜く気迫という現実には目をつぶり、ともすれば、かかる努力によってはじめて開花した平和という美しい花にのみ気をとられてきたきらいがないだろうか」と、スイスが長い間平和と安全を享受するために払った代償、民間防衛と軍事防衛をあわせた防御態勢樹立の努力を知り、「最悪の事態」に備える発想を喚起している。

余談になるが、本書は1995年の阪神淡路大震災後ただちに新装版『民間防衛　新装版―あらゆる危険から身をまもる』と題して、緊急出版されたが、自衛隊イラク派兵の議論が盛んになった本年(2003年7月)再度復刊された。平和愛好国スイス・イメージがかなり歪められてきたように思われる。

1970年代末には、経済界からもスイスをモデル化する論議が提示された。第36回西日本経済同友会大会における神戸経済同友会の「わが国の安全保障と共同体精神」と題する研究報告(1978年11月)である。そこでは、スイスの民主主義、自由と平和は、全国民の生命を賭けた努力の賜物であり、祖国防衛の精神と軍備の成果であるという主張がなされた。

9、終わりに　―新しいスイス像の模索―

スイスの歴史、あるいは政治のしくみを総合的に紹介せず、ご都合主義の部分的利用に対して、筆者は1980年に『スイス　歴史から現代へ』を書き、地域主義・直接民主政・武装中立の3本柱を立て、スイスの特徴を紹介した*49。80年代以降ジャーナリスト、スイス長期滞在者による多数のスイス紹介書が刊行された。現在も旅行書を含めて、スイス紹介書は百花繚乱といえる。

その中で注目されることはスイス憲法や政治のしくみに関する数多くの専門研究書の出版である。小林・国枝・関根・渡辺・美根の研究書であるし*50、新スイス憲法も翻訳されている。日本の憲法改正論議の中で、武装中立と同様に、ご都合主義的なスイス憲法の部分的つまみ食いには注意を払う必要を感じるところである。

註
*1日本史籍協会編『川勝家文書』東京大学出版会、1930年（1970年覆刻）。
*2加藤弘之『立憲政体略』植手通有編『日本の名著　西周・加藤弘之』中央公論社、1972年、339頁。
*3加藤『立憲政体略』341頁。
*4福澤諭吉『福澤全集』 時事新報社、1925年、211頁。
*5海後宗臣編『日本教科書大系』近代編第18巻、歴史（1）、講談社、1963年、722頁。

*6文部省『史略、西洋下』同上書、47頁。
*7田中義廉『萬國史略』『日本教科書大系』（近代編第18巻、歴史（1）、講談社、1963年、219一220頁。
*8西村茂樹『校正・万国史略』明治6年、師範学校編『万国史略』巻2、明治7年については、拙著『スイス　歴史から現代へ』36頁以下3照。
*9『日本教科書大系』往来編第9巻、地理（1)、講談社、1966年、542頁。
*10『日本教科書大系』近代編第18巻歴史(1)、 講談社、1963年、525頁。
*11柳田泉編『明治文化資料叢書』第9巻翻訳文学編、1959年、67頁。
*12山田郁治（譯述）『哲爾自由譚　1名自由之魁』（出版人　佐々木和亮）、明治15年、11－12頁。
*13植木枝盛『自由詞林』土佐國(出版人・市原眞影),明治2十年、8、12頁。
*14姉崎正治『花つみ日記』博文館、1909年、4頁。
*15姉崎、454頁。
*16姉崎、9頁。
*17安部磯雄『地上之理想國・瑞西』第1出版株式会社、　1947年[5月］（初版・明治37年、平民文庫)、 3 頁。
*18安部『地上之理想国』5一6頁。
*19安部『地上之理想国』97一98頁。
*20安部『地上之理想国』185一187頁。
*21高野善一編著『日本社会主義の父　安部磯雄』1970年、80頁。
*22安部『地上之理想国』33一34頁
*23片山哲『安部磯雄伝』大空社、1958年、131頁。
*24安部『地上之理想国』194頁。
*25大内兵衛『スイス紀行　世界の問題』朝日新聞社、1950年、99一103頁。
*26川崎三蔵『戦なき國の繁栄　スイス一過去と現在』成人社、3頁。
*27片山哲『回顧と展望』福村出版、 1967、 264頁。 なお、 同じ箇所は片山哲記念財団編『片山内閣』1980年、 236一237頁、 袖井林2郎『マッカーサーの2千日』中央公論社、 1976年、 217頁に引用されている。
*28高野編『安部磯雄』85頁に「マクアーサーが『平和憲法』の公布に際して、『日本よ東洋のスイスになれ』といった」と書かれているが、確認できない。
*29『参議院会議録』第11号（官報号外1949年4月8日）、古関彰1『『平和国家』日本の再検討』岩波書店、 2002、 61一62頁も3照。内山正熊『現代日本

外交史論』慶應通信、 1971年、 300頁では、3議院本会議と予算委員会の帆足の発言が混合している。
*30『参議院予算委員会会議録』第13号、 昭和24年4月15日。
*31帆足計「日本の永世中立と再軍備放棄」『世界評論』第4巻第6号、1949年、 26頁。
*32『衆議院会議録』第18号（官報号外1949年4月17日）。
*33『参議院会議録』第15号（官報号外、 昭和25年1月29日）内山『外交史論』302頁註21の日付は間違いであろう。
*34 J。P。マッキヴォイ「マッカーサー元帥日本を語る　偉大な司令官との単独会見記」『リーダーズダイジェスト』1950年6月号、 4頁。
*35『朝日新聞』昭和25年(1950年)4月20日の1面トップで『リーダーズダイジェスト』のマッカーサーの「極東のスイス」発言を紹介している。昭和25年6月2日には、ニューヨーク・タイムス紙の特派員がマッカーサー元帥に対して、かつて「日本は東洋のスイスであることを希望する」といった見解を質している記事が載っている。
*36田岡良一『永世中立と日本の安全保障』有斐閣、 1950年、 233頁。
*37坂西志保編『小学校の社会　めぐる機械』（5年生中巻）日本書籍、1952年、 85ー87頁。
*38馬場四郎編『日本の生活⑧日本と世界Ⅰ』(6年生上巻)教育図書出版、1955年、 79ー80頁。
*39『朝日新聞』昭和25年(1950年)1月1日に総司令部発表全文が掲載されている。
*40 A。シーグフリート、 吉阪俊蔵『スイス　ーデモクラシーの証人ー』岩波書店、 1952、 ii頁。
*41渡辺剛『スイス国民の偉大な精神に学ぼう＝自衛の努力なくして独立なし＝』国際経済新報社、 1956年、 1頁。
*42渡辺『スイス国民』7頁。
*43田岡良一「スイス」日本国際問題研究所編『中立主義の研究』上巻、1961、 155ー178頁。
*44田岡良一「中立のほんらいの意味　ースイス及びスェーデンの歴史に照らして」日本国際連合協会京都本部編『中立及び中立主義』日本国際連合協会京都本部、 1961年、 3ー61頁。
*45北村孝治郎『第2次大戦とスイスの中立』時事通信社、 1962年、 22頁。

*46宮下啓三『中立を守る　スイスの栄光と苦難』講談社、1968年、5一6頁。
*47杉田一次・藤原岩市共著『スイスの国防と日本』時事通信社、1971年、15一16頁、及び228頁。
*48原書房編集部訳『民間防衛』原書房、1970年、315頁。
*49森田安一『スイス　歴史から現代へ』刀水書房、1980年（3補版1994年）。
*50小林武『現代スイス憲法』法律文化社、1989年（旧憲法の翻訳あり）。
国枝昌樹『地方分権　ひとつの形』大蔵省印刷局、1996年。
関根照彦『スイス直接民主制の歩み一疑しきは国民に』尚学社、1999年。
渡辺久丸『現代憲法の研究』信山社、1999年。
美根慶樹『スイス　歴史が生んだ異色の憲法』ミネルヴァ書房、2003年(2000年の新憲法の翻訳あり）。
参議院憲法調査会事務局編(関根照彦・岡本三彦調査・作成）『スイス連邦憲法概要』参憲資料第7号、2002年。

SWITZERLAND'S ECONOMY THROUGH JAPANESE EYES – CHANGING PERCEPTIONS

By Prof. Dr. Takafumi Kurosawa

Summary (R. Mottini)

The first comprehensive Japanese report on Switzerland and the Swiss economy was compiled by the Iwakura mission visiting the country in 1873 (see article Mottini in this book). With regard to the economic conditions in Switzerland, the mission's report conveyed the image of an agrarian society with a strongly expanding industrial and commercial sector. Swiss industry was described as highly developed, dominated by textile production (cotton, silk and straw hat manufacturing), watchmaking, machine building, arms production as well as production of apparel and music instruments. The mission's report drew a very detailed picture of Switzerland's economy and society, characterized as a society of freelancing small farmers and petty bourgeois.

During the Meiji era, Switzerland served as an example for the bottom-up strategy of development in sharp contrast to the top-down approach favoured by the Meiji government.

From 1904 to 1924, Japan experienced a period of rapid industrial progress; during that time Switzerland was portrayed as a country with a highly developed social welfare and labour protection legislation. This image was mainly the work of Abe Isoo, a socialist leader with Christian beliefs (see article Meyer in this book).

Between 1929 and 1945, Japan went through a serious financial crisis (Shōwa crisis), experienced war economy and suffered economic collapse; meanwhile Switzerland managed to stay out of conflict and saw a decline of the textile production and the rise of the machine-building and chemical industry. In Japan, the politician and entrepreneur Ōkouchi Masatoshi (1878–1952) emphasized economic reforms taking Switzerland's economy as a model. In his view the Swiss economy maintained a healthy balance between preserving its agrarian production base and the development of high-tech industries. According to him, the reason for Switzerland's competitiveness was the systematic application of scientific and technological research by the Swiss industry.

Swiss economic topics treated in Japanese print media after the war dealt with the following sectors: 1. Finance, 2. Transportation and traffic networks, 3. Agriculture, 4. Watchmaking and precision-tools industry, 5. Post and telecom, 6. Tourism.

During the fifties, the Japanese image of the Swiss economy was basically reduced to the financial sector with industry hardly noticed. Connected to this image was the perception of Switzerland as a wealthy country but in the same time containing rather basic alpine settlements as depicted in the fairy tale of "Heidi".

After 1965 the mostly positive image of the Swiss economy turned sour after the translation of a book written by the American journalist Fehrenbach criticising the business practices of Switzerland's banks. The book became hugely popular in Japan and was followed by a flood of similar publications. In the seventies Switzerland's image in Japan was damaged and largely reduced to be a place for shady financial dealings; with the exception of watchmaking, Switzerland was hardly noticed as an industrialized country.

During the eighties, Japan's economy was booming to the point of overheating; with growing numbers of Japanese tourists visiting Switzerland the idyllic "Heidi" image saw a revival this time accompanied by a heightened interest in ecological issues and questions of lifestyle. Critical Japanese voices to Switzerland and its economy were inspired by a book written by Jean Ziegler in 1976 focussing on unsavoury financial dealings. This left-wing criticism in Japan was highly emotional and going as far as alleging that Switzerland has no "orderly state"; from 1985 on, this kind of critique gave way to a more differentiated and scientific approach to Switzerland and its economy.

In the nineties Japan's and Switzerland's economies shared a number of similarities; both economies showed weak, even stagnant growth and were considered unable to adapt to the changing reality of globalization. In Japanese eyes, the Swiss economy could not serve as an example how to cope with the challenges of a fast-changing world economy and its new players. In the Japanese discussion of "Anglo-Saxon capitalism" versus the "Rhineland model" only Germany was cited. Japanese reporting on Switzerland's economy increased nevertheless with these topics: 1. The "Swissification" of Japan?, 2. The role of Switzerland and its banks during the Second World War, 3. Increasing activities of Swiss firms in Japan.

The first topic appeared as a headline in the Japanese edition of "Newsweek" on May 5, 2002; the term "Swissification" served to characterize a stagnant economy dominated by a growing class of wealthy pensioners, inward-looking and politically isolated from the rest of the world.

The second issue about Nazi gold reserves and closed private accounts found its way into Japan also through Anglophone channels and damaged the Swiss image of idyllic innocence considerably.

The third topic has to be understood on the background of Japan's mounting economic trouble in the second half of the nineties. Just before the collapse of the Long-Term Credit Bank of Japan in 1997, there was talk about a takeover by Swiss Banking Corporation (Bankverein). The takeover was not thoroughly managed, however, and Japanese media blamed the Swiss bank for the collapse, speaking of "Swiss shrewdness" in "exploiting the troubles of a Japanese bank". News of large mergers in Switzerland (UBS, Novartis) were always good for headlines in Japan as well.

In 2001 Syngenta, a Swiss subsidiary of Novartis, succeeded in decoding the rice genom causing a feeling of defeat in Japan because this had been a national pet project. News like these obviously contradict the negative image conjured up by the term of "Swissification" of the economy.

As a conclusion one can say that from a Japanese perspective, Switzerland's economy as a whole is still largely unknown.

Takafumi Kurosawa, born 1969 in Hitachinaka/Ibaraki prefecture. 1997 PhD in economics from Kyoto University. Presently professor at Kyoto University; research in economic history of Switzerland.

日本におけるスイス経済像——その変容にみる近代像・経済政策認識の変遷

黒澤隆文

はじめに

日本にとって、スイスとの経済的関係はさほど重要なものではない。例えば輸入相手国としてはスイスは二一位、また輸出では二七位にすぎない。これはカタールやパナマよりも下位に位置する。歴史的にも、「富国強兵」や「経済大国」化をめざしてきた日本においては、関心はもっぱらアメリカ合衆国や英独仏など「主要国」に向けられてきた。

それにもかかわらず、日本人にとってスイスは比較的馴染みの深い国である。これは経済面においても変わらず、時計や「スイス銀行」をその代表とするが、スイス経済のその他の側面への言及も、それほど稀とはいえない。断片的でしばしば興味本位であるものの、ヨーロッパの小国との比較においては、——福祉国家として関心を引いてきたスウェーデンを唯一の例外として——スイス経済のイメージは、日本では意外なほど豊富である。

明治以来近年に至るまで、日本のモデルは欧米の「国民国家」、しかも一定の国家規模と均質性をもつ諸国家であった。スイスはそうしたモデルの対極に位置する。この点で、「スイス経済像」は、日本の同時代人の経済的認識のみならず、日本における「近代化」像をも浮き彫りにする格好の素材ともいえるだろう。以上の観点から、ここでは、日本におけるスイス経済像の変遷を両国の経済実態の変化を確認しながら検討する。その過程で、日本における経済的・経済政策的自己認識の変化も明らかになるであろう。

一国の経済に関する他国での認識を扱う場合、「経済」現象の幅広さと、その意味のいわば希薄性が障害となる[1]。両国の間の経済取引すべてを扱うことは不可能であるし、また無意味でもあるので、ここでは、スイス経済全体あるいは一部を対象に、意識的あるいは体系的に提示された認識のみを分析対象としたい[2]。

1. 戦前のスイス経済像

1.1 日本=スイス交渉史初期のスイス経済認識

日本とスイスの交渉史は一八五九年に始まる。初期の交渉の舞台は日本であり、スイス人貿易商人とその商品が日本人のスイス経済認識の唯一の窓口であった[3]。こうした中では、スイスを実際に訪れての最初の包括的な観察・紹介の事例は、岩倉使節団によるものと考えられる。久米邦武編、田中彰校注の『特命全權権大使　米歐回覧宴記』によれば[4]、同使節団は、アメリカ米欧各国を歴訪後、行程の最後近くに、一ヶ月弱にわたってスイスに滞在している(一八七三年六月一九日〜七月一五日)。このいわば公式の報告書では、スイス経済の特色はどのように把握されているだろうか。

スイスはまず、工芸に秀でた工業国として描かれる。スイスは農業国、それも牧畜国でもあるが、地形の点で農業に不利であるため、「やむを得ず」工業部門に力を注いだという[5]。工業国イメージが先に立っていることは、後の時代との比較で興味深い。また工業については、時計・オルゴール・楽器生産への言及の他、十九世紀工場制度の代表で当時絶頂にあったスイスの綿工業についても、「木綿ヲ紡シテ、纖細ノ糸ヲナスニ長ス、欧州ニテ甚タ名誉ヲ得タリ」とある。絹製品、麦藁製品生産など繊維工業に優れること、機械工業でも、「砲銃ノ軍器、水輪、鉄碓等、器械ノ製」に長じることが指摘され、さらに「瑞士ニ鉄十分ナラス、石炭モ不足ナリ、唯国中ニ急流ノ河多シ、瑞士人ハ其水力ヲ用ヒテ器械ヲ運転ス」とある[6]。

経済構造に関しては、「土地ヲ私有セルモノ、各家ニ普ク」、「ヨク財産ヲ平均シテ、貧疲ノ戸甚タ少ナシ」とあり、資産分配の平等性と、自作農的・小農経済的な農業構造が指摘されている。こうした指摘は、国の財政規模の小ささと民力の充溢に関する言及と対をなしており、全体として、いわば「下からの」発展を想起させる経済像を構成している。概して、「勤勉と工夫によって自然条件の不利を克服し、民富を基盤に工業国化した国」と認識されているといえよう。そのほか、交通基盤の充実ぶりが驚きを込めて紹介され、また、後の時代にはほとんど関心を持たれなかった州立銀行にも言及がされている[7]。

今日の経済史的通説に照らすと、上記の認識は非常に正確で多面的である。また後の時代のスイス像と比較すると、社会国家、高所得国等のイメージが欠けているが、連邦工場法成立以前の一八六八年時点では、スイスの「社会国家」としての性格は今だ萌芽的であったし、また所得水準の点でも、この時期のスイスは出稼ぎの送り出し国から受け入れ国にようやく転じつつある頃であり、非常に高い工業化水準にもかかわらず、他の西欧諸国に比していまだ特段に富裕とはいえなかった。いずれにせよ、日本におけるスイス経済像の最も基本的な要素が、すでにこの最初の概観においてほぼ出揃っていたといえるだろう。

1.2 「社会国家」スイスと安部磯雄(一九〇五〜三〇年頃)

二〇十世紀初頭は日本では産業革命期にあたるが、この時期は日本のスイス経済像にとっても重要な時期である。すでに森田安一が指摘しているように、この時期、キリスト教的社会主義者である安部磯雄により『地上之理想國瑞西』が著され[8]、日本におけるスイス像の形成に大きな影響を及ぼしたからである。この著書で安部は「政治」「教育」の次に「社会問題」の項目を設けており、そこからは以下のスイス経済像を読み取りうる。

第一にスイスは、交通・通信基盤が充実し、資産配分が平等な国である。「到る處坦々たる道路を通じ、汽車走り電線懸り、電話電燈の便一として備わらざるはな」く、「鐵道延長の割合如何を見れば欧羅巴の諸國一」であり、「驚くべき程の富豪もないが、又多くの貧人もな」い。これらの叙述は「回覧実記」と重なる[9]。

第二に、政府の歳入歳出は小規模で控えめである。しかしそれにもかかわらず、「州政府および中央政府が各巨額の公有財産を有」する。「多くの独占事業を政府にて経営」し、例えば「二十五州の中十八州は火災保険を政府事業と為して、私立会社の営業することを許さない」。税制においては累進課税方式が採用されており、かつ、「瑞西に於いては最も極端の度に於いて之を応用」している[10]。

第三に、こうしたスイスのもとで、労働者は極めて恵まれた状況にある。労働者の賃金は低廉であるが、「一たび同盟罷業を企てれば多く成功する」。工場法(一八七七年制定)による法定労働時間は十一時間(土曜は一〇時間)である。「婦人及び小児を保護するは工場法の主なる目的であるが,瑞西の工場法は此点に於いて殊に勝れ」、婦人の夜間労働・日曜労働は全面的に禁止され、また「満十四歳以下の者に労働を禁ずることは殆ど世界無比」である[11]。

その他、安部の著書は、半官半民組織としての労働局の活動、他国には見られない強制加入式の失業保険制度の存在等を紹介しており、スイスの社会政策の多様な要素に多くの紙幅をあてている。安部によれば、スイスでは「社会主義的の政策を大胆に実行」しているのであって、それだからこそ、「別段社会党なる団体を設くるの必要を感ぜぬ」のである[12]。

ここで確認しておくと、スイスでも、一八八〇年代以降、特に都市部を中心に、活発な労働運動がみられた(八〇年、スイス労働組合総同盟設立、八八年、スイス社会民主党設立)。これらは、地域によっては自治と相互扶助原則による素朴な共同体秩序の帰結であったが、ドイツ語圏の都市部ではむしろこうした旧秩序との対立の側面が目立っていた。しかし安部は、この両者をともに、社会改良的で相互扶助的なスイス社会の特質として把握していたようである。また、社会政策について多くの叙述があるにもかかわらず、政策の前提となるはずのスイスの経済的状態、産業の状況への言及がきわめて僅かである。この点で、安部のスイス経済像は安部自身の「社会主義」「民主主義」論の従属物であるということができよう。

今日、周辺の欧州諸国との比較では、スイス経済はむしろ政府部門の小ささで際だつ。そこで、社会国家的「理想国」というスイス認識の妥当性も検討しておこう。ここで工場法を例にとると、同時代の各国の状況は安部の認識を裏づけているように思われる。実際には、スイスの連邦工場法の先進性は、安部の指摘した婦人・年少者保護の点よりも、むしろ成人男子の保護を団体交渉に委ねず工場法の対象とした点にあった。しかしいずれにせよ、周辺国に比して早い時期に、広範囲の労働者に対する保護がスイスで実現していたことは否定しがたい。また失業保険も、部分的ながらすでに一八八〇年代から普及していた。保守的・農業的なカントンの事例を無視しているという点で部分的に均衡を欠いてはいるものの、総じて、スイスを先進的な社会国家として位置づける安部の視点は、この時期に関しては誤ったものとは言い難い[13]。

安部磯雄の著書の他、この時期には、社会保険に関する訳書、工場法立法の紹介、スイス滞在者による随筆などが出版されており[14]、いずれも「社会国家」としてのスイス像を根拠づけるものとなっている。

その他、この時期には①金融市場や通商関係の概況、②農林業、③観光業など各産業部門を対象とした文献が公刊されており[15]、第二次大戦後へも繋がってくるスイス関心の初期の事例と位置づけることができる。

1.3 昭和恐慌と大河内正敏のスイス認識(一九二九〜四五)

一九二〇年代から三〇年代にかけて、スイスと日本の経済状況は大きく変化した。スイスでは繊維工業が機械・金属・化学工業に基軸産業の座を譲った。二九年に発生した世界恐慌はスイス経済にも打撃を与えたが、外国人労働者比率が就業人口の二割近くに達していたために、雇用の調整は主としてこれら外国人労働者の自主的・半強制的な帰国によってなされえた。しかもスイスの経済成長率は、この時期低い数値ながら各国との比較では最も高い水準にあった。その結果、生活水準の大幅な低下や深刻な経済問題の発生は回避されたのである。

これとは対照的に、日本の経済情勢は遙かに深刻であった。日本の工業は第一次大戦時の好況を跳躍台に長足の進歩を遂げたが、いまだ欧米の先進工業国との間には埋めがたい懸隔があった。二七年の金融恐慌、三〇年の金解禁とその帰結である徹底的なデフレ政策、世界恐慌の国内への波及によって、日本経済は出口の見えない危機に突入した。この危機の時代は同時に日本における経済学の確立の時期でもあり、二七年の『労農』の創刊、三二年からの『日本資本主義発達史講座』の刊行によって、いわゆる日本資本主義論争が展開されたが、そこでは窮迫する農村の経済が重要な分析対象とされた。また三一年の満州事変以後、歩調を一段と速めた日本の軍事化傾向のもとで、植民地争奪を巡って政策論争も行われた。

こうした時代背景のもと、スイス経済に関して注目すべき言及を行ったのが大河内正敏(一八七八-一九五二)である。貴族院議員でもあった大河内は、技術者的企業家として、機械･金属部門の新興コンツェルンである「理研」グループを興した人物である[16]。多数の著作を残した大河内の思想は「科学主義工業」論や「農工両全主義」として知られる。このうち三四年の著作である『農村の工業』では[17]、農村への工業分散立地によって農村での雇用創出と生産コストの低減を図ること、さらに旧来的な工業から技術集約的工業への転換によって、農村救済と資源制約の克服を同時に達成すべきことが主張されていたが、その少なからぬ部分が、スイスを模範とした議論であった[18]。

大河内は、農村工業を家内工業に限定せず、「大工業組織の工場を、幾多の小工場に分解して地方に散在させしめ、更にその工場の作業の一部をその地方農村の家庭に、分散せしめ」ることを主張した。この主張は戦後高度成長期にみられた工場の地方分散の動きを先取りするものであったが、彼の発想の背景には、農村に基盤を置くスイスの高付加価値産業に関する知識があった。

大河内によれば、「少数の熟練工の手で、より多くの仕事をなし得る様、設備を改善するか」、あるいは「不熟練工でも間に合ふか、又は熟練工と同様以上の仕事をなし得る工作機械や、製造装置を考案する」こと、これが、イギリスの機械工業がスイスの精密機械工業に圧倒された唯一の原因である[19]。また原燃料の点で不利な地域においては、「工業の発展に最も多くの余地のあるものは特殊の技巧を要するものであるか、もしくは卓越した頭脳による発明、研究の結果を産業に応用する事」であり、その実例がスイスの時計工業や計測機器、各種精密機械である。また染料工業で世界に冠たるドイツを「質において凌駕せんとするものは実に瑞西」であり、「原料を悉く輸入品に仰ぐ」にもかかわらず、「科学を以って是を補充し、或いは科学によりて新しき資源を創造」している。さらに「驚くべきは瑞西における大機械類、重機械類の工業」であって、「タービンでも内燃機関でも或いは水力機械」でも、高価な原燃料と輸送費にもかかわらず高い国際競争力を維持している[20]。

「本邦天然資源の少なき憂ふるに足らず」との章題に明白であるように、彼の主張は、高付加価値の知識集約型・資源節約型工業の振興によって、資源制約の克服を目指す議論であった。造兵学者であった大河内の視点は、常に国防の経済的・技術的基盤の確保に置かれており、したがってこの技術革新による資源制約克服の論理は、戦争への協力的な姿勢にも結びつき得たが、スイスを引用しての立論に限るならば、技術革新による植民地獲得戦からの超越という解釈の余地をも残していた[21]。

こうした大河内の主張がどの程度の影響力を持ったかは確認しがたいが、三〇年代には、農村の疲弊を背景としたスイスへの関心を示す文献がその他にも見られた。スイス農民連盟の公刊物を翻訳した『瑞西国山村農民窮乏克服策』はそのひとつであり、食糧自給促進策、生産条件改善策、農業に対する補助金・金融支援策などを解説している[22]。しかしながら、東亜の盟主を任じて戦争への道をひた走る日本においては、小国スイスを模範とした政策論は、受容基盤を欠いていたといえよう。

2. 戦後におけるスイス経済像の変遷

2.1 雑誌記事名による戦後スイス経済像の概観

戦後のスイス経済像の分析に入る前に、戦後に限った数量的概観を試みておきたい。具体的には、国立国会図書館の蔵書検索・申込システム(NDL-OPAC)を用い、雑誌記事名を手がかりとした集計を行った。「スイス」を記事題目・キーワードに含む記事から、本来の検索意図に該当する二一六五件を抽出したうえで、表題・副題・掲載誌から判断される主題ごとに分類(複数の分類に跨がるものは重複集計)し、五年ごとに出版点数を集計した[23]

この簡単な概観の結果は以下に要約されよう。まず、戦後一貫してスイスへの関心は多面化・深化しており、七〇年代半ばと九〇年代半ばには記事点数が大きく増加している。これは部分的には出版市場の「雑誌化」の反映であろうが、同時にスイスに関する学術研究の多面化による紀要論文の増加の結果でもある。

次に、対象を経済面に限定し、産業分野ごとに分類すると、記事が多い順に、①金融、②交通運輸、③農林畜産、④時計・精密機械、⑤ＰＴＴ(郵便・通信)、⑥観光業という順位となる。交通運輸と郵便・通信では官庁の報告書が主体である。交通運輸は登山鉄道・観光関連記事を含む。あえて単純化するならば、戦後日本のスイス経済像は、銀行業、時計工業イメージと、広義の「アルプス」的経済像(農林畜産+鉄道)に代表されるのである。さらに、手工業的熟練のイメージを持つ時計工業を「アルプス」的スイス像に含めることも可能であろう。

時計工業以外の製造業への関心の低さが際だつが、その理由のひとつは、資本財と最終消費財では産業に対する認知度が一般に大きく異なることにあろう。スイスの機械工業や化学工業は大量生産型ではなく、しかも製薬を例外として資本財の生産を柱としており、一般消費者になじみが浅いのは当然である。実際、最終消費財を扱うネスレ、ロシュ両社に比し、機械製造企業の関連記事は少ない[24]。しかしその結果、いわば「普通の先進工業国」としてのスイス像は極めて希薄なものとなっている。

最後に、スイス経済の特質を基準に分類すると、①金融市場とスイスフラン通貨への関心が一貫して強いこと、②戦後当初には加工貿易立国への関心から、また後にはＥＣ・ＥＵとの関係への関心から、経済外交関連記事が多いこと、③農業・農山村関係では、戦前からの「豊かなスイス農村」への関心に加え、八〇年代半ば以降は、食糧安全保障、農業保護、食品の安全、環境配慮の農業政策等など、あらたな「アルプス」関心と呼ぶべき傾向が見られること、④匿名口座をはじめとするマイナス・イメージのスイス関心は七〇年代からみられ、また九〇年代後半の強まっていること、⑤日本での労働力不足を背景に八〇年代後半には外国人労働者に関する記事もみられること、以上が確認される。以下、各時代について、代表的なスイス経済論の傾向を検討してゆこう。

2.2 経済復興と小国論的スイス像(一九四五～六〇年代半ば)

戦後しばらくの間、スイス経済像を決定的に規定したのは、いうまでもなく敗戦の体験であった。軍事大国路線の挫折と植民地の喪失、それに、戦後自由貿易体制の成立は、日本人の認識の前提を大きく変え、小国スイスへの関心を呼び覚ますことになった。こうした中で、四七年には安部磯雄の著書が復刻再版された。またマッカーサー元帥による「東洋のスイス論」(本書森田論文参照)が強い影響力を持っていた一九四九年には、スイス駐在から帰国したばかりの新聞記者、川崎三蔵によって『戦なき国の繁栄――スイス　過去と現在』が著され、翌年には経済学者大内兵衛による『スイス紀行――世界の問題』が公刊された。また五二年には、大戦期スイスの独立・中立を主題とする『ヨーロッパのバルコニー』(ベガン著)と、包括的なスイス紹介である『スイス――デモクラシーの證人』(シーグフリード著)の二冊の翻訳書が公刊されている[25]。これらはいずれも、戦後初期のスイス像をつくりあげた基本文献であった。

大原社会問題研究所の元所員であり、マルクス主義者である大内の紀行文では、スイスに関する言及は旅行者としての観察の域を出ないが、安部磯雄以来の「社会国家」的スイス経済像が踏襲されている[26]。それに対し、川崎三蔵の『戦なき国の繁栄』はスイス自体についての体系的な知識・関心と政策提言を前面に出した文献である。特に食糧原材料輸入・工業製品輸出という貿易国スイスに関する言及には、植民地を失った日本への指針が書き込まれているといってよかろう[27]。この川崎の書は、二冊の翻訳書とともに、「敗戦国」「小国・貧困国」「資源小国」という日本人の自国認識を背景に読まれたと推定され、「独立と平和」「勤勉」により「貧しい山国・小国」から「豊かな工業国」になった模範例として、スイスを日本人に印象づけたと思われる[28]。いわば非戦を前提とした経済復興論的スイス経済像といえよう。

これらの文献に垣間見られる「豊か」で「金持ち」とのスイス像は、戦前にはない新しい要素であるが[29]、これはスイスの経済実態の変化の忠実な反映であった。この間スイスの所得水準は外貨換算では大幅に上昇していた。瓦礫の山に立ちすくむ周辺国との対比においては、戦禍を免れたスイスの経済的ストックの豊かさは、一層印象的であったろう。この「豊かで金持ち」としての新しいスイスの姿は、やはり戦後一般化した「アルプスの少女」の中の貧しいスイス像との整合性を問われることなく、戦後のスイス経済像の基本的要素となっていった[30]。他方、この時期にはほとんど認知されなかったが、スイスへの逃避資金とそれを支える匿名口座の役割も、この時期すでにジークフリードの著書で紹介されていた[31]。戦前においては専門家や研究者向けの金融事情紹介があったのみであるから、これは「スイス銀行」の特殊な性格について初めて紹介したものといってもよいが、その扱いはささやかで、また平和国家イメージと背反するものでもなかった。

2.3 「スイス銀行」の登場とスイス像の二面化 （一九六〇年代後半〜七〇年代末）

以上見てきたように、明治以来、スイス経済像は肯定的な印象に彩られてきたが、一九六〇年代末以降、この状況は一変する。従来の清廉なスイス像が、いわゆる「スイス銀行」ものの隆盛の中で大幅に相対化されるからである。

スイスの銀行業に関する一般の日本人のイメージは、六六年に英語からの訳書として刊行されたフェーレンバッハ著『スイス銀行——世界経済、影の巨大組織』によって初めて形成されたと考えられる[32]。この訳書は六七年には六刷を数え、七二年には改訂版が、さらに七九年には文庫版が出されており、その人気と影響力とが窺われる。著者はアメリカ国籍のジャーナリストであった。英米からのマイナスイメージの輸入というパターンは、その後も今日まで続く。

この本は、扇情的な日本語の副題や解説を付して販売され、また実際にもスイス銀行による各種の地下経済的な取引を赤裸々に描いていた。しかし著者のフェーレンバッハは、スイス側の「悪意」や「陰謀」、「犯罪性」については明確に否定し、スイスの安定性とスイス銀行の堅実性、スイス社会の特質こそがスイス銀行の繁栄の要因であるとして、外国のスイス銀行批判を、「的はずれ」と批判していた[33]。著者はその限りで抑制的にスイスの銀行を描いていたのだが、それにもかかわらず、「怪しげな取引を行うスイス銀行」のマイナスイメージは以後ひとり歩きしていった[34]。これ以降、「スイス銀行もの」と総称しうる様々な図書・雑誌記事が、今日まで切れ目無く刊行されている[35]。

このフェーレンバッハの著書は、日本におけるスイス経済像にとって大きな転換点を意味した。これ以降、スイス銀行による「汚れた」スイス像は、しばしば「武装」中立国の軍事的イメージとも結びついて現れたが、これらは、牧歌的で手工業的な「時計とチョコレート」のスイス像とは整合しない[36]。また銀行のイメージは、機械工業と化学工業を中心とする、いわば「普通の先進工業国」としてのスイス像とも遠い。そのため、銀行の印象が強まるにつれ、工業国としてのスイスイメージは、時計という特殊な製品イメージを例外に、これ以降決定的に後退していった。

それればかりではない。このフェーレンバッハの著書は、それまで日本で称揚されてきたスイスの民主主義や平等性には、極めて低い評価しか与えなかった。スイス社会は、「ヨーロッパ最後の前封建的な農民社会」と都市ブルジョワの同盟からなり、そこでは「階級もしくは地位の意識が強くて、生まれよりもカネがものをいう」。そして「商売のためにならないというので封建制に反対をしたスイス人は、同じ理屈で、専制主義、中央集権主義、社会主義、マルクス主義、そして婦人参政権のいずれにも反対する」[37]。こうしたスイス像は、安部磯雄以来の「社会国家スイス」像とも戦後の平和国家イメージとも相容れない。これ以後、「スイス銀行」論の隆盛の中で、社会国家としてのスイスの特質に注目するような視点は、ごく少数の学術的な研究を除いて姿を消していった。

スイスの銀行業が注目を集めた理由として、そのマイナスイメージが既存の理想化されたスイス像とあまりに鮮烈な対照をなしていたこと、また「陰謀もの」という特殊な市場に合致したことが挙げられるが、同時に国際経済秩序上の変化も見逃せない。七一年のニクソン・ショック以降のスイス金融市場の地位向上、日本の黒字国化を背景とした日本の銀行のスイス市場進出の動きは、スイスの金融市場を日本人にとってはじめて身近なものとしたからである。もっともここで、このスイス銀行への関心自体、ごく一面的なものであったこともつけ加えておかねばならない。「スイス銀行もの」が対象としたのは、当時「三(四)大銀行」と総称された少数の大銀行か、あるいは、日本人に縁遠いプライベート・バンキング(富裕層個人資産管理業務)を営む個人銀行であって、特色あるカントン銀行(州立銀行)や、競争力に富む保険・再保険業などについては、まったく顧みられることがなかったのである。

「スイス銀行」像の出現によって特徴づけられるこの時期にも、均整のとれたスイス紹介がなかったわけではない。七四年に日本語訳が刊行されたストゥッキの著書や、その翻訳者である吉田康彦の概説書、また少し遅れて八一年に出版された阿部汎克の著書は、その代表例といえよう[38]。ストゥッキはスイスの経済史をわかりやすく概説し、吉田と阿部の著書は当時のスイス社会の実情を多面的に紹介していた。特に後者は、冷静な洞察に富む社会観察をも含んでいた。しかし、スイスが競争力に富む工業国であることに触れている吉田の著書でも、全体的には武装中立国イメージが先にたっており、また阿部の著作では経済面への言及が少なく、スイスの富の源泉をもっぱら銀行業に求め、製造業については時計産業の苦境について紹介したにとどまった[39]。その結果、これらの冷静な分析も、一連の「スイス銀行もの」がつくりだしたイメージを相対化するほどの影響力を持ち得なかったのである。

2.4　日本における近代観・自国認識の転換　(一九八〇年年代〜九〇年代半ば)

一九八〇年代以降、前述のようにスイス経済像はより多面化し豊かになる。しかしその中核的な構成要素はそれほど変化していない。むしろ目立つのは、受容側、すなわち日本側の自国認識の変容、あるいはモデルとされてきた欧米社会に対する見方の変化である。この変化は、明治以来の近代(化)像の転換をも意味する。そこでここでは、対象をいったん「スイス像」全体に広げて、変化の内容を以下の三点に要約してみたい。

第一は、日本の自国経済認識の変化である。「敗戦国」から「自由世界第二の経済大国」、さらに限定なしの「経済大国」への変化は、スイス像にも影響を及ぼした。八〇年代後半には円高によって一人あたりの国民所得も欧米主要国を凌駕し、「先進国」との表現があたりまえとなった。生活実感と名目値の乖離は議論の対象となったが、経済力に基づく自負は、スイス社会に対する評価に反映されていった。これ以降、スイスを模範とするスイス論でも両国経済の懸隔を前提とした立論は姿を消し、スイスと日本を、同様の問題に直面している二つの社会と位置づけるようになってゆく。

立脚点の類似性が認識されるほど、関心は両国の現実面での差違へと向かわざるえない。この時期には、意識的にスイス経済に着目した文献があらわれたが、実際その大半は、スイスにおける農村と都市、農業と商工業の均衡に焦点をあてていた。むろん背景には、高度成長の終焉や、公害問題の発生、「列島改造論」の破綻とともに高まった経済成長・開発至上主義批判があった。

こうした文献の一例である高橋俊一の『飢えない国スイス』は、食糧安全保障の観点から、「したたかな」スイスを模範と位置づけていた[40]。七三年以降、貿易自由化交渉が断続的に続いたため、同様のスイス経済関心はその後も続く。さらに大谷健の『緑の経済学　新・東洋のスイス論』も、山村荒廃・都市過密解決のモデルをスイスに求めていた[41]。九〇年代には、こうした方向でのスイス関心は、食品安全性や環境を重視した農業・農村政策等へと多面化・深化していった。またこれとも関連しつつ、環境問題への関心にもとづくスイス紹介が顕著に増加してきた。

これらはいずれも、アルプスと結びついたスイス像の再生産に寄与したが、その半ばは、牧歌的にみえるスイスの知られざる「したたかさ」を強調していた。「東洋のスイス論」のいわば新しい形といえよう。またこの時期、円高の進行によって歴史上はじめて、スイスが一般大衆の身近な訪問先となった点も重要である。観光旅行客の大半の訪問先は、ごく少数の特定の山岳観光地に限られたから、スイスをアルプスと同一視するような一面的な認識は、この時期むしろ強まったとも考えられる。反面この時期は、社会科学・工学分野など多様な分野でスイスに関する研究が増加した時期でもあった。これを一般的な認識の深化と同一視することはできないが、正確なスイス情報を比較的容易に得る可能性が生まれたことは、無視されるべきではなかろう。

第二の変化は、日本における近代像に生じた変質である。明治以来模範とされてきた「近代」の諸価値と、それを体現するとされた西欧諸国の社会モデルへの疑問が、この時期明示的な形で提示されるに至った。しかもそれは、国粋主義や穏健な日本趣味の表明ではなく、欧米社会での自己認識・近代像の変化とも歩調を合わせるものであった。

第三に、以上の近代像の変質の結果、スイス認識の図式自体が変化した。この時期はじめて、近代化のモデルとされた典型的・理念的な西欧社会像と、「スイス的なるもの」の間に横たわる懸隔が明示的に意識されたのである。そしてその場合、二つの方向性がありえた。ひとつは、「近代」への評価はそのままに、そこからのスイスの逸脱を指摘し、否定的なスイス像を描くというものである。いまひとつは、両者の乖離を手掛かりに、近代の価値理念や近代世界像を見直そうという方向性である。後者はどちらかといえば学術的な著作で目立つので、ここではまず前者についてみてみよう。

スイス社会と、理念化された西欧社会像とのずれは、スイス銀行に関する前述のフェーレンバッハの著書ですでに指摘されていた。その限りでは、新しい認識の素地は、すでに一連の「スイス銀行」ものを通じて形成されていたのである。しかしここでは、転換期のスイス像の最も極端な事例として、八木あき子のスイス論を採り上げておこう[42]。

一九七九年、「二〇世紀の迷信『理想国家・スイス』」と題する八木あき子による論説が、月刊誌『諸君』に二回の連載として掲載され、翌年に単行本として出版された。この一連の著作は、一般化の可能性が不明瞭なスイスでの三年間の個人的体験と、現地における社会批判の紹介からなるが、その表現は激烈かつ感情的であり、スイス社会への憎悪が率直に表明されている。そのためもあってその直接の影響力は限定的であったとみられるが、それだけに否定的なスイス・イメージの構成要素をよく示している。

八木によれば、スイスは「部族的社会」であり、そこに蔓延するのは、ムラ社会的相互監視、外国人への差別と暴行、独善と吝嗇、拝金主義と倫理の欠如、「平和国家」の欺瞞(軍=財界癒着、武器輸出)、教育水準の低さ、「汚い方言」、男尊女卑、徹底したローカル性、「国家」の不在である。スイスでは、「政府機関とスイスの重要な産業部門や金融機関の間の人的交流や癒着が日常茶飯事」であり、民主主義は機能していない。また「事実上ストは不可能」で、労働者は無権利状態にある。さらに、外人警察の職務の一つは「外人労働者の数を需要に応じて調節すること」で、スイスの人権意識も見習うに値しない。端的には、「底の方にゲマインデという閉鎖的・排他的な単位が泥沼のように澱み、その上に一見、全く正反対の性格を持つ超国家的インタナショナルな企業と金融の支配体制が制圧するようにのし掛かっていて、この二重構造がスイスを掴みところのない国にしている」[43]。

こうした批判の半ばは、スイスの左派勢力によるスイス社会批判と軌を一にする。折しも七六年、ジュネーブ大学教授ジーグレールが、スイスの企業・銀行を徹底して批判する著書を公刊していた。この著書はスイスや欧州各国で衝撃をもって受け止められ、日本でも翌年には訳書が出された。それ以来、スイスに関するマイナスのイメージが各国にひろがっており、八木の主張もまた、こうした一連の文脈の中にあったのである[44]。

しかし八木の叙述には、そればかりでなく、スイス人が平然と「前近代的」体制を維持していることに対する、日本人としてのある種のいらだちが表れている。明治以来、「文明国」あるいは「先進国」として扱われるために一貫して西欧的・近代的理念へ自己を近づけることを自らに課し、欧米各国の目に映る自己像に右顧左眄してきた日本の側から、そうした規範から自由であるようにみえるスイス社会に対する割り切れなさが表明されているともいえよう。しかもこの八木のスイス論は、明治以来の「上からの近代化」や、これに接ぎ木された戦後民主主義を肯定する立場からのスイス社会批判でもある。これは、スイスの「汚い方言」が標準ドイツ語に劣るとする意識や[45]、男尊女卑や「ムラ社会」的特質への批判、「スイスは国家か」との雑誌記事の副題に如実に表れている。逆にここでは、日本社会が「近代」的であることは、ほとんど疑われていない。したがって八木においては、「スイス=先進、日本=後進」という構図が完全に解体している。

八木が描いた否定的なスイス像の構成要素は、純粋に個人的な体験や明らかな誤解に基づくものを除き、その後のスイス論においても繰り返し姿をあらわしている。しかし八木が前提としたような近代観・国家観は、八〇年代以降の日本では、はっきりと後退していった。むしろこの時期に関しては、さきに述べた第二の可能性、すなわち「スイス的なるもの」の積極的な価値づけによって、近代の価値理念や世界史像を見直そうという学術研究者による試みがみられたことを新しい現象として指摘すべきであろう。森田安一による連邦制・直接民主制・中立政策の紹介や、既存の国民国家形成史観を相対化する都市史研究は、その顕著な事例である[46]。九〇年代以降になると、政治史、行政学、経済史等の幅広い分野で、類似の問題意識による研究がみられるようになった[47]。

2.5 グローバル化とスイス経済像　(一九九〇年代半ば～)

戦前においては、スイス経済と日本経済の類似性は資源的・地形的条件など、いわば外生的な要因に限られた。しかし戦後、とりわけ高度成長期以降は、スイスと日本の経済面での類似性が目立ってくる。両国とも、安定したマクロ経済、高い国際競争力と経常収支黒字、低失業、健全な政府財政を誇り、日本は成長率の高さによって、またスイスは所得水準の絶対的な高さと低インフレによって、ともに戦後世界経済の優等生となったからである。

国際通貨体制の下でよく似た位置にあるこの両国は、八〇年代末にともにいわゆる「バブル経済」を経験し、またその破裂によって打撃を受けた。八七年頃から急騰して九一年頃に天井を打ち、その後一〇年かけて三〇年前の水準に低落するという両国の不動産価格指数の動きは、驚くばかりに酷似している。しかも九〇年代は、戦後の両国にとって未経験の経済的不振の時代であった。長期にわたる成長率の低迷、政府財政の悪化、歴史的な高失業に見舞われたのである。企業競争力も悪化し、製造業の国外脱出による空洞化現象が進行した。スイスでは、ヨーロッパ経済領域(ＥＥＡ)加盟の政府案が国民投票で否決されるというショックがこれに加わり、直接民主制に対する信頼も揺らいだ。対する日本は、長期の政治的混迷を経験した。その結果、スイスでは「スイス・モデル」の終焉が、日本では「日本的」な経済システムや経営の限界が語られるに至ったのである[48]。

しかしながら、両国経済のこうした類似性は、両国においてほとんど認識されることがなかった。九七年以降、日本経済が再度の金融危機に陥ったのとは対照的に、スイス経済は一足早く低迷を脱し復調を遂げたが、バブル後に経済政策的に参考とされたのは、もっぱら主要国あるいは英語圏諸国の政策か、あるいは北欧諸国の不良債権処理の例などに限られた。スイス経済についての学問的な蓄積は、金融市場分析などごく限られた領域に限定されていたからである。九〇年代後半に注目をあびた「ライン(型)資本主義」をめぐる議論でも[49]、「アングロ・アメリカ的資本主義」に対置されたのは、もっぱらドイツの社会的市場経済であり、スイス経済への言及はほとんどなかった。

それにもかかわらず、この時期、スイスの経済や企業に関する日本での言及は少なくなく、しかも増加する傾向にあった。それらは具体的には、①一部の批評家による「日本のスイス化」論、②戦後処理問題や「スイス銀行」像の肥大化によるマイナス・イメージの増大、③スイス企業の日本市場での存在感の高まりという形をとった。

「日本のスイス化」とは、アメリカ人ジャーナリストであるグロッサーマンが、構造改革を避ける日本に対する表現として九〇年代末に用いた言い回しである。その後、佐和隆光や船橋洋一など、日本の複数のエコノミストやジャーナリストがこの表現を模倣し、二〇〇二年五月には、「スイス化するニッポン——経済再生の夢断たれリッチで気楽な「引退国家」へ」との表題が『ニューズウィーク日本版』誌の表紙を飾った[50]。スイスの経済・社会を、豊かさと低成長、自己改革能力の欠如、内向きな姿勢による外交的な孤立によって特徴づけたうえで、経済システムの根本的な改革に消極的とされる日本の現状に、「スイス化」の語をあてたのである。その主張によれば、「日本は重要な地位からゆっくりと後退しつつも、居心地のよさのなかにある。スイス同様、伝統に縛られた内向きな平等社会」である[51]。

スイスの名を借用してのこの日本経済論は、しかし、スイス経済の実態を踏まえたものではおよそなかった。九七年以降のスイス経済の復調や財政の急速な健全化に関する認識は完全に欠落していたし、ＥＵとスイスの関係についての解釈も皮相なものであった。これらの論者が、そもそもスイス経済への関心を持っていたも疑わしい。そこそこ豊かだが世界の潮流には背を向ける引退国家との認識は、伝統的な「アルプス」イメージを無媒介に「金持ち」イメージに結びつけたものにすぎない。これはいわば、日本経済論の小道具的概念にすぎないのであって、日本の構造改革の「遅れ」に対する危機感を扇情的にかき立てるためには、小道具たるスイス経済像も、何人にも直感的に理解されうる、ステレオタイプ的なスイス像でなければならなかったのである。

スイス経済の露出度の高まりは、第二に、スイスの戦後処理問題と、それに密接に関わる「スイス銀行」イメージの肥大化という形をとった。中立国スイスは、戦中も戦後も、アメリカ合衆国からは敵国協力国・潜在的敵性国として、しばしば冷淡な扱いを受けてきたが、冷戦の終結後に表れたアメリカ発のスイス告発は、両国間の外交問題にまで発展した。その結果日本でも、九六年以降、ナチスへの協力や中央銀行によるナチス金塊購入の疑惑、スイスの銀行口座に残る虐殺されたユダヤ人資産の問題などが、英語メディアからの翻訳として頻繁に報道された。

こうした中で発生したのが、「長銀事件」である。九七年七月、不良債権処理にあえいでいた日本長期信用銀行(長銀)は、ＳＢＣ(スイス銀行コーポレイション、九八年にスイス・ユニオン銀行と合併しＵＢＳとなる)との提携と、ＳＢＣによる二〇〇〇億円の増資引受を発表した。しかしこの増資は実現せず長銀は破綻し、後には粉飾決算が明らかとなった。これは端的には企業買収の頓挫の一事例に過ぎなかったが、経済週刊誌などには、「はめられた長銀」「金融敗戦」といった見出しが踊った。さらに二年後には、クレディ・スイス・ファースト・ボストン社の日本法人が日本の銀行に対して不良債権の「飛ばし」サービスを提供していたことが発覚し、外資系銀行に対する初の行政処分に帰結した。新聞や経済週刊誌等、多くの読者を持つメディアによって、「窮状にあえぐ日本の銀行、それを手玉にとる外資」との構図が描かれ、「狡猾なスイス企業」のイメージが流布したのである。

以上の二つの事件の背景には、日本市場におけるスイス企業の存在感が、大型の企業再編と多国籍化の一層の進展によって高まったことがあった。ＵＢＳはその一例であるが、九七年には『エコノミスト』誌がプライベート・バンキング業務の特集を組み、スイスの銀行の独擅場であるこの分野について、事実上日本ではじめての顧客向けの紹介をおこなった。製造業でも、スイスの二大化学企業の合併によるノバルティス社の誕生(九六年)、日本の国家プロジェクトに先駆けてのスイス企業によるイネゲノム解読(シンジェンタ社、二〇〇一年。ただし解読はカリフォルニアの同社研究所による）といったにニュースによって、「ネスカフェ」や「ローレックス」といった既存の製品イメージとは異なるスイス企業像が、とりわけサラリーマン層に浸透していった。

「グローバル化」の尖兵としてスイス企業を描くこのようなスイス経済像は、スイス社会の退嬰性を前提とする「日本のスイス化」論のスイス経済像とは相容れない。このように、内的整合性を持つ統一的なスイス経済像は日本では今日もなお欠落しており、スイス日本商工会議所のスイス紹介書の副題のように、スイスは経済的には、依然として「誰も知らなかった国」でありつづけているのである[52]。

おわりに

以上みてきたように、スイス認識の前提となる日本の大状況の転換点は、敗戦にあった。植民地の喪失と世界的な自由貿易体制の確立によってはじめて、「小日本主義」的な加工貿易立国が現実となり、同時に経済民主化の実現が、社会国家論的なスイス論の根拠を部分的に堀り崩し、社会国家関心を弱めたからである。一方、明治以来総じて肯定的であったスイス経済像は、六〇年代半ば以降、「スイス銀行もの」の流布により大幅に修正された。これは工業国から金融国へのスイス経済像の変化でもあった。また日本の自己認識の変化は、八〇年前後にみることができる。「経済大国」意識の定着とともに、スイスは同じ土俵に立つ国へと立場を変え、時には前近代的な社会とさえ認識されるに至った。しかしそうした中でも、「アルプス」的なスイス像経済像は依然として健全であり、スイスはしばしば、「生活小国」日本が学ぶべきモデルとして位置づけられたのである。

しかしこれらのスイス「経済」像は、スイス・イメージ全体の中では、むしろ政治像や自然像の従属物という性格を持っていた。戦前の社会政策関心は「民主国」関心の、また「貿易立国」は「小国」関心の派生物といえるからである。「スイス銀行」の汚れたイメージも、スイスの国家・政治像に規定された「小国」「民主国」イメージと、「アルプス」の牧歌的で肯定的なスイス認識を大前提として、これを反転させた写像と解釈しうる。牧歌的で肯定的なイメージが定着しているからこそ、それを裏切るスイス像が、「知られざる」スイスの実像として人目をひくのである。その内容の豊富さにもかかわらず、経済像が自立性を持つにほどには、スイス経済への認識は深くはなく、また体系的でもなかったのである。

	経済総記	マクロ経済事情	スイスの個別産業への関心：農林畜産業	時計工業・宝飾品・精密機械	繊維工業	金属・機械工業	化学・製薬工業	その他工業・工業一般	銀行・証券・保険業	流通・サービス	交通・運輸・鉄道航空道路	郵便・電信・電話	観光・旅行業 旅行記除く
1948－50	3	1	1	1	0	0	0	0	2	0	0	0	1
1951－55	17	3	9	5	1	3	1	4	4	1	4	0	4
1956－60	2	2	0	2	0	0	0	3	7	0	2	0	0
1961－65	2	2	0	2	0	0	0	3	7	0	2	0	0
1966－70	1	0	3	1	1	0	0	0	3	0	9	0	1
1971－75	2	3	6	1	0	0	0	0	6	2	4	15	0
1976－80	4	4	1	8	1	2	0	0	16	0	4	12	1
1981－85	2	1	7	3	0	0	2	0	6	0	8	9	1
1986－90	5	2	8	2	1	1	2	1	3	0	7	0	6
1991－95	1	0	4	1	3	1	0	2	3	0	8	0	2
1996－00	8	1	38	8	3	4	9	1	65	4	26	3	7
2001－02	4	0	16	3	0	2	1	2	15	0	9	2	3
合計	51	19	93	37	10	13	15	16	137	7	83	41	26

	その他のスイス経済の側面への関心：企業・経営 社名含むもの	経済政策	財政・税法・租税論	経済法	労使関係・労働市場・技能養成	社会保障・福祉政策・社会政策	経営学・会計学	消費者問題その他	その他	スイス経済に関する主題：農村・農村工業・地場産業	貿易立国・経済外交・欧州統合	スイス金融市場とスイスフラン	秘密口座・地下市場・ナチ疑惑	外国人労働者・移民	食料安保・農業・農山村政策
1948－50	0	1	0	1	3	0	0	0	1	2	1	1	0	0	0
1951－55	7	4	0	6	12	0	4	0	1	6	9	6	0	0	0
1956－60	5	7	15	21	5	0	2	0	0	0	3	3	0	0	0
1961－65	5	7	15	21	5	0	2	0	0	0	3	3	0	0	0
1966－70	3	3	1	9	10	2	3	0	3	2	2	6	0	0	0
1971－75	2	5	1	13	6	1	8	2	0	3	5	10	1	0	0
1976－80	2	1	4	21	3	2	4	0	0	2	1	5	7	0	0
1981－85	6	1	4	16	4	3	9	1	0	0	4	6	0	0	0
1986－90	6	1	11	8	7	1	7	0	1	5	5	9	2	4	5
1991－95	4	5	12	12	3	0	6	0	0	4	6	6	3	2	4
1996－00	56	11	15	9	14	8	9	6	10	5	8	9	39	0	30
2001－02	13	1	1	1	2	2	1	2	2	1	3	4	3	3	8
合計	109	47	79	138	74	19	55	11	18	30	50	68	48	16	47

	スイス一般に関する主題：連邦制・多言語・地方自治	直接民主制・住民自治	景観・環境・空間政策	外交・防衛・中立・スイス軍	国際機関・国連・亡命者受入	スイス論・スイスモデル	人文社会各分野ごとのスイスへの関心：観光案内・紀行・登山・文化論	哲学・言語・文学・芸術	宗教学・宗教史・宗教事情	歴史学・歴史叙述	文化交/日本・スイス関係	地理学・地誌・山岳・防災論	教育学・教育制度・教育事情	政治学・政治情勢	司法・警察・行政	法学一般	その他の人文・社会科学	理系諸分野での関心：医学薬学・心理学・保健・福祉	理学・工学・農学・自然科学	環境防災工学・山岳水利土木	建築・工芸文化・産業デザイン	分類不能・不明	5年ごとの小計 重複集計
1948－50	0	0	1	2	0	4	3	0	0	0	0	1	2	0	0	1	1	0	0	0	0	2	36
1951－55	0	1	9	13	1	6	19	13	0	1	0	2	9	1	4	5	0	0	1	0	1	4	201
1956－60	1	0	1	15	4	4	3	5	0	6	0	2	2	2	3	27	2	0	0	0	0	5	161
1961－65	1	0	1	15	4	4	3	5	0	6	0	2	2	2	3	27	2	0	0	0	0	5	161
1966－70	1	0	1	3	0	1	3	7	0	5	0	2	7	4	1	8	7	0	1	2	1	2	119
1971－75	2	3	7	4	0	1	6	9	3	5	1	0	8	4	2	29	4	2	3	1	1	2	193
1976－80	3	3	8	4	0	3	6	10	3	5	1	4	4	3	11	47	3	2	20	1	1	0	247
1981－85	3	1	4	10	0	4	17	21	2	9	4	9	5	8	11	51	4	4	7	2	1	0	270
1986－90	0	8	8	4	5	1	13	14	2	17	4	7	3	17	7	33	8	4	11	3	11	1	291
1991－95	21	18	9	13	2	1	7	19	1	11	4	7	6	14	12	38	0	4	8	2	1	0	290
1996－00	17	19	34	22	2	6	26	22	4	38	7	11	17	29	22	51	11	21	29	30	34	1	859
2001－02	8	13	11	12	6	2	36	14	7	17	2	2	6	7	13	24	6	5	14	4	2	0	315
合計	57	66	94	117	24	37	142	139	22	120	23	49	71	91	89	341	48	42	94	45	53	22	3143

[1] この点は、「中立」「直接民主制」「連邦制」など、理論化・抽象化の産物を分析対象としうる政治像の場合と比較するとわかりやすい。もちろん経済面においても、たとえばドイツの社会的市場経済のように比較的明確に定式化された事例があるが、スイスの場合はそうした明瞭な政策モデルを持たない。

[2] 戦前については図書のみを、また戦後に関しては書名にスイスの名を冠した図書と雑誌記事を対象とする。なお経済像の場合にも学校教科書は非常に重要であるが、十分な資料が得られず、ここでは断念せざるをえなかった。

[3] 中井晶夫『初期日本=スイス関係史』風間書房、一九七一年。

[4] 久米邦武[編]、田中彰校[注]『特命全権大使　米欧回覧実記(五)』、岩波書店、文庫版、一九八二年

[5] 前掲書、三三-三四、五八-五九頁。

[6] 前掲書、三四、六〇、七〇-七一頁。

[7] 前掲書、五八-七一、七九頁。

[8] 安部磯雄『地上之理想國瑞西』大原社會問題研究所編纂、初版平民社、一九〇四年、一九四七年第一出版より再版。引用は再版本による。

[9] 前掲書、一頁、一〇〇頁。

[10] 前掲書、二三-二六頁。

[11] 前掲書、四九-五〇頁。

[12] 前掲書、一〇〇頁。

[13] 世界に先駆けて制定されたとされるドイツのビスマルク社会立法(一八八三年〜八九年)は、①疾病保険法、②災害保険法、③廃疾・養老保険法からなり、失業保険を欠く。これが実現したのは一九二七年である。強制的な国家失業保険が世界で初めて成立したのは，一般的には一九一一年のイギリスとされている。

[14] クルト・クルンビーゲル[著]、簡易保險局[編]『瑞西社會保險』簡易保險局、一九二二年。松澤清編『瑞西工場勞働制限制　：　日獨對照』有斐閣、一九二七年。なお、初期のスイス関連図書の一つにバーゼル滞在の新聞記者による随筆があるが、そこでは、「当地の学校は小学校はもとより、工業学校、商業学校、各種女学校等、全て無月謝である」と指摘されている。守田有秋『瑞西より』日吉堂本店、一九一八年。四九頁。

[15] 星埜章[編]『瑞西國「スヰス・バンクフェライン」見學報告書』　[出版社不明]、一九一三年、商工省商務局貿易課編『瑞西経済事情』商工省商務局貿易課、一九二九年。農商務省山林局　[編]『瑞西森林事情』農商務省山林局、一九二二年、片山茂樹[著]『瑞西ノ林業トKontrollmethode』興林会、一九三〇年。『瑞西觀光事業概觀』[鐵道省]國際觀光局、一九三三年。

[16] 大河内正敏は、東京帝国大学工科造兵学科を卒業し、同大学の教授を勤めた後、二一年に理化学研究所の所長となった。同研究所の所有特許の企業化を担ったのが、二七年に設立された理化学興業である。その後、同研究所の傘下に多数の企業が設立され企業集団をなした。なお今日のリコー株式会社は、理化学興業から独立した企業である。

[17] 大河内正敏『農村の工業』鐵塔書院、一九三四年。

[18] この時代の農村工業への着目は、戦後のいわゆる「大塚史学」や、周辺の経済史的研究に継承される。柳澤治「大塚久雄の農村工業論の背景――同時代日本の論争をめぐって」住谷一彦・和田強[編]『歴史への視線――大塚史学とその時代』日本経済評論社、一九九八年。

[19] 大河内正敏、前掲、五-六頁。昭和九年一月になされた朝日新聞への寄稿の再録。

[20] 大河内正敏、前掲、一〇七-一一二頁。

[21] 大河内の思想については、戦前から近年まで経済学者・経済史家による多くの解釈があるが、ここではスイスに関する言及に論点を限定する。一般的には、斎藤憲「大河内正敏による経営理念の形成――貴族院議員としての活動を中心に」『経営史学』一八巻三号、一九八

三年、五〇～六八頁、および、太田一郎「地方産業振興問題の展開――大河内正敏の農村工業論を中心にして」『帝京経済学研究』二一巻一・二号、一九八七年、一五七～一九二頁を参照。
22 農村更正協会［訳］『瑞西国山村農民窮乏克服策』農村更正協会、一九三七年。
23 「本来の意図」に合致する記事とは、以下の記事を除いたものである。①発音の一致にすぎないもの。②商品・製品名、物質名等、「スイス」関連語を持つが記事自体はスイス社会に関係ないもの。③地名としてのみスイスが言及されているもの。④スイスの企業名を含むが、企業自体が記事の主題でないもの。⑤スイス企業の出版物であるが、単に発行元にすぎないもの。ここでの集計は、雑誌発行部数や記事の長短を無視したごく大雑把なものに過ぎないが、本稿の目的に限定すれば有効であると考えられる。
24 ネッスル／ネスレ社の名を関する記事は六三件、そのうち大半が一九八〇年代以降の、かつ日本法人に関する記事であった。それに対して、重電・エンジニアリング大手のＢＢＣ／ＡＢＢ社はわずか三件、機械製造のスルザー社では一五件であり、化学分野では、チバガイギー社が五件、日本法人の活動が目立つロシュ社では三四件となっている。
25 川崎三蔵『戰なき國の繁榮』成人社、一九四九年。大内兵衛『瑞西紀行――世界の問題』朝日新聞社、一九五〇年。Ｐ・ベガン［著］、鶴岡千仞［訳］『ヨーロッパのバルコニー』岩波書店、一九五二年。Ａ・シーグフリード［著］吉阪俊蔵［訳］『スイス――デモクラシーの證人』、一九五二年。
26 「ここにはアメリカのような豪奢はないが、もし中流だけとって考えればここの中流のほうが落ち着いた立派な生活をしている」「ここには全く貧民がない」「スイスには世界にまれな厚生保険と養老保険があり、今もなお失業は全くない。スイスは労働者の天國である」大内兵衛、四八、一〇一-一〇二頁。
27 川崎は、「日本を東洋の工場にすべきか、世界の観光国にすべきか」と自ら問いを立てたうえで、スイスの観光業を、国家的な長期投資の産物であり、アルプスの自然が当然に生みだしたものではないと指摘し、観光国スイスが同時に工業国であることをも忘れず、日本は工業立国を目指すべきだと結論している。「東洋のスイス」論の当時における影響力の強さを示す事例であるが、同時にこれは、「東洋のスイス」論が受け手によりかなり多様な形で解釈されたこと、その限りで一般大衆にとってのスイス像がいまだ多分に曖昧であったことを示すものといえる。
28 「ただ戦争を避けて、国民がよく働き、よく貯蓄したことが、逸早くスイスを富める国にし」た。川崎三蔵、七〇頁。「繁栄の主要な原因は一世紀以来スイスがヨーロッパの如何なる戦争にも巻き込まれず、したがって国富の絶えざる増強を阻害されなかったことである」ジークフリード、一二九頁。ベガンの著書では戦時経済体制を除けば経済への言及は少ない。ジーグフリードの著書は経済面にも詳しく、スイスの工業が大量生産ではなく「量より質」の特殊・注文・高級品生産を基軸としている点、またスイス企業の多国籍企業化傾向、具体的には生産の国外移転と本社機能の残存、財の輸出とともにサービス輸出（「無形の輸出」）が重要であることを指摘している。
29 「スイスはヨーロッパ随一の債権国である。全世界七〇数カ国の中でも米・ソ・英に次ぐ第四番目の金保有国である」「米国に次ぐ高額な個人所得で、戦後は更に戦前をしのいでいるだろう。しかも米国のように極端な金持ちも貧乏人もなく、富の程度が平均している」川崎三蔵、前掲書、三、七一頁。
30 このヨハンナ・スピリ原作の童話は遅くとも一九二〇年には日本語に翻訳されているが、児童向けの出版は戦後において著しい。高畑勲演出・宮崎駿場面設計によるアニメーションの初回放映は七四年で、絶大な人気を誇った（本書増本論文参照）。
31 「しかしながらスイス銀行の真の特色は（中略）スイスに逃避地を求めて入ってくる異常に巨額な資本の量にある」。というのもスイスでは、「秘密はあくまで守られる」。「これらの外資により、スイスは国内の鐵道を拡張、維持し、その保険会社を発展させ、土木事業政策を実施することができた」。「納税の正直をあれほど誇っているこの国が、この場合には正真正銘の国際的脱税者の保護者となっている」。ジークフリード、前掲、一二四一二六頁。

32 フェーレンバッハ『スイス銀行——世界経済、影の巨大組織』早川書房、一九六六年。

33 前掲書、 三九、五四、七三、七六頁。

34 フェーレンバッハの著書の原題は ” The Swiss Banks” であり、「スイスの諸銀行」の意であるが、この書は「スイス銀行」と訳され、定着した。また今日のＵＢＳの前身の一つ、Schweizerische Bankgesellschaftも、しばしば「スイス銀行」と訳された。そのため「スイス銀行」を特定の一銀行と捉えるような誤解は日本では珍しくない。

35 草柳大蔵「世界の二宮金次郎——スイス銀行(世界王国論)」『文藝春秋』五一(十)、一九七三年、一八四-二〇〇頁、吉田康彦「スイス銀行、七七年の大破局」『諸君』九(一一)、一九七七年、一六八-一八五頁、ジャン・ジーグレル[著]、上杉聡彦[訳]『驚くべきスイス銀行——多国籍企業を含めて』竹内書店新社、一九七七年。ロバート・キンズマン[著]、佐瀬隆夫[訳]『スイス銀行のすべて』日本経済新聞社、一九七八年、草柳大蔵[ほか]著『スイス銀行の怪——鉄壁の”銀行秘密”を誇る金融聖域』大陸書房、一九八二年。高橋俊一『飢えない国スイス』家の光協会、一九八二年。ニコラス・フェイス[著]、斎藤精一郎[訳]『秘密口座番号スイス銀行の秘められた世界』日本放送出版協会、一九八二年。ジャン・ジーグレル[著]、萩野弘巳[訳]『スイス銀行の秘密——マネー・ロンダリング』河出書房新社、一九九〇年。アダム・レボー[著]、鈴木孝男[訳]『ヒトラーの秘密銀行——いかにしてスイスはナチ大虐殺から利益を得たのか』ＫＫベストセラーズ、一九九八年。クリフトファー・ライク[著]、土屋京子[訳]『匿名口座』(小説)講談社、一九九八年。ダニエル・ジュフュレ[著]、長島良三[訳]、『スイス銀行の陰謀』(小説)中央公論新社、二〇〇一年。福原直樹『黒いスイス』新潮社、二〇〇四年。

36 ネスレ社による日本での生産・販売活動は戦前に遡る。戦後の比較的早い時期に、チョコレート、チーズ等の商品イメージによるスイス像が定着していたと考えられる。

37 フェーレンバッハ、前掲書、二七頁。

38 ロレンツ・ストゥッキ[著]、吉田康彦[訳]『スイスの知恵——経済王国・成功の秘密』サイマル出版会、一九七四年。吉田康彦、『不思議の国スイス』駸々堂出版、一九七四年。阿部汎克『特派員の目　スイス　虚像と実像』毎日新聞社、一九八一年。この阿部の著書は、スイスの「高福祉国」ぶりについても数値を挙げ、その基盤を、高い税負担にではなく、スイスの経済的な豊かさの絶対量に求めている。なおこの時期には、社会保障制度に関する翻訳もなされている。Ａ. ザクサー[著]佐口卓・春見静子[訳]『スイスの社会保障制度』光生館、一九七五年。

39 なお八〇年代以降、「スイスの時計工業がクォーツ技術によって日本の時計工業に敗れた」との見方が日本で一般化し、今日まで残っているが、これは当時も今も誤った認識である。七九年に日本の時計産業がスイスのそれを凌駕したのは出荷個数においてであり、出荷額では当時もスイスの時計産業が優位を保っていた。クォーツ技術が市場の激変をもたらし、その結果スイスの時計産業が一時危機に陥ったのは事実であるが、その後の回復もあって、ここ二十年は就業者数はほぼ横ばいで推移している。対照的に日本では、八五年以降の生産額の低迷が著しい。二〇〇三年の統計では、スイスの時計輸出額は日本の時計輸出額の実に七二倍の規模に達する。http://www.fh-tokyo.com/Production/ production2003.pdf

40 高橋俊一、前掲書、一三一頁。

41 「戦後の日本経済はまさに『臨海立地型工業』によって世界を制覇した」「『白砂青松』の海岸は各地で姿を消し」、「山はさびれ果て」た。「それでよいのだろうか。スイスには海岸がなく、臨海工業地帯もない。険しい山地と盆地に立地し、それでいて付加価値の高い製品を生産し、高い所得を維持している。日本にそれができないか。」大谷健『緑の経済学——新・東洋のスイス論』潮出版社、一九八〇年。一八-一九頁。

[42] 八木あき子「二十世紀の迷信「理想国家・スイス(一)」」『諸君』一一(八)、一六〇-一九九頁、一九七九年、同、「「二十世紀の迷信「理想国家・スイス(二)第二部　スイスは国家か」」、同誌、一一(九)、一五四-一七七頁。八木あき子『理想国家スイス——二十世紀の迷信』新潮社、一九八〇年。

[43] 前掲雑誌論文、(一九七九年(二))、一六一頁。一六九-一七〇頁。

[44] ジャン・ジーグレル[著]、上杉聡彦[訳]、前掲書。

[45] 八木を批判した屋山太郎の論説(「スイス良いとこ一度はおいで」『諸君』一一(一一)、一二二-一三七頁、一九七九年)においてさえも、「標準」語と方言の間の価値序列意識自体に対しては明瞭な批判がなされていないこと、むしろそうした価値序列を前提としつつ、自らのドイツ語の「美しさ」を鼻に掛ける八木の尊大さがスイス人に反発を引き起こした可能性を指摘するにとどまっていることは、今日の視点からすると興味深い。

[46] 森田安一著『スイス ： 歴史から現代へ 地域主義・直接民主政・武装中立』、刀水書房、一九八〇年。森田安一、『スイス中世都市史研究』、山川出版社、一九九一年。

[47] 関根照彦『スイス直接民主制の歩み——疑わしきは国民に』尚学社、一九九九年。岡本三彦「スイスの行政制度」、土岐寛・加藤普章[編]『比較行政制度論』、法律文化社、二〇〇〇年、一二一〜一五〇頁所収。世利洋介『現代スイス財政連邦主義』(財)九州大学出版会、二〇〇一年。黒澤隆文『近代スイス経済の形成——地域主権と高ライン地域の産業革命』京都大学学術出版会、二〇〇二年。なお研究書ではないが、スイス経済に関する数少ない概説書として、佐多直彦『スイスは、いま。——金融・情報大国の素顔』ダイヤモンド社、一九九〇年がある。

[48] 黒澤隆文「スイス」財務省財務総合政策研究所　「経済の発展・衰退・再生に関する研究会」報告書第六章、二〇〇一年六月、一三九〜一六五頁。

[49] 「ライン資本主義」の語を広めたアルベールの著書にはスイスについての言及がかなりあるが、その後の議論ではスイスはほとんど言及されていない。ミシェル・アルベール[著]、小池はるひ[訳]『資本主義対資本主義』、竹内書店新社、一九九六年。

[50] ジョージ・ウェアフリッツ／高山秀子「スイス化するニッポン——経済再生の夢断たれリッチで気楽な『引退国家へ』」『ニューズウィーク日本版』、二〇〇二年五月一五日版。

[51] ジョージ・ウェアフリッツ／高山秀子、前掲、一八頁。

[52] 八幡康貞[編]『スイス——誰も知らなかった国』スイス－日本商工会議所、一九九八年。

SWISS AND JAPANESE PERCEPTIONS OF FINANCIAL CONSULTING SERVICES TO JAPANESE HIGH NET WORTH INDIVIDUALS

By Dr. Katsura Suzuki

Introduction

This article addresses the needs of wealthy Japanese, their families and successors who are seeking to realise their visions on the global platform from the research paper the author recently completed. It aims, in part, to compare financial consulting services in Japan and Europe in order to find where there are strengths and weaknesses and, additionally, to identify the perceived technical and cultural gaps that may exist between European and Japanese advisors serving wealthy Japanese and their families. This could then lead to the provision of more appropriate advisory services for their clients.

Family companies play a very important role in the Japanese economy. Some 95% of Japanese companies are family companies and approximately 40% of the listed companies are family businesses (Kurashina 2003). Wealthy Japanese families and their asset management companies demand that their professional service teams work for them internationally. Company owners should be able to act independently, leaving behind the constraints of historical, political, and economic systems such as banks, insurance companies, the Ministry of Finance and the Government of the United States of America. This should encourage them to think more freely and openly and to act globally when making decisions. Such freedom requires them to engage independent service teams and to be innovative and entrepreneurial.

It is not just established family businesses that need a comprehensive range of financial services. Young entrepreneurs and wealthy individuals who are setting up new companies, which will eventually be passed on to a second generation, also demand international solutions.

Additionally, there is limited knowledge about the services provided to and required by wealthy Japanese who work in overseas locations. This includes a significant number of Japanese women who marry non-Japanese and live outside Japan. They also want to invest outside Japan in different assets, including businesses, and to protect their wealth. This article aims to address this important area and the findings should provide the basis for further research as well as the provision of more appropriate services.

A review of the literature relating to family wealth management reveals the existence of firms offering financial planning, in the form of family office services, in the USA as well as private banking services in Europe. However, it appears that a recent history of formal centres like these for managing and preserving the wealth of a family in Japan at an international level does not exist. Additionally, there is little published academic research on such services, with even less written in Japanese (Goffee 1996).

As a result of the lack of published information, there is therefore a need to identify the characteristics and components of the advice that meets the requirements of wealthy Japanese and their families.

This article attempts to:

- increase the understanding and awareness of differences so that Japanese clients can obtain advice from European advisors
- identify what advice is required so that advisors can provide appropriate services
- increase the intercultural awareness of Japanese and European advisors.

Walker and Schmitz (2003), among others, agree that Japan is a high-context communication culture, which means that communication is implicit and indirect and advisors from different cultures have to understand the implications of this. Yoshida (2002, p. 2) states, 'a critical agenda for the Japanese will be to improve communication with the rest of the world'. Japan is the country of Zen Buddhism, and in order to understand the Japanese, their spiritual values should be acknowledged and understood, too (Beer 1997, Neubauer 1998).

Outline

Wealthy Japanese are increasingly looking for financial-planning services outside Japan in order to protect their wealth. Additionally, many Japanese reside or wish to reside in Europe and seek investment advice from European as well as Japanese advisors. However, because of differences in cultural perceptions, this advice may conflict. As a result, the services provided might not be appropriate for the clients.

This paper reviews concepts that will contribute to a conceptual framework for the research study the author has made. Based on the 200-literature review, important characteristics of the services provided for wealthy individuals and their families are identified. These characteristics can be divided into five categories: technical aspects, independence of advice, trust between advisors and clients, intercultural aspects of the Japanese and future generations. It attempts to improve, validate and justify the theoretical characteristics derived from the literature with the development of a framework designed to identify gaps in cultural perceptions of services. These perceived gaps between advisors and services are investigated using the questionnaires and interviews. Finally, the author discusses the contribution this research makes to the academic field and to consultants in the field.

Background

In order to understand wealth in Japan today, it is necessary to know something of the country's rich and varied history.

Japan experienced a long period of feudal conflicts ending in the late 1500s. However, stability was restored in about 1600 when Ieyasu Tokugawa, who had achieved great wealth and virtually unlimited power, was appointed Shogun ('chief warrior') by the emperor. The Shogun was the effective ruler and Ieyasu Tokugawa and his familial successors led the country as a military dictatorship for the next 250 years. This period became known as the Edo period and the country was at peace during this time. The Samurai warriors, who no longer had to prove themselves as fighters, began to educate themselves in other areas such as martial arts, literature and the arts. However, at the same time, Japan became isolated from the rest of the world (Lehmann & Turpin 2002) and overseas travel and the reading of 'foreign' books was forbidden. The long period of isolation from the rest of the world, together with Japan's geological location as a group of isolated islands, is still a factor that contributes to the closed Japanese mentality.

The stability of the Edo period came to an end as other countries began applying pressure to Japan to establish international trade links. Imperial power was re-established in 1868 and this change, known as the Meiji restoration, saw the capital move from Kyoto to Tokyo (Gomi et al. 1998 pp. 311–313). Political power was given to a group of former samurai and a small number of the aristocrats. Kyoto, however, remained as a symbol of the Empire (Japan Guide 2005).

Some of the merchants, although they came from the fourth tier of the Edo-period class system, became very wealthy and started to form financial cliques known as zaibatsu. These were family enterprises with official status, which, during the Meiji period, diversified, grew and gained in importance. One family, the Mitsui, introduced money changing shops and a system of promissory notes, which was safer than transporting money from town to town. This service also enabled them to act as intermediaries between the government and traders and saw the introduction of lending services. In 1876 the Mitsui Bank was formed and had powerful influence with the government. The Mitsui Trading Company still exists today (Kasuya 2002, Yasuoka 2002).

Emperor Taishō succeeded Emperor Meiji and Japan entered a period of conflict and economic decline, which was aggravated by the devastating earthquake of 1923. Furthermore, Emperor Taishō was weak and unhealthy and died at an early age in 1926. He was succeeded by Emperor Shōwa who faced a period of popular unrest, aggravated by the worldwide economic depression of 1929. The 1930s saw the beginning of a long period of hostilities with other countries (Gomi et al.). The Allied Forces occupied Japan until 1952 during which time they tried to reduce the power of the Emperor and they introduced measures to boost the economy. This was stimulated further by the Korean War in 1950 when Japanese industry developed rapidly, led by heavy industry such as ship building, steel as well as the chemical and oil industries (Gomi et al. 1998 p. 485). There then followed a boom period during which

Japan achieved trade surpluses and dominated markets such as electronics, car making and computer technology[1] (Japan Guide 2005, Okazaki 1993 pp. 183–207).

One impact of the occupation was the breakup of monopolies and the introduction of privatisation. Large concentrations of power were broken up by the dissolution of the powerful zaibatsu cliques (Yasuoka 2002, Japan Guide 2005) as the Allied Forces sought to introduce a system of equality. The measure was only partly successful as the groups soon regrouped and emerged, with popular support, as keiretsu ('system or series'). The keiretsu pooled their resources and established intricate networks instead of having a single line of control through one family. They were a major part of Japan's economic boom and its emergence as a global power.

As a result of the postwar boom, a new segment of wealthy individuals was born, who had made their wealth from employment in the large companies involved with the reconstruction of the Japanese infrastructure, such as construction, banks, department stores and real estate. These people accounted for some 25% of jobs, which guaranteed employment for life (Yashiro 1997 pp. 34–36) and there was economic stability (Yamane 2005 p. 61). Employees were expected to pledge loyalty to their firm and this was rewarded with pay rises based on their length of service. At this time, unemployment had been practically eradicated (Werner 2003 pp. 19–20).

The wealthy were now typically large company owners and salaried presidents who had made their way to the top rather than landowners with inherited

[1] According to Werner (2003), key parts of the postwar economic structure of Japan had already been established during the war by the Japanese Government itself, with the emphasis on 'public before the individual' and the shift from agriculture to industry. The USA urged the West to buy Japanese goods, pushing some companies out of business and raising unemployment in these countries still further. At the same time, Japan imposed high import tariffs to discourage exports to Japan even though they were themselves exporting to these countries. The driving force was not profit but the desire to create huge trade surpluses. The influence of the USA, under General MacArthur, resulted in greater social equality through the breakup of the *zaibatsu* (not entirely successful as they regrouped as *keiretsu*) and the reallocation of land.

wealth. Others were prominent within the government, with positions of political, governmental and financial power (Abe 2001, JTB 1996, Yoneyama and Nathan 1998, 2001).

From the end of the 1980s a different segment of wealthy individuals emerged. These included entrepreneurs, who were not necessarily highly educated, in businesses offering services, as well as educated people such as medical doctors. Their status is linked to occupation, education and income rather than to inherited wealth and position (Oshita 2005).

The old elite does not necessarily accept this new generation of wealthy individuals, which includes highly successful and often well-educated women, and, as a result, these groups tend not to hold positions of political power at the present time. They are, however, beginning to exert more influence in society through their increasing economic power and are responsible for driving the Japanese economy forward (Tachibanaki & Mori 2005 p. 220). The cartels established by the keiretsu groups have presented a huge barrier to outsiders, both Japanese and foreign, but liberalisation of policy is helping to break down these barriers (Werner 2003 p. 185).

Liberalisation of economic policy, starting in the 1980s (MoF 2003, Okazaki 1993, p. 38), has allowed people to seek investment opportunities outside Japan and to extend their entrepreneurial businesses abroad. In 1980 capital flows were deregulated, followed by a process of almost two decades of liberalisation and continuing deregulation[2] (Werner 2003 p. 187). Finally, in 1998, major reform, popularly referred to as Japan's 'Big Bang', saw the removal of foreign exchange restrictions. This globalisation has affected the lives of wealthy families, leading to higher international mobility and diversification into real estate and company holdings.

[2] This liberalisation of policy coincided with a period of negative growth in Japan – a situation which still taxes analysts today (Werner 2003 p. 278).

Accordingly, the need for international tax advice has increased, and estate planning has had to adapt to take account of international rules. Dedicated Japanese consultants are necessary to offer support services in the Japanese language, law and intercultural aspects (Beer 1997, Hofstede 1980, Walker, Walker & Schmitz 2003, Yoshida 2000). An increasing number of young Japanese are willing to take risks and set up new businesses, creating additional wealth (Swiss-Japanese Chamber of Commerce 2003). Whilst overall tax revenue, as a percentage of national income, in Japan is relatively low in comparison to countries such as the United Kingdom, the United States and Germany (OECD 2005), inheritance tax rates are very high (Hauser 2001, Kurashina 2003, MoF 2005) and people are looking for more tax-efficient ways of saving abroad, whilst remaining inside the law.

The literature review

Gaps between European and Japanese advisors include different perceptions about private banking and different attitudes toward the authorities, independent service, bank secrecy and the family office. European advisors better understand the technical aspects of the international services provided and can offer independent advice, but they may have difficulties in understanding Japanese characteristics, such as high-context communication, and values. Japanese advisors may have difficulties in understanding the value of international solutions and the relationships with authorities in Europe. As a result of tight government controls, Japanese advisors in Japan tend to be more afraid of taking risks than their European counterparts, meaning that there are certain difficulties in giving independent advice. However, Japanese advisors seem better able to build trusting relationships with their clients because of the homogeneous culture and their understanding of Japanese characteristics. Overall, Japanese advisors appear to be weaker when it comes to advising future generations of wealthy Japanese families than European advisors.

After reviewing the literature it appears that there are five significant characteristics to be considered when advising wealthy Japanese families. These characteristics can be categorized as: technical aspects, independence of advice, trust between advisors and clients, intercultural aspects of the Japanese and future generations.

The literature review revealed that many important characteristics should be considered when advising wealthy Japanese families. The most important issue to emerge was that of cross-cultural understanding. It is not sufficient for an advisor to offer a range of services; he must also understand the needs and expectations of his client. Differences in high and low contextual perceptions can lead to misunderstandings and inappropriate advice. The literature review doesn't take into account the link between cross-cultural differences and other critical issues such as problems in Japan, which are not necessarily related to cross-cultural understanding but rather to the problems of the Japanese system and their historical impact on wealthy Japanese families.

European technical competence has so far not been utilised to any great extent although it would seem to offer financially advantageous solutions for Japanese clients. On the other hand, Japanese advisors understand the social problems in Japan as well as the Japanese mentality. The literature review did not find how these issues are interrelated and this will be investigated using questionnaires and interviews with both European and Japanese advisors to wealthy Japanese and their families.

Research design

This research asks the questions: 'what are the gaps in perceptions between European and Japanese advisors to wealthy Japanese and their families and how do they affect the type of Swiss-based European-style services provided?' Particular attention is paid to the services offered in Switzerland.

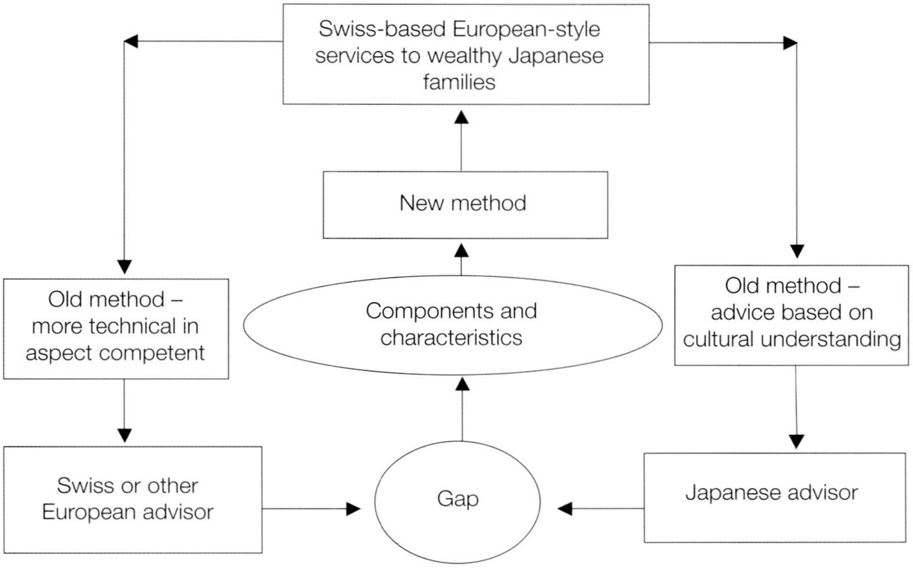

Figure 3.1. Conceptual Framework

Figure 3.1 above shows the existing situation, whereby European advisors, who are highly competent, offer services to clients which are more technical in aspect. Japanese advisors, on the other hand, give advice based on cultural understanding, trust and knowledge of the Japanese system.

This framework demonstrates the gap revealed in the literature review that exists between the advice given by Japanese and European advisors. Research and analysis of the missing characteristics and components should lead to the provision of more appropriate services for Japanese families.

A set of research questions were developed to test whether the identified factors were currently those most used in providing advisory services to wealthy Japanese families and to identify the gap between practice and the literature findings. Questions then identified those factors that are critical in advisory services so that a methodology could be developed which could be applied to wealthy Japanese family advisory services.

Three main research questions were developed, namely:

- the problems faced by wealthy Japanese and their families under existing Japanese financial systems
- the gaps in advisory services that are attributable to cultural differences
- the critical success factors necessary for providing appropriate advisory services in Switzerland to wealthy Japanese families

Methodology

The perceived gaps, arising from the literature review, between advisors and services were investigated through questionnaires and interviews with 100 advisors in Japan and 100 advisors in Switzerland. All participants, regardless of nationality, were asked the same questions and the interviews explored these in greater depth. The responses were then analyzed and compared, leading to suggestions for improvements to the services offered. The criteria for selection were: 1) professional qualification, 2) experience in Japan business, 3) experience or knowledge in the area of international financial advisory services.

The respondents included tax specialists, lawyers, CPAs, private bankers, bank officials, consultants, businesspersons and university professors. Interviews were undertaken with a sample of those who completed the questionnaire and who expressed their willingness to be interviewed.

Demographic profile of respondents – Questionnaires

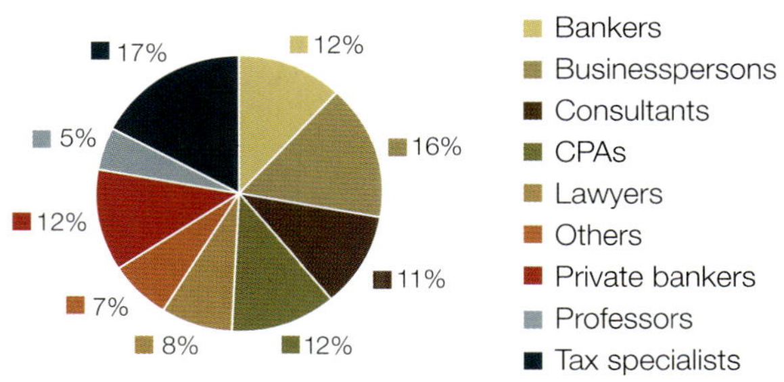

Demographic profile of respondents – Interviews

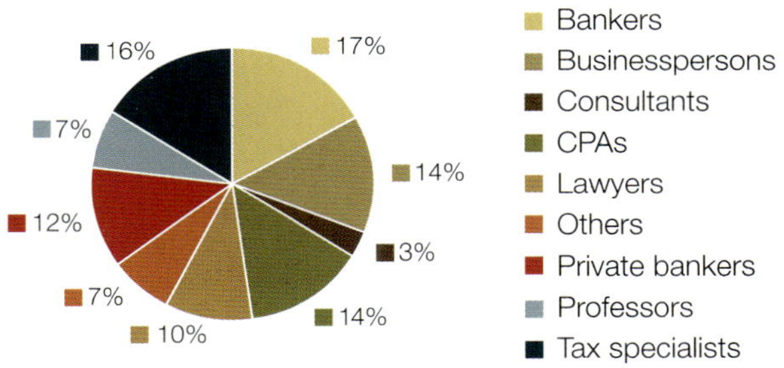

Figure 4.1. Demographics of the respondents (Some of the interesting graphics can be found in Appendix I)

The response rate to the Japanese questionnaires was 52% and 32% for the responses in English, giving an overall rate of 84 out of 200 or 42%. From these respondents 70%, or 58 out of 84, were selected to become interview participants. Questions of the questionnaire and interview can be found in Appendix H.

The average number of years of experience of Japanese advisors in Japan-related business is 18 years and for European advisors 14 years, with an overall average of 17 years.

198 **Findings from the research questions**

This section brings together and summarizes the detailed results of the questionnaire questions and the interview questions. It addresses the three research questions and seeks to confirm the propositions.

RQ1: What problems do wealthy Japanese and their families face under existing Japanese financial systems?

The problems can be summarised as the high taxes, lack of clarity, strong governmental controls and the risk of scandals. There is no bank secrecy, with little concept of the need for privacy. Additionally, rich people cannot be openly rich because of the system of equality adopted after the Second World War. The Japanese financial system lacks stability and there are not enough independent international advisors in Japan. This could contribute to the trend seen by advisors of wealthy Japanese families wishing to adopt the ways of wealthy Western families, although they are largely unable to do so. This point was also identified in the literature review.

Wealthy families still control many fields in industry and they still have a considerable influence in politics. As the literature review discussed, they have their own asset management companies, controlled internally under the terms of their own businesses. One solution is that these could be replaced or complemented by working together with firms offering family office type services in Switzerland. Clients need the expertise of international advisors to optimize their tax and investments but many of these possibilities are closed to them. As a result of stock market controls and reductions in the value of real estate following the burst of the economic bubble, the Japanese economy has been in a weak situation for a long time and many families have seen their wealth lose value, making opportunities overseas seem more attractive.

The fear of scandals comes from the lack of corporate governance and a general lack of trust in the mass media and politicians. The companies within the clans are not open enough and they avoid situations leading to any sort of scandal, which could result in loss of face. The hidden but acknowledged power of the mafia is also an influence. If someone criticises the system they risk being pulled down by it, such is the power within many families.

As discussed in the literature review, the 'modernization' of Japanese society has included some controversial changes such as the termination of the cross-share holdings of the banks. This has had a negative impact on group companies and can create an unstable situation in terms of the shareholding structures of the owner companies. However, on the positive side, it has opened up the markets for new enterprises and entrepreneurs.

A new law in 2006 concerning the share exchange process will make it easier for mergers and acquisitions of Japanese companies by foreign companies and company owners need to protect themselves from such potentially unwelcome takeovers.

There are many social issues and problems in Japan, such as the aging society facing a shortage of pension funds. As a result of government bond issues, unemployment and bankruptcies, the government cannot introduce active measures for improving the standard of living in Japan; on the contrary, they create a heavier burden through tax increases. Not only the current economic climate but also the complicated controls covering all aspects of the economy have led to an inefficient social system.

A further problem is linked to culture. It is possible for a Japanese client to have a relationship with both a European and a Japanese advisor. The European advisor might view it as a good, strong relationship but it will never be on the same level as that of one with a Japanese advisor purely because of the implicit and instinctive levels of understanding which have their roots in cultural understanding.

Proposition: there is no difference between European and Japanese advisors in advising wealthy Japanese families.

The results show quite clearly that there is a difference. Japanese advisors are ill informed and lack understanding of the opportunities available in the European market. This is due in part to the differences in systems as well as in products and services and also in part to the language barrier. However, they understand the needs of their Japanese clients well but, because of their lack of knowledge and their limited understanding of cultural and legal differences, it is difficult for them to offer appropriate advice and services. Additionally, the strong controls of Japanese law present a further barrier to giving appropriate advice. Conversely, European advisors cannot reach Japanese clients easily because of the cultural distance between them, the restrictions on soliciting business in Japan and because of their limited knowledge of the Japanese system and client needs. Although both sides acknowledge these gaps, the problem remains a very difficult one to overcome for the reasons stated above. Advisors, regardless of nationality, have to win the trust of their clients to ensure a good relationship and to make sure that their clients are kept well informed.

RQ2: What are the gaps in advisory services that are attributable to cultural differences?

Although the Japanese tax and legal regulations are clearly an obstacle for clients wishing to optimize their tax bills and investments, the system itself is not the only problem in Japan. Differences in high and low contextual understanding, as discussed in the literature review, can lead to ambiguities and lack of understanding. A European advisor might interpret a 'yes' in Japan as an agreement or sign of understanding whereas to the Japanese advisor it might only mean that the client is listening but does not necessarily imply agreements. Hierarchical levels in Japan mean that there are different levels of accountability, which can differ from European models. This can lead to long processes of decision making and this can prove very frustrating to the European advisor whilst being normal for Japanese advisors. Japanese tend to have a group mentality and are unwilling to be different in situations where European advisors might expect to be able to offer a tailor-made individual solution to a client's requirements.

Trust is the key word, as seen repeatedly throughout the questionnaires and interviews and in the literature review. Both the literature and the results from this research show that Japanese high net-worth individuals are reluctant to trust the Japanese financial and political systems. On the other hand, they are also reluctant to trust non-Japanese advisors largely because of their apparent strangeness in terms of language and cultural differences. The gaps, therefore, are not only in the services provided but also in the cultural differences and relationships of trust required by both clients and advisors.

Proposition: European advisors perceive that they can provide better advice to wealthy Japanese families.

This proposition is confirmed in that European advisors perceive that Japanese clients should be better informed and educated about the international financial products and opportunities available and that they are qualified to offer these services. However, because of the cultural gap and legal difficulties, it can prove very difficult reaching and winning the trust of potential clients.

Proposition: European and Japanese professionals perceive the problems of serving wealthy Japanese families in the same way.

This proposition is only partially confirmed in that both groups acknowledge the problems of the Japanese system with its strict governmental controls, lack of clarity, ambiguity and high tax rates. Additionally, since the system of equality introduced after the war, there is the additional problem that Japanese clients feel that it is wrong to admit to their wealth and to openly look for tax-saving possibilities. This can make it difficult for advisors to reach potential clients. Once again, the European advisors often fail to understand the huge importance of mutual trust and long-term relationships, an issue well understood by the Japanese advisors. Government controls and frequently changing laws mean that a mentality is created in which people are unwilling to take responsibility for decisions, to take risks or to be the first to try something new and European advisors are not necessarily used to these attitudes.

Proposition: European and Japanese professionals do not perceive the problems of serving wealthy Japanese families in the same way.

This proposition is confirmed in that both sets of advisors acknowledged different problem areas when serving their clients. European advisors felt that they could work well with Japanese clients. However, due to their backgrounds there are certain limitations in that Japanese do not trust them fully because of the lack of cultural and language understanding or simply because they are not Japanese. On the other hand, the Japanese advisors understand these cultural problems but acknowledge their lack of the international experience necessary to provide the appropriate services for their clients. Japanese advisors also realise that their clients tend to feel more secure with a Japanese advisor. As was seen in the literature review, although the Japanese welcome Western technology and ideas they choose to keep their ethos and tradition intact – an approach known as *wakon yōsai,* which accounts in part for their resistance to change.

RQ3: What are the critical success factors for providing appropriate advisory services in Switzerland to wealthy Japanese and their families?

It is a fact that gaps and differences in terms of language and culture do exist and these are acknowledged by both Japanese and European advisors. It is therefore necessary to find ways of weakening and bridging those gaps.

Trust is again the key word and the question of how to persuade the client to trust the advisor. This requires both cultural understanding and technical competence – but it also needs more. A country such as Switzerland has a competent financial system and proven ability in protecting people's privacy, making it a favourable location for such services.

As discussed earlier, a solution might be for advisors in Europe, who are technically skilled, and those in Japan, who understand the intercultural communication aspects, to cooperate with each other and form mutual relationships in which they can fully meet the needs of their clients. Once again, the high level of taxation and strict government controls are a major barrier. Critical success factors are that Japanese advisors and clients should become more informed about and develop greater understanding of the advantages of European financial schemes and investment opportunities suitable for their wealth management needs. Conversely, European advisors have to be better educated in terms of the Japanese system and matters concerning intercultural communication.

Japanese advisors could learn technical expertise and product awareness through seminars, with products adapted for the needs of the Japanese market. Additionally, clients have to be well informed in their own language about the possibilities available to them.

Proposition: European and Japanese advisors place different importance on the critical success factors necessary for providing services in Switzerland to wealthy Japanese.

This proposition was not fully confirmed as the results show that there are several areas of equal concern to advisors, regardless of nationality. Both groups state the need for a good, reliable product, which meets the needs of the clients as well as political and economic security and the need for confidentiality in relationships. However, Europeans place high importance on technical ability but less on intercultural issues whereas this is of great importance to their Japanese counterparts. Surprisingly perhaps, Japanese advisors did not rate the importance of mutual trust. The researcher attributes this to the fact that as it is such an intrinsic part of any relationship it was not considered an issue.

Conclusion

At the beginning of this research, it was clear to the author that, despite well-intentioned and skilled advisors, wealthy Japanese clients are not always being given the comprehensive advice they require.

The findings show that Japanese advisors are more aware of the Japanese system and problems in Japan than European advisors but they do not fully understand the technical aspects of providing services for wealthy Japanese and their families. Europeans, whilst technically skilled, have difficulties in intercultural communication with Japanese clients.

The importance of trust was emphasized repeatedly in the interviews and questionnaires and this would seem to be paramount in all relationships with Japanese clients. The literature review revealed the long history of family groups and the importance of cooperation and understanding within these groups. In this way, trust is built on many years of tradition and understanding.

Even though Japanese clients expect their advisors to be multi-disciplined experts, the issue of trust is still paramount. From the questionnaires and interviews, it seems that many clients prefer to consult Japanese advisors even when they lack expertise in specialist areas and indeed, specialist international solutions are lacking in Japan. European advisors find this attitude hard to comprehend and they don't understand why Japanese clients appear reluctant to optimize their tax bills and investments. According to one of the Japanese interviewees, "Japanese society requires that social relationships are taken care of before talking about technical issues. If the social relationships are not taken care of then business people in Japan will not accept each other.

One of the difficulties faced by private bankers is that the Japanese people still have no 'private' feelings. This comes from the aftermath of the Second World War when hierarchy was replaced by equality and the historical ideal of the group ethic rather than individualism. People learned that tax is a social obligation and that it is not considered correct to think of oneself and use one's wealth for personal gain. The Japanese need to learn that they can optimise their tax burdens and use the saved money in some other way, whether for personal gain or philanthropic purposes. Another difficulty is that the country is isolated as a group of islands and the people are historically not used to foreigners, which makes it more difficult for them to trust non-Japanese people working for them."[3]

[3] Translated from Japanese.

European advisors are aware that they have many skills to offer, as well as broad international experience, but they are frustrated in their attempts to attract Japanese clients because of the obstacles presented by the Japanese legal and financial systems, cultural differences and language. They realize that Japanese clients need to be made aware of what services are available in Europe.

Another problem for European advisors is that they are used to clients who, on the whole, are able to think independently and to seek solutions to suit their particular requirements. Japanese clients often react with a herd instinct (Beer 1997). When they know that everyone else is doing the same thing, then it must be the right thing to do and this in turn builds a sense of security. Interviewees acknowledge that there is, of course, a small segment of Japanese clients who are able to think independently and who are frustrated by the lack of appropriate services for their particular needs. Japanese advisors commented that European advisors have to be very careful with this group of clients because fundamentally they are still Japanese although their expectations are not the same as those of other wealthy clients.

According to one interviewee, "Japanese 'baby boomer kids' are now managing companies and in the next five to ten years many of them will retire. This will bring a lot of changes in Japanese society. Many old systems will disappear and skilled young people will be free to be much more active in the business world. At the moment, very skilled young people are not speaking out [about the Japanese system] since they risk being pulled down, which is a great pity for the development of Japanese society. Japan is stuck [within its own system]."[4]

Some Swiss banks and financial companies such as UBS, Credit Suisse and Pictet are already trying to reach Japanese clients by hiring Japanese advisors. Although this removes the problems of language and cultural understanding, it still leaves the actual problem of reaching the clients and satisfying the requirements of the tax and legal systems. A problem noted by Europe-based advi-

[4] Translated from Japanese.

sors is that Japanese law does not allow them to sell services in Japan if they are not qualified and licensed in Japan. Additionally, clients are still wary about investing in Europe because of uncertainties about the tax and legal implications. The advisors best placed to optimize taxes are the firms and advisors who are actually based in Japan, but Japanese law, as previously discussed, strictly controls their activities.

It would therefore seem that the ideal solution for bridging the gap in the conceptual framework between European advisors and their potential clients would be to improve the cooperation and trust between advisors within Europe and those within Japan. This would combine the superior technical skills and international understanding of the European advisors with the cultural understanding of the Japanese advisors and their knowledge of the Japanese systems.

The main point to come across from this research/study was that advisors have to understand each other better and to learn how to work together in order to reach Japanese clients and provide them with appropriate services. This needs time, effort and trust on both sides. It is not enough for an advisor just to win a client. All advisors have to be aware of cultural and language differences and to recognize the strengths of their coworkers. When clients see that there is trust between advisors, then they will be more likely to trust them. This would suggest that the mutual trust between advisors in Japan and Europe is more important, at least initially, than the trust between clients and advisors.

One person said, 'We as [Japanese] clients are very sensitive to feel whether the advisors are cooperating only superficially or whether they are working well together. We want to see that they trust each other – before giving us any advice. In particular, private issues are more sensitive than corporate issues. We have to reveal very private matters, which we would otherwise not disclose to a third party. So trust is the key issue.'[5]

[5] Translated from Japanese.

Advisors have to be able to identify the needs and match the individual expectations of clients as well as supply information in Japanese. Mutual cooperation between advisors in Europe and Japan should be able to satisfy these needs. Long-term mutual, non-competitive relationships can be built, leading to long-term solutions for the clients.

Following the writing of this chapter, the researcher became aware of a new venture between a corporate financial advisor in Switzerland and a private financial advisor whereby a facilitator brought the two parties together. In this way the corporate financial advisor can offer his clients the skills and competences needed in all areas of their businesses and the private financial advisor has access to a wider customer base. The cooperation established between them should lead to greater trust, strong relationships and a wider range of services for clients. The relationship effectively removes any competition between the advisors and the clients can see for themselves the trust and synergy between the representatives from both sides of the business.

Although this would seem to offer a solution to the problem of communication between advisors, it is necessary to bear other important factors in mind. It must be acknowledged that there are some wealthy Japanese clients who wish to keep their corporate and private affairs totally separate due to their lack of trust in both the Japanese system and in advisors. Once again the issue of confidentiality is a major factor, as confirmed by one of the interviewees who commented that, whereas a Japanese client might trust his advisor in Switzerland, when covered by Swiss bank secrecy laws, he might not be able to trust the same advisor should he, in other circumstances, come under Japanese jurisdiction.

In short, advisors must take a multitude of factors into account when advising their wealthy clients. Not only do they have to conform to the legal requirements of the different countries they operate in, they have to be able to communicate with each other and, of paramount importance, they must view each customer as an individual with his own unique set of requirements.

The findings show clearly where there are problematic areas, which is what this research set out to prove. However, it is difficult to gauge the actual level of success, as the researcher believes that the confidential nature of advisors' expertise prevented them from being as open as they might have been.

Implications

As seen, there is a need for Switzerland-based European advisors to form close relationships with advisors in Japan. Each group has particular skills to offer and they can therefore inform and support each other. This could involve Japanese advisors being based in Switzerland or European advisors working in Japan.

How this could be accomplished is by Switzerland-based service providers, such as the private banks, lawyers, tax experts, consultants, family office and accounting firms reinforcing their services with Japanese advisors in their advisory teams. Similarly, Japan-based service providers could come to Switzerland and provide their services alongside European experts as part of their advisory team.

Advisors working in mutually beneficial relationships should be able to develop a range of products and services specifically for the needs of wealthy Japanese families. These should take into account the tax and legal requirements of the Japanese system and should be flexible enough to react to changes in the law. For example, there is a need for practical solutions that create liquidity, as wealth is often tied up in real estate and in the shares of own group companies. Possible solutions to this problem include forming trusts under, for example, New Zealand law but administered in Switzerland and the securitization of real estate in real estate investment trusts (REIT 2004) so that it is possible to trade in it as an asset. Clients should be kept informed in their own language and should have a reachable contact person who is also their mentor. Using mutually beneficial working relationships, this would provide services that are more acceptable than in organizations from both countries acting alone.

There is a great resource that can be tapped by service providers, particularly in Europe, in the many mixed couples, who have experience of both cultures.

Many of these have a professional background and it should therefore be possible to train them and place them in situations where they can explain the extensive technical knowledge of European advisors whilst acknowledging cultural aspects and differences, thus bridging the gap between advisors and clients.

Main limitations

Japanese people living in Japan could not provide a lot of detail about services in Switzerland as it was usually beyond their experience. Similarly, European people could not always respond authoritatively about the problems of the Japanese system.

The research did not differentiate sufficiently between types of wealth in Japan. The "nouveaux riches" are entrepreneurs but are not necessarily in positions of political and economic power and influence. Their expectations of advisors may prove to differ from the requirements of traditionally wealthy families.

Although the response rate was good, the sample size was limited because its requirements were that suitable candidates were advisors with both a professional qualification and experience in Japan-related business. Although the average length of experience of respondents in Japan business was 17 years, this did not necessarily reflect the true length and depth of experience of all candidates.

The original questionnaire was in English. This was translated into Japanese, with a Japanese context, for Japanese advisors. The responses were then translated into English but in an English context. Due to language and cultural differences it must be acknowledged that some of the responses might have lost part of their original meaning in the translation, even though every care was taken to ensure an accurate interpretation of them.

Future research

Up-coming generations are very important and it is a fact that the successors of traditional wealthy Japanese families are becoming more international and open-minded. They could have different attitudes to those of their predecessors and this would be an interesting area for further research.

Philanthropy, mentioned under the spiritual values of the Japanese, is also a field requiring further research. Whilst the idea of philanthropy is deeply rooted in Japanese society at the moment, this is changing with the emergence of the newly rich generation. There has to be a motivating factor for wealthy people to contribute to the needs of the world and it is important to look at how this could be organized, managed and developed.

Another segment is that of wealthy, highly successful women who are unmarried or without children. Others marry non-Japanese and many become clients of private banks in Europe. If they do indeed form a wealth segment of their own, this would be an interesting area of future research, as their attitudes may also differ significantly from those of the traditional wealthy families.

A further area, which warrants greater investigation, is the question of how to improve access to Japan for Swiss firms. There are already cooperation agreements in place and the issue of double taxation has been addressed but there remains the necessity for greater liberalisation of the financial markets in Japan.

Katsura Suzuki, 1962
Doctor of Business and Administration at the University of South Australia – Title for the Dissertation *'Identifying the differences in perceptions in financial consultants providing advisory services: An exploratory study of European and Japanese advisors to wealthy Japanese and their families'* and Master of Business Administration at the European University – Thesis: *'Private Banking for Japanese financial institutions in Switzerland'*

She has been 16 years in Japan Business Services, at Ernst & Young Switzerland from 1989 to 1997, and then as an independent consultant with her own company, Katsura Suzuki Consulting. She is back to Ernst & Young again from 2006, to make Swiss market known and active for Japanese multinational corporations, based in Zurich and Geneva with a focus on Japanese large corporate clients and HNWIs.

Appendix H: **Questions of the questionnaires**

Q1. Your profession or qualification

Tax specialist, Lawyer, CPA, Private Banker, Banker, Consultant, Business-person, Researcher at a University, Other:

Please put your rating: 4 – high, 3 – medium, 2 – low, 1 – not relevant or 0 – not aware

Q2. To what degree do each of the following characteristics and components (some of the items below are components) of Japanese financial systems cause problems for wealthy Japanese families?

1. Serious long economical recession
2. International Accounting Standards
3. Current market price accounting method
4. Inheritance tax rate
5. Over-complicated, often changing tax law
6. Ambiguity of the law and a lack of written precedent
7. Control of overseas fund transfers
8. Absence of bank secrecy
9. Central Government policy and the politico-economic system
10. Bureaucratic power to change existing arrangements
11. Manipulation of the financial market
12. Risks of the financial sectors such as banking and insurance
13. Motivation of Japanese banks for self-survival rather than service to clients
14. Manipulation of public opinion through media (risk of scandal)
15. Inter-company relationships

16. Others: If you are aware of any other characteristics and components, which you think are relevant, please write a short comment here:
17. Comments: If you would like to make any comments about this question please write them here:

Q3. How important do you rank the following services, which are currently not provided in Japan?

1. Internationally objective financial advice
2. Bank secrecy
3. Independent services which focus on family interests
4. History and know-how of private banking and infrastructure
5. Possibilities for creative international solutions to financial problems
6. Education system and possibility for Family Business
7. Consolidated reporting services of several financial institutions
8. Overseas Emigration or Immigration services
9. International trust and foundation schemes
10. International life insurance schemes
11. International Estate Planning
12. Others: If you are aware of any other services, which should be included, please write a short note here:
13. Comments: If you would like to make any comments about this question please write them here:

Q4. How important do you rank the following advisory services in Switzerland to wealthy Japanese families?

1. Japanese-style service
2. Services provided in Japanese language
3. Japanese legal and tax expertise
4. Understanding of Japanese culture by advisors
5. Personal trust relationships with advisors
6. Advisors having Power of Attorney to deal with banks and third parties

7. Independence of service provider
8. Reachable contact person
9. Multi-disciplinary team of advisors
10. Others: If you are aware of any other services, which should be included, please write a short note here:
11. Comments: If you would like to make any comments about this question please write them here:

Q5. How would you rank the following issues as concerns of your Japanese clients?

1. Scandals (for example, money laundering)
2. Services provided are not in a Japanese style
3. Risk-taking attitude
4. Abiding by the Japanese legal system
5. Control by authorities
6. Rapid changes in laws
7. Others: If you are aware of any other issues, which should be included, please write a short note here:
8. Comments: If you would like to make any comments about this question please write them here:

Q6. For those who already serve, or have an interest in serving, wealthy Japanese families with their expertise, how important are the following Swiss characteristics and components for these families? Characteristics are more cultural in aspect and components are more technical.

1. Political and economic safety of the country
2. Safety and security of the scheme
3. Legal differences between Switzerland and Japan
4. Bank secrecy
5. Confidentiality
6. Developed Swiss Banking system

7. Others: If you are aware of any other characteristics and components, which you think are relevant, please write a short comment here:
8. Comments: If you would like to make any comments about this question please write them here:

Q7. If you have any further comments about any aspect of this questionnaire, please feel free to state them here.

Questions of the interviews

Q1. Your profession or qualification

Tax specialist, Lawyer, CPA, Private Banker, Banker, Consultant, Business-person, Researcher at a University, Other:

Please respond in your capacity as an expert advisor who provides services to wealthy Japanese families.

Q2. What characteristics and components of Japanese systems cause problems for wealthy Japanese families?

Q3. What important advisory services do you think need to be made available, which are currently not provided in Japan?

Q4. What important advisory services do you think need to be made available in Switzerland to wealthy Japanese families?

Q5. What are the critical issues of wealth management for Japanese families?

Q6. What are the Swiss characteristics and components of advisory services that are important to wealthy Japanese families? Characteristics are more cultural in aspect and components are more technical.

Q7. If you have any other comments, please feel free to make them.

Q6. For those who already serve, or have an interest in serving, wealthy Japanese families with their expertise, how important are the following Swiss characteristics and components for these families?

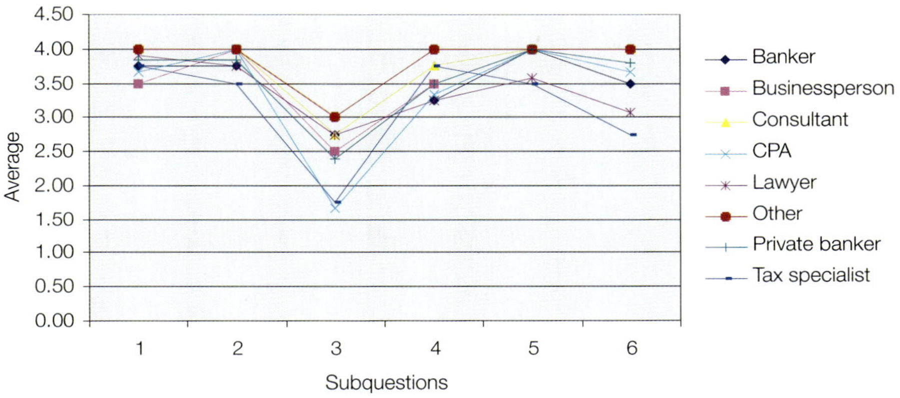

Question 6.	European Responses					
Banker	3.75	3.75	2.75	3.25	4.00	3.50
Businessperson	3.50	4.00	2.50	3.50	4.00	
Consultant	4.00	4.00	2.75	3.75	4.00	4.00
CPA	3.67	4.00	1.67	3.33	4.00	3.67
Lawyer	3.92	3.75	2.75	3.25	3.58	3.08
Other	4.00	4.00	3.00	4.00	4.00	4.00
Private banker	3.83	3.83	2.40	3.50	4.00	3.80
Tax specialist	3.75	3.50	1.75	3.75	3.50	2.75

1. Political and economic safety of the country
2. Safety and security of the scheme
3. Legal differences between Switzerland and Japan
4. Bank secrecy
5. Confidentiality
6. Developed Swiss Banking system

Q3. What important advisory services do you think need to be made available, which are currently not provided in Japan?

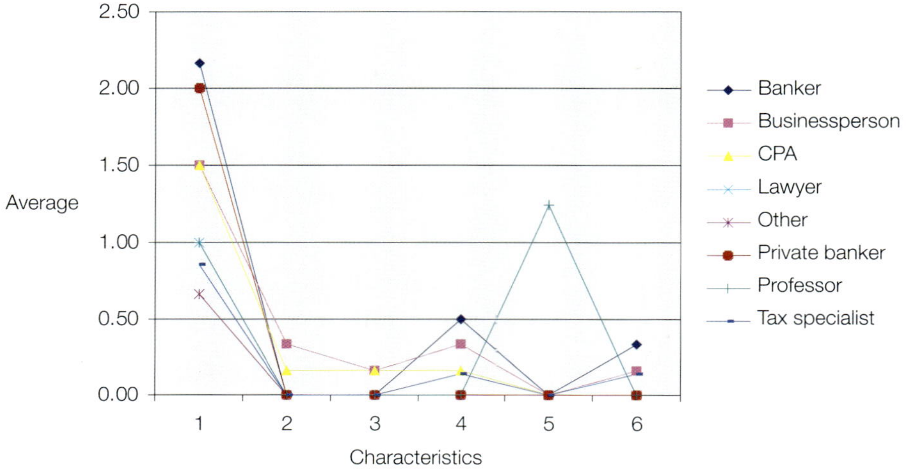

Interview Q3	Japanese respondents					
Banker	2.17	0.00	0.00	0.50	0.00	0.33
Businessperson	1.50	0.33	0.17	0.33	0.00	0.17
CPA	1.50	0.17	0.17	0.17	0.00	0.00
Lawyer	1.00	0.00	0.00	0.00	0.00	0.00
Other	0.67	0.00	0.00	0.00	0.00	0.00
Private banker	2.00	0.00	0.00	0.00	0.00	0.00
Professor	1.00	0.00	0.00	0.00	1.25	0.00
Tax specialist	0.86	0.00	0.00	0.14	0.00	0.14

Characteristics
1 technical aspects 2 independent advice 3 mutual trust between advisors and clients 4 intercultural aspects of the Japanese 5 future generations 6 others

Q4. What important advisory services do you think need to be made available in Switzerland to wealthy Japanese families?

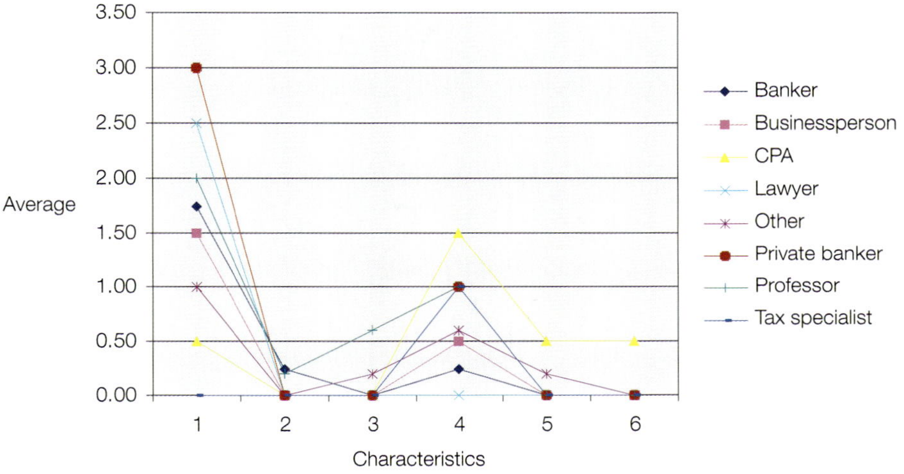

Interview Q4	European respondents					
Banker	1.75	0.25	0.00	0.25	0.00	0.00
Businessperson	1.50	0.00	0.00	0.50	0.00	0.00
Consultant	0.50	0.00	0.00	1.50	0.50	0.50
CPA	2.50	0.00	0.00	0.00	0.00	0.00
Lawyer	1.00	0.00	0.20	0.60	0.20	0.00
Other	3.00	0.00	0.00	1.00	0.00	0.00
Private banker	2.00	0.20	0.60	1.00	0.00	0.00
Tax specialist	0.00	0.00	0.00	1.00	0.00	0.00

Characteristics
1 technical aspects
2 independent advice
3 mutual trust between advisors and clients
4 intercultural aspects of the Japanese
5 future generations
6 others

Q5. What are the critical issues of wealth management for Japanese families?

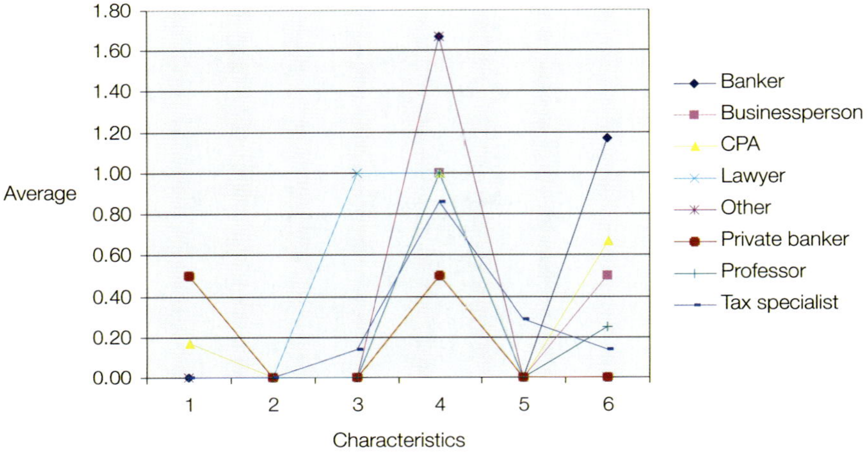

Interview Q5	Japanese respondents					
Banker	0.00	0.00	0.00	1.67	0.00	1.17
Businessperson	0.50	0.00	0.00	1.00	0.00	0.50
CPA	0.17	0.00	0.00	1.00	0.00	0.67
Lawyer	0.00	0.00	1.00	1.00	0.00	0.00
Other	0.00	0.00	0.00	1.67	0.00	0.00
Private banker	0.50	0.00	0.00	0.50	0.00	0.00
Professor	0.00	0.00	0.00	1.00	0.00	0.25
Tax specialist	0.00	0.00	0.14	0.86	0.29	0.14

Characteristics
1 technical aspects
2 independent advice
3 mutual trust between advisors and clients
4 intercultural aspects of the Japanese
5 future generations
6 others

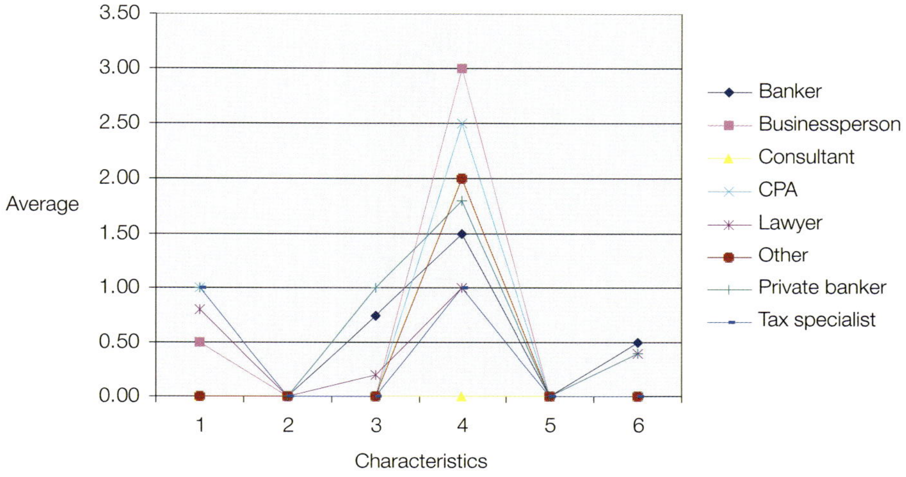

Interview Q5	European respondents					
Banker	0.00	0.00	0.75	1.50	0.00	0.50
Businessperson	0.50	0.00	0.00	3.00	0.00	0.00
Consultant	0.00	0.00	0.00	0.00	0.00	0.00
CPA	1.00	0.00	0.00	2.50	0.00	0.00
Lawyer	0.80	0.00	0.20	1.00	0.00	0.40
Other	0.00	0.00	0.00	2.00	0.00	0.00
Private banker	1.00	0.00	1.00	1.80	0.00	0.40
Tax specialist	1.00	0.00	0.00	1.00	0.00	0.00

Characteristics
1 technical aspects
2 independent advice
3 mutual trust between advisors and clients
4 intercultural aspects of the Japanese
5 future generations
6 others

Reference List

Abe, N., & Takahashi, T. (2001) *The 100% Complete Illustrated Guide to Japanese Systems,* Kodansha International Co. Ltd. Tokyo.

Beer, J. E. (1997) Communicating Across Cultures, Japanese Culture, 19.01.2005 www.culture-at-work.com/highlow.html.

Goffee, R. (1996) *International Journal of Entrepreneurial Behavior & Research, Understanding Family Business: Issues for Further Research* 2, pp. 36–48.

Gomi, F., Takano, T., & Toriumi, Y., (1998) *Nihon Rekishi Kenkyu (Study of Japanese History),* Yamakawa Press.

Hauser, B. R. (2001) *The Journal of Wealth Management, The Family Office: Insight into Their Development in the U.S., a Proposal Prototype, and Advice for Adaptation in Other Countries* Fall 2001, 15–22.

Hofstede, G. (1980a) *Culture's Consequences,* Sage, Beverly Hills, CA.

Hofstede, G. (1980b) *Organizational Dynamics,* Motivation, Leadership and Organization: Do American Theories Apply Abroad? 9, 42–63.

Japan Guide (2005) History of Japan, 06.06.2005 www.japan-guide.com/e/e641.html.

Japan Travel Bureau (1996) *"Salaryman" in Japan,* Nippon Shuppan Hanbai, Tokyo.

Kasuya, M. (2002) *Change in the Relationship among Owners, Managers and Employees around the Meiji Restoration*, 18.01.2005.

Kurashina, T. (2003) *Family Business (Japanese),* Toyo Keizai Shinpoh Sha, Tokyo.

Lehmann, J. P., & Turpin, D. (2002) *Japan missed the first globalization train: will it catch the next?* Perspectives for Managers January 2002.

Ministry of Finance Japan (2003a) *Inheritance and gift taxes – Update*, 18.01.2005 www.mof.go.jp/jouhou/syuzei/syuzei.htm.

Ministry of Finance Japan (2003b) *Inheritance Tax and gift tax have been differently structured* (Japanese), 18.01.2005 www.mof.go.jp/jouhou/syuzei/pan1503-1/contents/02/body.html.

Ministry of Finance Japan (2005) *History of Japanese Foreign Currency Policy,* 31.10.2005 www.mof.go.jp/jouhou/kokkin/kawase.html.

Neubauer, F., & Lank, A. G. (1998) *The Family Business,* Routledge, NY.

OECD (2005) *The OECD Factbook, Economic, Environmental and Social Statistics,* OECD, Paris.

Okazaki, T., & Okuno, M., (1993) *Gendai nihon keizai shisutemu no genryu,* Nihon Keizai Shinbun-sha, Tokyo.

Oshita, E. (2003) *DreamMaker – The Real Face of the New Generation Company Owners,* Softbank Publishing Inc.

REIT 2004 World REIT Market.

Swiss-Japanese Chamber of Commerce (2003) *Swiss-Japanese Chamber of Commerce, Japan-Switzerland Towards Global Partnership in the 21st Century*, p. 6–15.

Tachibanaki, T., & Mori, T. (2005) *Who are the Rich?,* NIHON Keizai Shinbu Sha, Tokyo.

Walker, D., Walker, T. & Schmitz, J. (2003) *Doing Business Internationally, The Guide to Cross-Cultural Success,* McGraw Hill, London.

Werner, R. A. (2003) *Princes of the Yen,* M.E. Sharpe (East Gate) Inc., New York.

Yamane, T. (2005) *Keiei no Taikyoku wo tsukamu Kaiei (Accounting from which we understand overall management),* kobunsha, Tokyo.

Yashiro, N. (1997) *Nihonteki Kanko no keizaigaku (The Economics of Japanese Employment Practices),* Nohn Keizai sha, Tokyo.

Yasuoka, S. (2002) *Families in Business, Japanese Zaibatsu,* 50–54.

Yoneyama, M., and Nathan, R. (1998, 2001) *Frequently Asked Questions on Corporate Japan (Japanese),* Kodan sha, Tokyo.

Yoshida, S. (2000) *Management Japan, Can the West Understand the East? And Vice Versa?* – Issues of Cross-cultural Communication Vol. 33, 2, 5, 6, 8–11.

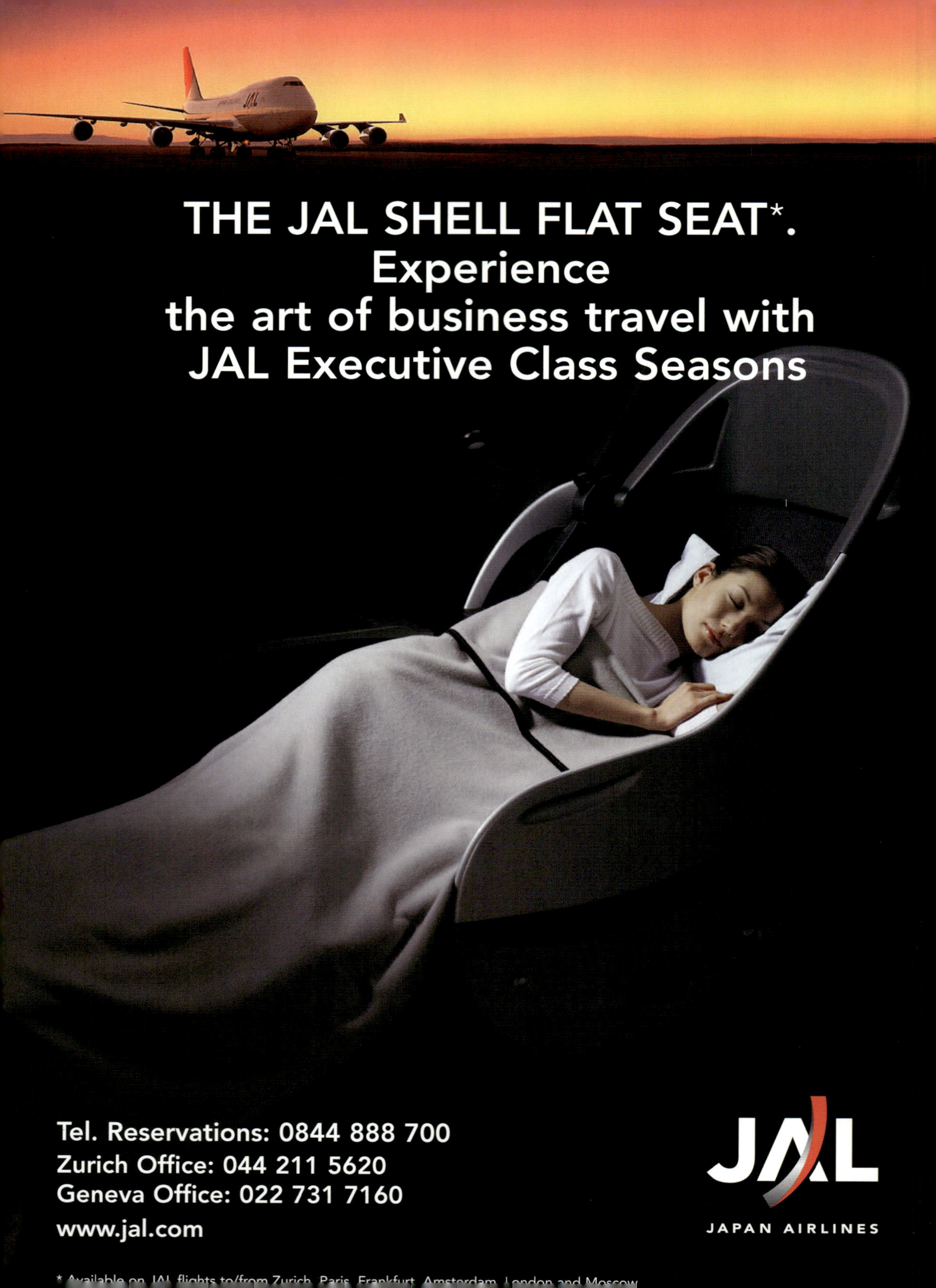

THE JAL SHELL FLAT SEAT*.
Experience
the art of business travel with
JAL Executive Class Seasons
Tel. Reservations: 0844 888 700
Zurich Office: 044 211 5620
Geneva Office: 022 731 7160
www.jal.com
JAL
JAPAN AIRLINES
* Available on JAL flights to/from Zurich, Paris, Frankfurt, Amsterdam, London and Moscow

SWISS PRESENCE AT THE EXPO 2005 AICHI, JAPAN
By Philippe Neeser

World Exhibition

The concept of World Exhibitions has changed over time, ever since the first one opened its doors in London in 1851. They have continued to play a role until today, even though nowadays, in our contemporary world of Internet and widely spread means of mass communication, some people have begun to challenge the very need for a World Exhibition.

A World Exhibition is a global marketplace. Countries join to sell ideas, images and products. They join to network. Expo 2005 Aichi was no different in that it was both a forum of ideas and a bazaar for merchandise. At the same time, it had to be entertaining, attractive, and playful – an ongoing celebration, a festival in the best Japanese "matsuri"-tradition.

I took an active part in the Swiss presence at the Expo 2005 in Aichi, and I can definitely say that this was a great opportunity for visitors to encounter both the world as a whole, and specifically to allow Japan and the world to rediscover Switzerland. At the same time, it offered me personally a unique way to discover some aspects of my own country, Switzerland, which I didn't know, and to find new aspects of my host country, Japan, yet unknown to me even after my 33-year stay.

In the run-up to the Expo, there was a debate in Switzerland, with some citizens wondering why Switzerland had to join this time again. To those, who, like me, have spent their entire professional careers abroad, it seems obvious that our country depends much more on the world than the world depends on us. This means that Switzerland, as a small nation, constantly needs to make itself known to and understood by the world community. What is also certain is that the Japanese people and most of the other participating countries would not have understood Switzerland's absence at Aichi.

Unlike previous World Exhibitions, Aichi was particular in the sense that Japan offered modular pavilions to the participating countries, allowing them to decorate them as they wished. Therefore Expo 2005 Aichi had less space for fancy architecture, these possibilities being left to the corporate pavilions.

"Nature's Wisdom" was chosen as the theme of Expo 2005 as an attempt to address the growing concerns of humanity and of most governments about our environment, offering all participants an opportunity to reflect. Switzerland took the key elements of its pavilion from its long relationship with nature.

Swiss Presence

While addressing the general theme of "Nature's Wisdom", Presence Switzerland, the organization responsible for the Swiss Pavilion, also specifically aimed to renew and to rejuvenate the traditional image of Switzerland in Japan in particular, and in Asia in general. The Swiss Pavilion was to demonstrate that our country is not only mountains, Heidi, cows, cheese, watches, permanent neutrality and chocolate, for which Switzerland is famous in Japan. The Mountain was there to show that Switzerland was that too, but, at the same time, much more, and that the country was indeed very much in movement.

Since I had not been involved in the concept phase of the project, I, like any other visitor, discovered the "Mountain" and its content as the Expo began.

The actual Mountain itself was a fascinating piece of art. The more I saw of it, the more I liked it, and the better I found it fitting the purpose of the Swiss presence in Aichi. I liked its shape, its flora and its sounds. After eating a raclette at the "Alpenrose" restaurant with a glass of Aigle "Les Murailles" white wine, most of my senses were satisfied, but for my nose, which missed the smells and perfumes of the Alps, of its flowers, of the hay being dried on its slopes, and the flavour of the omnipresent cow dung. But I may have been asking for too much.

Holding the iconic military pocket lamp and riding into the Mountain to the sound of a mountain train to discover the 140-odd items of "Swiss Myths", "Vision", "Risk and Caution", "Top of Science" was an experience worth repeating, as you discovered new aspects with every visit. The interactive aspect of our voice guide pocket lamp proved extremely popular with all generations.

When I entered the Mountain, on the right-hand side, Hans Erni's big Landi (Swiss national exhibition of 1939) painting was the first to strike my heart. It reminded me of my grandfather René telling his grandchildren stories of the great Dixence and Chamoson dams, for which his company was supplying the Pelton-type turbines.

With the number and diversity of the items exhibited, I believe, almost every visitor found at least one item to which he or she could strongly relate.

These exhibits told the visitors about Switzerland's diversity, its capacity to accept and integrate outsiders, becoming richer by their contact. They spoke about Switzerland's narrow territory, urging courageous boys and girls of all generations – people like Ella Maillart, Auguste, Jacques and Bertrand Piccard – to seek space, challenge and adventure outside her borders. They further demonstrated the eagerness of our people to face problems and seek answers to the challenges of nature with the help of nature's wisdom.

Human touch

One of the main reasons for the popularity of the Swiss Pavilion at the Expo 2005 Aichi was certainly the quality of our guides. Our guides had been recruited mainly in Switzerland among students of Japanese. Most of them therefore had mastered the Japanese language to some extent, along with English and at least one of our national languages. Some of our guides were from Swiss-Japanese families. Some were Japanese-born but raised in Switzerland, speaking our dialects like native Swiss. These young men and women performed their role as hosts and hostesses of the Mountain with enthusiasm, amazing resilience and an ever-smiling charm, posing for pictures with visitors, giving autographs, and answering questions. The shifts were long. The weather was freezing cold at the beginning, swelteringly hot later on. The commuting conditions were far from easy and at times exhausting, but nevertheless good humour prevailed all the time. The same can be said of the staff of the Alpenrose Restaurant, whose popularity was demonstrated every day by the long queue, or of the "Best of Switzerland" pavilion shop. The professionalism, modesty and kindness of our staff have proved once again to be solid Swiss values.

The Imperial visit

As I had the unique privilege to guide Their Imperial Majesties the Emperor and Empress of Japan through the "Mountain" on July 11, I can bear witness to the deep interest Their Majesties manifested, through the many questions They were asking. I felt that They would probably have preferred to stay longer, if only They had been given such opportunity. The restoration of Hans Erni's Landi paintings using Japanese "funori" techniques, further developed in Switzerland, attracted Their attention. Looking at the portrait of Johann Kaspar Horner, the first Swiss ever to reach Japan in 1804, as member of a Russian expedition, They recalled receiving a reproduction of one of Horner's paintings of a Japanese landscape in the fall of 2004 from Federal President Joseph Deiss. Despite tight time constraints, the research of Prof. Schwab's team in Zurich on the successful regeneration of central nervous tissues in rats and its potential and revolutionary implications for the treatment of traumatic lesions of the spine in humans seemed to fascinate Them, inviting a number of further questions.

When entering the last bubble "Monte-Rosa-Hütte", Their Majesties could see the screen providing live pictures transmitted from the Monte-Rosa-Hütte via internet. Unfortunately, given the seven hours time difference, it was still pitch dark in the Alps, when I guided Their Majesties, and They had to believe me when I explained that the previous day, weather had been fine in Switzerland. I also explained that with the help of our sponsor Sika AG, the refuge had undergone a complete restoration in full respect of environmental requirements.

Their Majesties also seemed delighted at the view from the terrace, and, true to Their reputation as lovers of nature, asked questions about the flowers and plants, so naturally gracing the man-made slopes of our Mountain, while listening to the distant echoes of yodelling, cow bells, the chirping of alpine birds or the discrete murmur of a mountain stream.

The Swiss pavilion was certainly most grateful and proud to count Their Majesties among the more than one million people that visited its Mountain.

Swiss Day and other events

The Swiss Day, on April 15, was honoured by the presence of Federal President Samuel Schmid, his wife and a strong delegation from Switzerland, including some members of the Federal Parliament. The Swiss Army Band, or at least a selection of its best members, provided the musical entertainment, together with the Group "Stimmhorn" and a school band from Shinshiro City, our Aichi Prefecture friendship partner town. Led by Mayor Yamamoto, some 500 citizens had come from Shinshiro City to support our event. The following day, the Swiss delegation paid a courtesy visit to Shinshiro City in eastern Mikawa, where they enjoyed a hearty welcome, contributing to further the friendship between Japan and Switzerland.

On August 1, the Swiss Pavilion was also the gathering place of some 200 Swiss residents from all over Japan and their friends for a unique joint celebration of our national foundation day, the musical entertainment being provided by an alphorn group from St. Moritz.

Throughout the duration of the Expo, the globalisation effect was demonstrated by various performances of music, alphorn and yodel by outstanding Japanese artists, being highly recognised in Switzerland.

Conclusion

Japan and Switzerland had just celebrated the 140th jubilee of the first Treaty of Amity and Trade in 2004. It had been the opportunity for the two countries to reassess the quality of their bilateral relationship. The steady popularity of the Swiss Pavilion at Expo 2005 Aichi confirmed the fact that a great number of Japanese citizens are attracted to, know and like Switzerland. I also felt that many of them might be even more attached to the traditional image of Switzerland than some of the Swiss people themselves.

The Swiss Pavilion, however, also gave our visitors the possibility to expand their perception of our country and to discover a dynamic Switzerland, some aspects of which they had not heard of before. When asked, the majority of our visitors declared their eagerness to visit our country. This alone was worth the trust and budget granted by the Swiss Federal Parliament to Presence Switzerland for this purpose.

In compliance with the theme “Nature’s Wisdom”, the organisers fulfilled their pledge and today, almost half a year after closing the Expo 2005 Aichi, all the buildings that were built for the Expo have been dismantled, and – with the exception of the remarkable Japanese Garden and the Tea House – the site of the Expo has returned to its original condition and purpose as a public park.

Philippe Neeser, 1947, from Geneva, graduated 1972 from Geneva University with a Master’s degree in law. 1973 on a Japanese Government scholarship in Japan. Since 1975 for Ciba-Geigy in Japan, Board member since 1994. Master of Tea, lives in Kyoto.

JAPAN'S ECONOMY RETURNING TO NORMALITY

By Thomas Fuster,
correspondent of the Neue Zürcher Zeitung

Thanks to strengthening private domestic consumption, reduced capacities and a reformed banking sector, Japan is currently enjoying robust growth. Policies implemented during the crisis can now be discarded, namely the extraordinary loose monetary policy.

Japan's economy is transforming itself from chronically sick patient into a standard bearer of hope: the Nikkei gained 40% during the last year, the strongest increase since 1986. Foreign investors returned in droves to Tokyo buying Japanese stock in order to strengthen their portfolios. For months in a row, Japan's domestic economy is enjoying a healthy growth.

The last quarter of 2005 showed an impressive growth of 5.4% on an annual base. This was nearly five times as much as the USA achieved in the same period. After a long period of absence, Japan is resuming its role as a growth engine for the world economy. If this is to continue during 2007, Japan is enjoying its longest recovery after the war.

Recovery 'Made in Japan'

Until very recently no observer of Japan's economy would have dared to think of such a comeback. The main reason for optimism lies in the fact, that domestic factors play a key role in the current upturn. This time it's not government money in the form of stimulus packages so popular during the nineties that is fuelling growth. Now Japanese enterprises are the driving force investing heavily in order to strengthen their competitiveness. Japan's consumers have overcome their reluctance to spend as well. Their mood is upbeat thanks to a stronger labor market. Nippon's companies are hiring again and salaries (including bonuses) are slightly increasing for the first time after five years.

These positive changes are not casual. They came as a result of structural reforms which strengthened Japan's economy considerably. Practically gone are the "three excesses", burdening the country in the past: an excess of company debt, overcapacity and staff. In 1996, interest payments on company debt achieved a level of 125% of GDP, nowadays this percentage is down to 80%. The financial situation of the companies is now as solid as in the early seventies. This allows the companies to put their cash flow to more productive use than paying back debt, they are now able to realize strategic investments for the future.

Overcapacity in manufacturing has come down as well. The numbers are as low as in the late eighties immediately before the bursting of the bubble. New production lines are increasingly built, mainly in Japan. The outsourcing euphoria towards China has considerably eased and is giving way to a more sober view. Problems with legal practice and intellectual property rights in China as well as with infrastructure, suppliers and local staff have led many companies to rediscover the qualities of the domestic business environment. This in turn has helped to reduce the third excess: labor. Now the situation is reversed with some companies already complaining of a shortage of labor.

Healthy banking sector
One can confidently say, equally gone is the banking crisis. The financial institutions are still operating with razor thin margins due to the zero-interest policy of the Bank of Japan and competition from the powerful postal savings bank (in the long term to be privatised after a lengthy political battle). However, the balance sheets of the major banks show a reduction of the number of nonperforming loans down to a manageable level. As a result of the liquidation of cross-share holdings, resistance towards the ups and downs of a volatile stock market has been improved. Their capital base has been strengthened by a reduction of insecure positions like Deferred Tax Assets (DTA) and by paying back government loans taken out during the crisis in the nineties.

The year 2007 is to mark Japan's return to normality. This holds true for the money policy as well. The policy of quantitative easing as an "emergency measure" whereby the banking sector had been amply supplied with liquidity while upholding a zero-interest policy, has come to an end in March. A successive tightening of the monetary policy will follow, as rising consumer prices continue to ease deflationary pressure. This change of direction, however, will most likely be accompanied by political stirrings; given the record high public debt of 150% of

GDP the government's interest lays with the continuation of loose monetary supply and zero-interest policy. The danger of a political destabilisation remains low, however. As convenient as a policy of free money might seem to some politicians, the government is aware that such a policy can not be upheld indefinitely.

Older people as an economic opportunity

It is obvious, that export-oriented countries like Switzerland can profit from an increasing domestic demand in the second-largest economy in the world. Switzerland is among the few nations running a trade surplus with Japan, its most important trading partner in Asia. Japan's ongoing policy of deregulation is creating new opportunities as well. Japan's market for pharmaceuticals is an example in case; this market is of special importance for Switzerland constituting a third of its exports to Japan. Access to the pharmaceutical market has traditionally been blocked by complicated bureaucratic procedures. In the past few years these regulations have gradually been eased. Another factor are the ambitious goals set by the government of Mr. Koizumi with regard to Foreign Direct Investments, although these are still far from being realized. Swiss companies eager to profit from a newly invigorated Japan are well advised to pay attention to the country's demographic structure. The share of people over 65 years constitutes alredy 20% of the whole population and in the future this segment will increasingly influence economic decision making. With considerable savings at their disposal Nippon's grey-haired generation is well equipped to spend for a comfortable and pleasant life in retirement. In 2007 the "baby boomer" generation, born between 1947 and 1949, starts to retire owning about 10 percent of national wealth. Little wonder, that this wealthy generation has come to the attention of Japan's marketers. For savvy entrepreneurs the ageing of the population is not a threat. Those who know how to cater to the needs of this "Silver Market" will find ample and rewarding opportunities.

Thomas Fuster, born 1967 in Appenzell, graduated from St. Gallen University with a PhD in economics. 1998 redactor at the "Neue Zürcher Zeitung"; Tokyo correspondent since 2001.

THE JAPANESE CORPORATE ENVIRONMENT ADAPTS ITSELF TO NEW REALITIES

By Charles Ochsner

Today, the Japanese economy is strong again, as planned.

Three years ago, many foreigners were skeptical about the revitalizing methods adopted. The vigorous critics repeated by the foreign financial press influenced many in their opinions about the chances to see Japan come out of recession. When faced with such pressure, Japanese officials were often on the defensive, showing only limited interest in recommendations received from abroad. Today, Japan is still led by the same politicians, bureaucrats and scholars who three years ago were being accused of not understanding globalization and market economy.

This situation is comparable with the respectful but distant attitude adopted by the Japanese legal professions towards the foreign law firms establishing themselves in the country, and willing to bring with them ways to practice law not suited to prevailing social rules and local practices.

Bad Loan Issue Solved

Resolution of the bad loans took 15 years but did not generate social crisis. Tokyo never looked like the capital of a country in recession. This was mainly due to typical Japanese values like endurance and social cohesion, but also for the unique distribution of wealth with an immense well-built middle class. Today, as a result, Japan is enjoying limited unemployment and an economy that not only has accomplished a turnaround but also the leap out of deflation.

Furthermore, the Bank of Japan has recently decided to terminate the quantitative easing policy, which had been maintained during the five years since March 2001. In other words, we will see a raise in interest rates in the near future.

New Breed of Young Investors

One of the basic principles that allowed Japan to remain such a strong economic power is the sense of priority adopted in the way to manage a business. The customers come first, then the employees, then the tax office, and, finally, the shareholders. This is pure common sense when one thinks and sees in the long term.

The modern societies of the instantaneous, emphasizing immediate return are, however, also influencing Japan today.

As a result of its regained economical prosperity, we are witnessing in Japan a young generation of investors, quite active in new technologies and services. Some are challenging the traditional order of priorities. Some are even cheating in their pursuit of gains ... and make the headlines in the media.

Change in Corporate Law

This renewed economical growth will also be supported by a change in the Japanese Corporate Law, one more indication that Japan adapts its legal environment to its constant evolution.

Japanese law on corporations was until recently based principally on the Japanese Commercial Code. However, this part of the Code and related pieces of legislation were radically revised and are reorganized into the new Corporate Law, which will enter in force around May 2006. The Yugen Kaisha (limited liability company, or GmbH, S. à r. l.) will be abolished and absorbed into the Kabushiki Kaisha (joint-stock corporation).

The new law will simplify the maintenance of subsidiaries of foreign companies in good corporate standing. For instance, the minimum capital requirement will be abolished, as well as the minimum number of three directors.

The law should also allow more flexibility for mergers and acquisitions.

Tax Reforms

Tax reforms are regularly set in place by the Ministry of Finance that takes measures in areas including corporate taxation, taxation of land and housing, international taxation, liquor tax and tobacco tax.

The challenge is to initiate for the years to come a smooth transfer of private wealth into public funds to contribute to a sustainable strength of the economy and society.

Here again, the powerful links existing between bureaucrats and the private sector will certainly allow finding successful solutions.

Charles Ochsner, Attorney-at-Law and Tokyo Resident Partner of Python Schifferli Peter.

Establishing Japanese business
in the heart of Europe.
A quality of Ernst & Young.

STARTING A BUSINESS IN JAPAN

A 33-year old Swiss with JPY 3 million capital on a risky adventure

By Martin Stricker

"How many employees do you have?" is one of the most frequent questions I encountered during my numerous sales calls in the first year of business. Some companies are more discreet than others and ask only towards the end of the meeting, while others go straight to the point and pop this question even before the customary small talk has come to an end. In any case, this question is on everybody's mind when dealing with start-up companies like the one I founded in 2004. Size does matter, at least in Japan. No matter how good the business idea may be; no matter how good my presentation during the customer visit is, Japanese companies still find great assurance or cause of concern in the size of their business partner. My business card is scrutinized from the same perspective.

Gaipro

マーティン・ストリッカー
Martin STRICKER
代表取締役

Gaipro有限会社
〒140-0015 東京都品川区西大井1-1-2
Ｊタワー 206室
Tel: 03-3777-2717
Fax: 03-3779-6992
E-mail: martin.stricker@gaipro.com
URL: www.gaipro.com

Most likely the following thoughts will be running through my customer's head:

- *"This company is not a K.K. (Joint stock corp.) but a Y.K. (LLC). He probably did not have enough money ..." (Note: Capital requirements are lower for Y.K.)*
- *"The phone number and fax number is different. At least the company can afford two lines ..."*
- *"Judging from the address it does not look like a home office. Ok."*
- *"He is a president. If the president is going on sales calls, that means the company must still be small."*
- *"They have their own home page and domain name. Good."*

Cold Calls and Customer Visits

As you can imagine, it is an uphill battle for start-up companies in Japan if the company's acceptance and success depends on its size. What is more, the above mentioned comments only outline what happens on a customer call IF a meeting could be set up. And that is a big capitalized IF because securing appointments with potential customers in Japan is no easy task. Let me illustrate this with the following table. The data presented is purely based on Gaipro's in-house experience and in no way does it pretend to be scientifically accurate.

Success ratio of securing meetings in the case of Gaipro, Inc.

Method	Cold calls	"Skilled" cold calls	Third-party introduction
Success ratio	1% or less	5%	100%

No matter how polite Japanese people are known to be, companies and individuals clearly draw the line when a (yet) unknown company like Gaipro requests a meeting. On the other hand, if I can find one single person who introduces me to my potential customer, the meeting is normally secured in a matter of days if not hours, no matter how big the potential client may be. Therefore, I made use of all my connections, both business and private, to secure meetings. Needless to say, even that has its (numerical) limitations, so Gaipro also has to make use of cold calls. But instead of wasting my limited time with odds of 100:1, I soon learned that the odds could be increased somewhat by applying minor modifications to my cold-call strategy.

Firstly, I would start by mentioning that I had previously worked for four years at T. Corporation, a Japanese chemical company (which happens to be listed on the 1st section of the Tokyo Stock Exchange). Hearing a big-company name is reassuring for the potential client and in turn secures me at least 30 seconds of conversation time. Secondly, instead of requesting for a meeting up front, I would ask in the politest possible form if sending a company brochure would not be creating too much trouble. My Japanese counterparts would have no trouble refusing meetings, but accepting a brochure seems harmless and thus most of the time they would give in to my request. Thirdly, when I place a follow-up call a few days later, no matter how busy or uninterested the potential client would be, he/she would at least acknowledge the receipt of the brochure. And more importantly, I would have become less unknown by then, which would increase my chances of securing some meeting time in the future.

Banks

"This is the list of documents you need to prepare if your company wants to open a bank account with us", the lady of the major Japanese M. bank said in the politest possible form. Secretly she had hoped that I would pack my things and leave. After all here was this young foreigner, who came without any referral asking to set up a corporate account. You see, even Japanese banks operate based on the concept of personal introductions. Companies cannot just ask to open an account. They need to be introduced by someone. I did not follow this custom and thus the lady sensed trouble. Unfortunately for her, I had done my homework and knew exactly which documents I needed to submit. She was obviously taken aback when I took out the folder with all the completed documents. As the next line of defence, she called in the deputy head of the branch to take care of my irregular case. After understanding my request, the deputy head emphasized that this was an "application" process, which means that the bank has no obligation to accept it. But then I got lucky. While screening my documents, he realized that I had worked for T. Corporation in the past, which happens to be a major corporate client of M. bank. Suddenly, the deputy chief changed his tone of voice and added that my application would most probably be accepted in a matter of a few days. And so it happened. Although I had come without referral, the corporate standing and size of my former employer had again saved my day.

Office Facilities

Fortunately, Japan had started to embrace start-up companies with great enthusiasm in the last few years, after coming to realise what effect they have had on the US economy. For example, in terms of office space, many districts in Tokyo had begun to set up offices specifically designed for venture companies. Some of them are even offered for free, although they have an endless waiting list. Gaipro was fortunate enough to be selected to enter a new facility run by Shinagawa ward. To attract future investment into its district, Shinagawa ward had set up a brand-new facility located just 1 minute away from the closest railway station, offering modern office space for 10 start-up companies. For under CHF 400 a month, companies are provided with office space sufficient for two people, as well as shared infrastructure such as meeting rooms and copy machines. The maximum rental period is three years. After this period of "incubation", the start-ups are expected to move out and get their own office so that other new promising ventures can take their place.

The Shinagawa Municipal Government cleverly distinguishes between "venture charity" and "venture support". It does not just want to provide cheap office space, since that would be abused quickly. Instead, it would like to support ventures only during the difficult start-up phase, and only after they have undergone a careful screening and assessment process.

With much anticipation, I attended my first inter-company meeting at the facility. I was looking forward to meeting my fellow entrepreneurs and was expecting to meet young individuals like myself who were pursuing their dreams and visions with fire in their pants. Looking around the meeting room, however, I soon realised that I was by far the youngest. The next senior was probably in his early forties. This to a certain extent is characteristic for Japanese start-ups. They are run and managed by people who have already had at least one extensive career in the past. For some of the entrepreneurs, running their own company was more a matter of necessity rather than a personal choice. Nevertheless, over the course of the next year, I would discover that irrespective of age, many of them were indeed driven by passion and very much young at heart.

Future Outlook

Just half a year ago, a company at the Shinagawa venture facility decided to move out and liquidate as it had run into financial difficulties. No matter how enthusiastic Japan had become in embracing start-up companies, the day-to-day reality of the market is still a tough one to survive in. Gaipro has had its share of luck and good fortune in coming this far. If anything, it is thanks to the extensive support of both personal and business contacts. It is no exaggeration to say that to a great extent, survival and success in Japan for start-up companies depends on personal network. And even then, just like in Switzerland or in the US, it remains a risky adventure!

Martin Stricker was born in 1973. After graduating from the University of St. Gallen, he attended Sophia University in Tokyo. He entered a Japanese chemical company at its headquarters in 2000, supporting the corporation in its overseas operations. In 2004, he established Gaipro, Inc., a company dedicated to Human Resources Consulting and Recruiting. He is married to a Canadian of Chinese ancestry and lives in Tokyo.

THE SCHOLARSHIP FUND OF THE SWISS-JAPANESE CHAMBER OF COMMERCE – BUILDING BRIDGES TO JAPAN

By Paul Dudler, Chairman

Understanding Japan, its culture, language and way of doing business is key to succeed in this large and sophisticated market. A truism? Yes, of course, but often ignored by new foreign business entrants who shy away from investing in time-consuming and costly efforts to acquire the necessary knowledge and expertise. Even worse, sometimes they sidestep this important success factor out of a misguided belief, that their time-honoured Western ways of doing business might work just as well with Japanese partners and customers.

"When in Japan, do it the Japanese way" is the SJCC credo reflecting years of experience of many members as residents and businessmen there. Consequently, the SJCC Scholarship Fund has set itself the goal of promoting knowledge of Japan beyond the common stereotypes. We hope to achieve this with an educational program focussing on encouraging and supporting young, well-educated residents of Switzerland in their efforts to acquire a thorough knowledge about Japan, its culture, language, social, political and business environments. Our concept is largely but not exclusively oriented towards the needs of business. It requires from scholarship recipients a commitment to study Japanese intensively and to acquire practical work experience during internships with a company in Japan for at least a whole year. The opportunity of this unique learning experience is well received by Swiss educational institutions and students. During the last 5 years we counted more than 50 serious applications per year on average.

Thus, our Chamber hopes to develop a growing pool of professionals who can build bridges between our two cultures. Their language proficiency and work experience will facilitate access to Japan's business world. Their practical Japan experience and familiarity with Japanese work practices will serve their Swiss employers as well. Likewise, their ability to ensure good communication between partners will remove many barriers and build credibility and trust. In a broad sense, therefore, our scholarship program is expected to make a lasting contribution to the Swiss economy and to the further development of bilateral trade relations between Switzerland and Japan.

Since the establishment of our Scholarship Fund at the end of 1988, approximately 150 male and female scholarship recipients have benefited from our career development program – 15 to 20 p.a. since 2002 when increased funds became available. The Swiss-Japanese Chamber wishes to express its gratitude and deep respect to its far-sighted sponsors, Stiftung Mercator Schweiz and its Chairman, for their continuous and generous donations without which our Scholarship Fund could not operate.

In addition to financial support, our Fund also provides practical assistance to scholarship recipients ranging from advice on living conditions and household budgets to finding the appropriate schools and – much more difficult – suitable internships. The intensity of this nonfinancial support and guidance depends on the individual needs of each scholarship applicant. It forms an integral part of the total activities of the SJCC Fund with the objective to help candidates optimize their learning experience and to apply their gained competence successfully in their subsequent careers.

A Typical Profile of a Scholarship Recipient

- Female or male graduate from university or qualified professional with apprenticeship
- Age less than 35 years, resident of Switzerland
- Has already acquired good basic knowledge of spoken and written Japanese
- Highly motivated and committed to a "Japan Year" consisting of intensive language training and internship in a Japanese or international company
- Well-balanced and positive personality with clear goals
- Displays an entrepreneurial spirit and risk tolerance.

In close to 100 personal interviews with scholarship candidates/recipients which I conducted since 2001 I have come to the conclusion, most of them showed a healthy spirit of adventure and a fascination for Japan; furthermore they were driven by a strong determination to succeed in a "new and unfamiliar environment". These are traits contradicting the stereotype of "the pampered young generation". One of the grantees put it this way: "A dream stays a dream until you take the first step to turn it into reality …!"

Equally strong is the desire to acquire professional experience, to broaden their mindset with a more global perspective as well as to test own strengths such as the ability to apply their academic know-how on the job. Not to forget, a willingness to adapt to and familiarize themselves with the cultural, social and economic environment of the host country without loosing their own identity. In short: building the first important stepping-stone towards a successful international career.

The subsequent excerpts from some reports of scholarship recipients provide the reader with a snapshot of their daily life and experiences (for selected full reports visit our website www.sjcc.ch, click "Scholarship Fund – Reports"):

"Novartis Tsukuba Research Institute" – Photo by Roger Getzmann.

On life in Japan: "… Most people work until 10 p.m. and then either go drinking with colleagues at work or spend time at home. I usually spend my evenings by playing sports at the local gym, chatting, cooking in the dormitory and studying Japanese. Life is sometimes difficult in this foreign culture and even frustrating but, at the end of the day, it is more personally rewarding than anything I have experienced before …" (Stephan Schmidlin at Fujitsu).

A rich personal experience: "… My stay in Japan is proving to be an exceptional and rich personal experience. A significant number of views I had about Japan before coming have certainly changed, which I see as a result of a better understanding of Japanese people and their culture. I also developed technical competence and could gain insight into Japanese standards and procedures ..." (Guillermo Fernandez Castellanos at Toshiba).

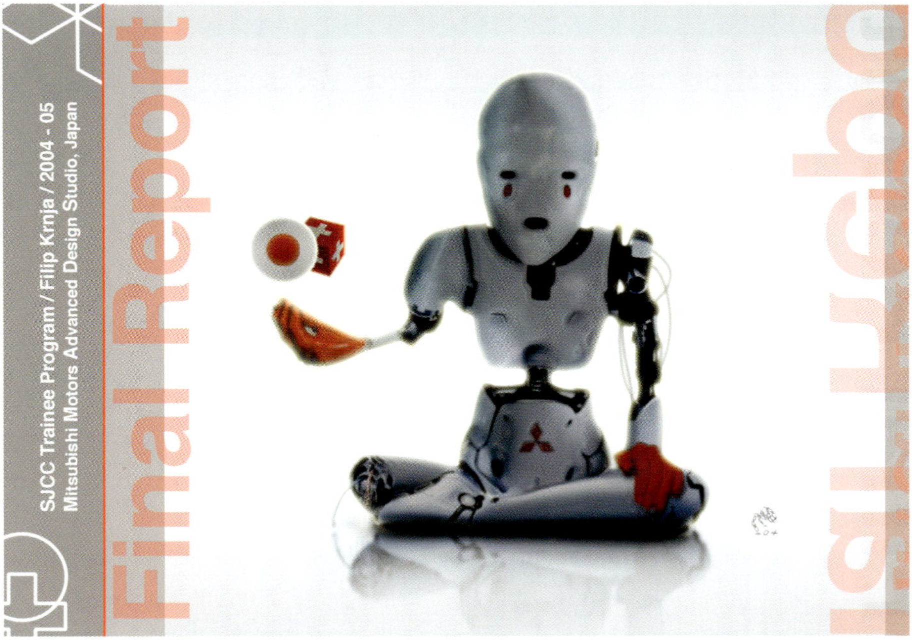

"Attracted by Japan's Robot Technology" – Report Cover by Filip Krnja.

On cultural differences: "… Remain yourself and think objectively. Japanese will accept culture differences without any problem as long as you respect them! ..." (Blaise Fracheboud at Koyo Seiko).

Performance Appraisal: "... Filip Krnja was the first trainee ever at Mitsubishi Motors design studios and I hold him in highest esteem both personally and professionally. He adapted quickly to the Japanese environment. Despite the immense challenges of joining a uniformly Japanese team, Filip integrated himself extraordinarily well. During his time at Mitsubishi, Filip was involved in the design of currently developed series cars as well as in deriving new concepts for future series- and show cars. He was perfectly able to communicate his envisioned concept ..." (Noboru M., direct supervisor of scholarship recipient Filip Krnja, whose model car has won the international competition of Mitsubishi's design studios and will be put on the market in 2007! Filip has meanwhile joined Daimler-Chrysler Design Studios in Yokohama and is currently on a sabbatical leave studying at the Royal College of Art in London).

Intra- and interpersonal skills, the key factor in Japan: "... In summary, in Japan, probably more than in any other foreign country, you have to pay special attention to your interpersonal skills. Some people speak about EQ, our emotional quotient or how we manage our emotions and the way we relate to others. Our EQ is the ability to establish and deepen connections at three levels: with ourselves, with another person (one-to-one), and within groups/teams. The Japanese experience is a question of whether you can endure frustration or not. The language is so difficult to learn and to use (leading to misunderstandings), and the culture and way of life is so different from ours that you will inevitably be confronted with conflicts and frustration. At this point your intra- and interpersonal skills come into play. They must be developed well enough in order to manage the huge emotional flow you will be confronted with. ..." (Vincent Sennhauser at Hilti Japan).

The Alumni Association – Building Social and Business Networks

- Assisting newly arrived SJCC scholarship recipients in Japan
- Platform of former scholarship recipients for sharing experiences and further developing knowledge of Japan
- Contributing to SJCC activities and benefiting from its network
- Promoting friendship and kinship among members through organizing events in both countries

Contact in Switzerland: Alex Renggli, President (alexrenggli@hispeed.ch)

Contacts in Japan: Dr. Felix Moesner (felix.moesner@eda.admin.ch)
Mike Zingg (mpzingg@yahoo.co.jp)

"The Founding Members" – Photo by Mike Zingg.

The Alumni Association has been founded in 2002. Its President is elected to the SJCC Board and all members are also automatically registered in the Membership List of our Chamber. We thus hope that our common bond Japan will become a source of inspiration and knowledge from which the Chamber can draw.

In Japan – thanks to the initiative of 2 alumni in Japan: Mike Zingg (former chairman of Hilti Japan) and Dr. Felix Moesner (Science Attaché at the Swiss Embassy) – a branch was established in Tokyo in December 2003. An impressive inaugural event provided motivation and ideas for planning future activities. It was made possible by the generosity of the Swiss Ambassador, Dr. Jacques Reverdin, who invited alumni and current scholarship recipients in Japan for dinner at his residence. I would like to express our warmest thanks to Ambassador Reverdin and his team for their support and continuous encouragement.

Educational, cultural and social events are being organized as part of the alumni program to help the newly arrived. Examples are cherry blossom viewing and barbecue parties, visits to Toyota Research Laboratories and Nestlé Japan in Kobe as well as a forum for exchange of experiences and self-help ideas.

In addition, the Swiss Chamber of Commerce & Industry (SCCIJ) in Tokyo is extending a standing invitation to our grantees to participate in their monthly luncheon events with prominent speakers that offer good networking opportunities. And last but not least, the SCCIJ Board members are most helpful in providing internships. The President and Board of the SCCIJ deserve our highest appreciation for this most welcome and valuable cooperation.

Conclusion and Summary

- The economic presence of our country in Japan is already significant – an estimated CHF 20 billion in local sales by Swiss companies (close to 3 times our exports to this biggest Asian market!) with yet a considerably higher potential for our innovative and strategically orientated companies

- Companies seeking to strengthen their Japan knowledge and/or engagement can take advantage of the growing pool of young and talented professionals with solid Japan experience
- SJCC considers its Scholarship Program as one of the pillars of its activities because it can provide tangible benefits to its members and the business community at large
- Interested in the Scholarship Fund? For more information contact its Chairman, Paul Dudler (pdudler@intergga.ch)

Appendix 1

250

Honorary Chairman
H. Exc. Ambassador Nobuyasu Abe

Honorary President
Bosshard Rudolf

Former Presidents

Bosshard Rudolf	1986–2000
Jaccoud René L.	2000–2005

President

Wegmann Heinrich	Privatbank IHAG Zürich AG

Members of the Board

Bischof P. Daniel *	White Eagle AG
Blechner Markus *	BFO Family Office
Borner-Mouer Elizabeth *	EFG-Eurofinancière
Bossert Felix *	soliswiss
Dudler Paul A. *	Chairman Scholarship Foundation
Friedl Richard A. E.	ABB
Hofstetter Bernard	Sony Overseas SA
Jaccoud René L.	STS Information Technology
Kaelin Alfred	Nestlé S.A.
Kron Oswald	Toyota AG
Moriwaki Seisuke	Brother (Switzerland) SA
Pictet Ivan	Pictet & Cie
Renggli Alexander	President Alumni Organization
Sata Nao *	NS Consulting
Schaad Hans-Peter *	CMS von Erlach Henrici
Schmid Peter R.	Credit Suisse
Segawa Tomihiro	Swiss Re
Suzuki Takashi *	Japan Airlines !nternational Co.
Trinkler Thomas P.	BSI AG
Walch Gerhard	LGT Bank

* *Members of the Executive Committee*

Standing Invitation Board Meetings

Hirai Yasuo	Japanese Embassy
Rechsteiner Alfred F.	Osec

Managing Director

Herb Martin	Herb Takata Attorneys at Law

Appendix 2

Member	City
ABB Switzerland Ltd	Baden
Aerni Victor	Zollikon
AISA Atomation Industrielle SA	Vouvry
Althaus Hans-Ulrich	Buchs SG
Alveo AG	Lucerne
Ameco FS AG	Zollikon
AMI Asian Management Institute Ltd.	Berneck
Ammann Marco	Kanagawa
Araki Olivier Jun	Zurich
Aschwanden Alain	Basel
Baker & McKenzie	Geneva
Bank J. Vontobel & Co. AG	Zurich
Bär & Karrer Rechtsanwälte	Zurich
Barfuss Andreas	Basel
Bassi Sirio	Savosa
Baumgarten Mark-Oliver	Zurich
Bedenig Florian	Zurich
Belimo Automation AG	Hinwil
Berning Anke	Lucerne
Bischof P. Daniel	Chur
Blechner Markus	Zurich
BMG Engineering	Schlieren
Bonetti Gianmarco	Oberuzwil
Borner-Mouer Elizabeth	Würenlingen
Bossard AG	Zug
Bossert Felix	Meilen
Bosshard Rudolf	Gümligen
Briner & Brunisholz	Geneva
Brother (Schweiz) AG	Baden Dättwil
Bruderer AG	Frasnacht
Brunner Roman	Jona
BSI AG	Zurich
Büchel Christine	Zurich
Bühlmann Laboratories AG	Schönenbuch
Buschmann Oliver	Neerach
Canon (Schweiz) AG	Dietlikon
Centerseas Hotel Management AG	Widen
CH Projects Management Ltd.	Geneva
Chemtob Nathalie	Saint-Julien
Chiesa Raphael	Lohn
Chocolats Camille Bloch SA	Courtelary
Chromos AG	Glattbrugg
Ciba Speciality Chemicals Inc.	Basel
CMS von Erlach Henrici	Zurich

Member	City
Contreva Management AG	Baar
Coret Ltd	Zurich
Corti Sascha	Kilchberg
Coutts Bank von Ernst Ltd.	Zurich
Credit Suisse Group	Zurich
Crettol Gilles	Geneva
Danzas (Switzerland) Ltd.	Geneva
Deisen Thomas	Bern
Deloitte & Touche AG	Zurich
Desco de Schulthess Holding Ltd	Zurich
Diener Patrick	Rütti
DIGITANA AG	Horgen
DKSH Management AG	Zurich
Dolder Hotel AG	Zurich
Dr. Bjorn Johansson Associates	Zurich
Dr. Egon Zehnder & Partner AG	Zurich
Dr. Marc Rutschmann AG	Zurich
Dr. Peyrot Paul	Zurich
Dreamcom Corporation	Chur
Dressler Martin	Greifensee
Dudler Paul	Arlesheim
Ed Jobin AG	Brienz
Egli Fischer & Co Ltd.	Zurich
Ernst & Young	Zurich
Erowa AG	Reinach AG
ESGE AG Ltd	Mettlen
Etienne Blum Stehlé Manfrini & Associates	Geneva
Evac AG	Buchs
F. Hoffmann-La Roche AG	Basel
Feintool International Holding	Lyss
Flueckiger Alexandre	Nyon
Flueckiger-Obayashi Remo	Tokyo
FM Acoustics Ltd.	Horgen
Fontanet Jeandin & Hornung	Geneva
Forbo Holding SA	Eglisau
Fritschi Stefan	Winterthur
Fritz Gegauf AG	Steckborn
Fritz Studer AG	Thun
Fry Fabian	Volketswil
Fujifilm (Switzerland) AG	Dielsdorf
Genevalor Benbassat & Cie	Geneva
Georg Fischer AG	Schaffhausen
Gerber Rolf	Luterbach
Gessner AG	Wädenswil

Member	City
Giger Paul	Uetikon am See
Gimpert & Bischof Ltd.	Küsnacht
Glanzmann Gregory	Dürnten
Glanzmann Walter	Dürnten
GMC Foto Optik AG	Dielsdorf
Gmünder Bruno	Ennetbaden
Gondrand AG	Basel
Greater Zurich Area AG	Zurich
H. Moebius & Sohn Inhaber Gallian & Cie	Allschwil
Hakki Ahmed	Zurich
Haltiner Markus	Carona
Hammer Thomas	St-Légier
Hämmerli Peter	Kilchberg
Hansen Niels	Aarau
Harris Kiyoko S.	Tokyo
Hartmann Benjamin	Basel
Hartmann Melanie	Arlesheim
Hartmann Muller Partner	Zurich
Hasler Daniel	Yokohama
Helbling Mangement Consulting Ltd	Dietikon
Helmut Fischer Elektronik und Messtechnik AG	Hünenberg
Herb Martin	Zurich
Hess Martin	Zurich
Heusser Marc	Zurich
Hilti AG	Schaan FL
Hirai Yasuo	Bern
Hirano Mariko	Münchenstein
Hoffmeister Meike	Zurich
Honda (Suisse) SA	Vernier
Hostettler AG	Sursee
Hostettler Thomas	Zurich
Hotel Management School Les Roches	Randogne
Hotz Gregor	Zug
Huber Ueli	Zurich
Hunkeler-Holding AG	Wikon
Hüppi & Von Sprecher	Zurich
Imlig Norbert	Munich
International Business Communications	Frauenfeld
Itschner Patrick	Küsnacht
Ivoclar Vivadent AG	Schaan FL
Jaccoud René Louis	Paris
JALPAK International (Europe) B.V.	Zurich
Janson Nicolas	Zurich
Japan Airlines International Co., Ltd.	Zurich

Member	City
JETRO Geneva Office	Geneva
Jinnai Yoko	Stäfa
John Lay Electronics AG	Littau
Josef Binkert AG	Wallisellen
Kaba Management & Consulting AG	Rümlang
Kaegi Rahel	Wädenswil
Kanaï Masaki	Zurich
Kistler Instrumente AG	Winterthur
Knecht & Müller AG	Stein am Rhein
Koenig Verbindungstechnik AG	Dietikon
Komax AG	Dierikon
KPMG private	Aarau
Kuederli Yves B.	Dübendorf
Kuhn Rikon AG	Rikon
L. Kellenberger & Co. AG	St. Gallen
Laine Andrea	Zollikon
Lamprecht Transport AG	Basel
Landert-Motoren AG	Bülach
Laurastar SA	Châtel-St-Denis
Lehner Melk	Zurich
LEM SA	Plan-les-Ouates
Leuenberger Matthias	Basel
Leuzinger Fridolin	Basel
LGT Bank in Liechtenstein	Vaduz FL
Loosli Urs	Zurich
Lottanti von Mandach Stefania	Zurich
Mächler Stefan	Forch
Magnin Dunand & ASS.	Geneva
Märki Yoshiko	Niederweningen
MAT SECURITAS EXPRESS	Kloten
Matherly John	Meilen
Maurer Thomas	Bern
Meier Anton	Oberwil-Lieli
Meierhans Evkarin	Suhr
Mepha AG	Aesch
Metrohm	Herisau
Mettler Tobias	Kirchdorf
Meyer Rudolf	Basel
Mizuho Bank (Switzerland) Ltd.	Zurich
Mock Jürg	Manaus-AM
Moesner Felix	Tokyo
Mottini Roger	St. Moritz
Natural AG	Basel
Neff Michael	Zurich

Member	City
Nestlé S.A.	Vevey
Neutrik AG	Schaan FL
Niederer, Kraft & Frey	Zurich
Niklaus Erik	Fällanden
Nishi's Japan Shop	Zurich
Nomura Bank (Switzerland) Ltd	Zurich
Notter Monika	Huttwil
Novartis International AG	Basel
Oba Koichi	Jona
Oeda Hiroshi	Düdingen
Omura Sachikazu	Zurich
Panalpina Ltd	Glattbrugg
Paris Miki (International) SA	Geneva
Pentapharm AG	Basel
Pentax (Schweiz) AG	Dietlikon
Pentel Papeteriewaren AG	Egg bei Zurich
Perréard, de Boccard, Kohler, Ador & Associés	Geneva
Pestalozzi Lachenal Party	Geneva
Pictet Ivan	Geneva
Pricewaterhouse Coopers AG	Zurich
Privatbank IHAG Zürich AG	Zurich
Probala Rolf	Kilchberg
Publicitas (Service International) AG	Zurich
Rauper Roman	Oberglatt
Rausch AG Kreuzlingen	Kreuzlingen
Reinfried Dr. Heinrich	Zurich
Reisebüro Harry Kolb AG	Kilchberg
Reishauer AG	Wallisellen
Renggli Alex	Zurich
Richoz-Zogg Emanuelle	Corsier GE
Rickenbach & Partner	Zollikon
Ricola AG	Laufen
Rieter Automotive Management Ltd.	Winterthur
Riken Yamamoto & Beda Faessler Architects GmbH	Zug
Robinson Max	Lachen
Roellin Martin	Zug
Rovelli Diego	Zurich
Ruettimann Remo	Effretikon
San-Ei Gen F.F.I. (Schweiz) AG	Zurich
Sarnafil International AG	Sarnen
Sata Nao	Cully
Sato.Schlaf.Räume	Zurich
Schalcher Urs	Greifensee
Schindler Alexander	Winterthur

Member	City
Schindler Niels	Geneva
Schleuniger AG	Thun
Schmid Ralph	Horgen
Schneider & Cie AG	Basel
Schneider René	Zurich
Schnider Peter	Dübendorf
Schoechli Hansueli	Spiegel
Schroder Salomon Smith Barney	Zurich
Schwarzenegger Christian	Zurich
Sekotac GmbH	Pfäffikon
Sennhauser Vincent	Rapperswil
Siegfried Ltd.	Zofingen
Siegrist Andreas	Regensdorf
SKAN AG	Allschwil
SMC Pneumatik AG	Weisslingen
Sony Overseas S.A.	Schlieren
Spescha Jose	Zurich
Spiegel Cornelia	New York
Spiess Hans	Winterthur
Stalder Roman	Bern
Stöckli Marc O.	Küsnacht
Stoll Giroflex AG	Koblenz
Storz Medical AG	Kreuzlingen
Strauss Alexandra	Greppen
Stuhlträger Erich	Zurich
Subaru (Schweiz) AG	Safenwil
Sugimoto Satoshi Jean-Paul	Therwil
Sulzberger Franz	Hasle-Rüegsau
Sulzer Metco Holding AG.	Winterthur
Suzuki Haltinner Katsura-Rie	Wädenswil
Swiss Re	Zurich
Swiss-ASIA Consulting Ltd.	Zurich
Takata Herb Arisa	Zurich
Tan Daniela	Zurich
Tavernier Tschanz	Geneva
Telion AG	Zurich
Thar Daniel	Eschlikon
Théry Lionel	Clarens
Thouvenin Rechtsanwälte	Zurich
TKB Medical AG	Lucerne
Toyota AG	Safenwil
Trepp Gian	Fribourg
Tucker John	Horgen
UBS AG	Zurich

Member	City
UFJ Bank (Schweiz) AG	Zurich
Unaxis Management AG	Pfäffikon SZ
Unisto AG	Horn
Urscheler-Kinugawa Michiyo	Zurich
Usunier Jean-Claude	Lausanne
Vandex International Ltd	Solothurn
Victorinox AG	Ibach
Vischer & Bolli AG	Dübendorf
Vitra (International) AG	Birsfelden
Volkswirtschaftsdirektion	Zurich
Von Roll Environmental Technology Ltd.	Zurich
Weber-Thedy Wolfgang	Zurich
Wegmann Heinrich	Winterthur
Wehrle Sigvald	Jona
Weidmann Transformerboard Systems AG	Rapperswil
WEKA AG	Bäretswil
Welti Hansjürg	Langenthal
Wiederkehr & Co.	Küsnacht
Wirz Werbeberatung AG	Zurich
Wirz Werbung AG	Zurich
WMH Walther Meier Holding AG	Pfäffikon
Yanku Stefan	Adliswil
Yazaki Corp. Swiss Office	Zurich
Zangger Eric	Binningen
Zehnder Dominik	Bäch
Zimmermann Karin	Zurich
Zingg Mike	Tokyo
Zwald Stefan	Zurich

Appendix 3

Events from 1.1.2005

12.1.2005 Luncheon, "The Swiss Business Hub in Japan: Supporting Companies to Open the Japanese Market"
Speech by Mr. Hermann Escher, Head of the Swiss Business Hub Japan, Tokyo

18.2.2005 Luncheon, "Selling Swiss (Technical) Goods in Japan, an Impossible Task?"
Speech by Mr. Walter Graf, Sales & Marketing Manager of WST Winterthur Schleiftechnik AG

16.3.2005 Japan Seminar, "Some Guidelines for Behaviour when Visiting Japan"
by Dr. Elizabeth Borner-Mouer, Ostasiatisches Seminar der Universität Zürich/EFG-Eurofinancière d'Investissements, Monaco

26.5.2005 Annual General Meeting, "Switzerland and Japan in the System of Global Development and Cooperation"
Speech by Mr. Walter Fust, Ambassador, Director-General of the Swiss Agency for Development and Cooperation (SDC), Federal Department of Foreign Affairs, Bern

31.5.2005 Sake Tasting and Seminar, "What You Always Wanted to Know About Sake"

30.8.2005 Luncheon, "Twelve Crucial Challenges Ahead – Are We Really Coping?"
Speech by Dr. Hans-Ulrich Doerig, Vice-Chairman of the Board of Directors, Credit Suisse Group

23.9.2005 Luncheon, "Japan Facing the Challenge of the XXIst Century: A New Partnership with China"
Speech by Naohiko Sata, NS Consulting

16.11.2005 Luncheon, "How Japanese Multinational Companies Could Fully Benefit from Headquarters and Principals Status in Switzerland"
Speech by Mrs. Katsura Suzuki and Mr. Jean-Marc Girard, Katsura Suzuki Consulting, Japan Business Representative of Ernst & Young Switzerland/International Tax Partner of Ernst & Young Global

8.12.2005 Dinner, "Swiss-Japanese Economic Relations in a Multilateral Context"
Speech by Ambassador Luzius Wasescha, Delegate of the Swiss Government for Trade Agreements, Swiss Chief negotiator in the WTO-Doha Round and Member of the Executive Board of the State Secretariat for Economic Affairs (seco).

16.1.2006 Shinnen Kai and visit to the Foundation Emil G. Bührle Collection
Introduction by Dr. Lukas Gloor

15.2.2006 Investment Seminar, "Basel meets Japan", Basel
in cooperation with JETRO, the Basel Chamber of Commerce and OSEC

7.3.2006	Luncheon, "Tokyo Stock Exchange: Where next? Is Japan's Recovery Sustainable?" *Speech by Mr. Arun Ratra, Managing Director and Chief Investment Officer, Credit Suisse*	
9.5.2006	Annual General Meeting *Speech by Samuel Schmid, Federal Councillor/Bundesrat*	

Application for Membership

I/we, the undersigned, hereby apply for membership in the Swiss-Japanese Chamber of Commerce.

Membership Category: COMPANIES

☐ small company	CHF	330.–
☐ medium company	CHF	550.–
☐ large company	CHF	1100.–

INDIVIDUAL

☐ individual	CHF	100.–

Company/Name: ______________________

Address: ______________________

Phone: ______________ Fax: ______________

E-mail: ______________________

If company:
Name of Representative: ______________________

Title/Function: ______________________

Type of Business or Activity: ______________________

Place/Date: ______________ Signature: ______________

Swiss-Japanese Chamber of Commerce, Kappelergasse 15, Postfach 2400, 8022 Zürich 1
Tel. +41 44 381 09 50 / Fax +41 44 381 09 54
info@sjcc.ch / http://www.sjcc.ch